P9-DTC-925

PACIFICO, INC.
2145 THE ALAMEDA SUITE B
SAN JOSE, CA 95126-1141

Developing
A Winning
Marketing Plan

Wiley Series on Business Strategy

William A. Cohen

DEVELOPING A WINNING MARKETING PLAN

William A. Cohen

JOHN WILEY & SONS

New York   Chichester   Brisbane   Toronto   Singapore

Copyright © 1987 by William A. Cohen.

Published by John Wiley & Sons, Inc.

All rights reserved. Published simultaneously in Canada.

Reproduction or translation of any part of this work
beyond that permitted by Section 107 or 108 of the
1976 United States Copyright Act without the permission
of the copyright owner is unlawful. Requests for
permission or further information should be addressed to
the Permissions Department, John Wiley & Sons, Inc.

This publication is designed to provide accurate and
authoritative information in regard to the subject
matter covered. It is sold with the understanding that
the publisher is not engaged in rendering legal, accounting,
or other professional service. If legal advice or other
expert assistance is required, the services of a competent
professional person should be sought. *From a Declaration
of Principles jointly adopted by a Committee of the
American Bar Association and a Committee of Publishers.*

Library of Congress Cataloging in Publication Data:

Cohen, William A., 1937–
    Developing a winning marketing plan.

    (Wiley series on business strategy)
    Bibliography: p.
    1. Marketing.   I. Title.   II. Series.

HF5415.C54247   1987   658.8′02   86-32402
ISBN 0-471-84529-9

Printed in the United States of America

10 9 8 7 6 5 4 3 2

SERIES PREFACE

Peter Drucker has said, "The future will not just happen if one wishes hard enough. It requires decision—now. It imposes risk—now. It requires action—now. It demands allocation of resources, and above all, human resources—now." The Wiley Series on Business Strategy is published to assist managers with the task of creating the future in their organizations.

Creation of the future requires application of the art and science of strategy. Strategy comes from the Greek word *strategia* which means generalship. It has clear military roots which defined how a general deployed the available forces and resources to achieve military objectives. But business and military strategy, though similar, are not identical. Business strategy is the allocation of resources to achieve a differential advantage at the time and place of decisive importance. Resources may be human, financial, promotional, unique know-how, or they may have a psychological emphasis. But to be effective, these resources must be concentrated so as to be superior where it counts. This achievement is the essence of any successful business strategy and the theme of this series.

v

The series will investigate strategy in all its many facets in business, including marketing, management, planning, finance, communications, promotional activities, leadership, and corporate culture—to note only those topics under preparation or planned. Its aim is to equip the practicing manager with the techniques and tools he or she will need for the most competitive and exciting period in business.

William A. Cohen
Series Editor

PREFACE

In many of my previously published business books, I have emphasized the importance of the marketing plan for business success. And why not? More than 500 marketing plans have been prepared under my supervision in the classroom. One of my students sold his plan for $5000. Several have gone into the business of preparing marketing plans for others, and many have used their marketing plans to start their own businesses, some of which have reached several million dollars in annual sales.

Nevertheless, I was unprepared for the overwhelming response when I presented information having to do with marketing plans at various conferences beginning in 1985 and when some of the forms contained in this book were published in a leading journal for marketing educators. At one conference, not knowing what to expect, I brought along a limited number of copies of my presentation. I was mobbed! Dozens of people gave me their business cards and pleaded with me to send them a copy of the information I presented. At a presentation in Kansas City, two consultants in the audience who examined several student plans I had with me stated positively that the plans were not worth $5000 as I indicated but $25,000—and these consultants knew, because their profession was the preparation of marketing plans. Yet these plans were prepared by undergraduate and graduate students. An article in *Marketing Educator* kept both me and my secretary busy for weeks fulfilling requests for additional information.

This is the era of marketing. Major articles in not only *Business Week,* but also *Time* and *Newsweek* and other journals, attest to this fact. Every organization needs marketing to be successful. And the key to marketing is the marketing plan.

This book will lead you through a sequence of step-by-step procedures and forms, all of which are explained in some detail. When you complete the book, you will not only know what to do, but also how and why. And you will have a professional plan. This procedure is not theoretical or someone's half-baked idea. It has been action-tested in hundreds of cases. It works!

WILLIAM A. COHEN

Pasadena, California
March 1987

OTHER BOOKS BY WILLIAM A. COHEN

The Executive's Guide to Finding a Superior Job, 2nd ed.
Principles of Technical Management
How to Sell to the Government
Successful Marketing for Small Business (with Marshall Reddick)
Building a Mail Order Business, 2nd ed.
The Entrepreneur and Small Business Problem Solver
Top Executive Performance (with Nurit Cohen)
Direct Response Marketing
How to Make It Big as a Consultant
Winning on the Marketing Front
High Tech Management
The Student's Guide to Finding a Superior Job

CONTENTS

Developing
A Winning
Marketing Plan

THE MARKETING PLAN
MYSTIQUE

Not long ago two Harvard Business School students, Mike Wigley and Jerry De La Vega, were talking about how to promote record sales. Basically their idea was to enable people to order any record they wanted right from their own living rooms. Twelve months later the idea caught fire. Joined by a third classmate from Harvard, David Ishag, these entrepreneurs used a cable television network that airs rock 'n' roll videos 24 hours a day to advertise their business, Hot Rock, Inc. By the seventeenth day Hot Rock, Inc., had received 50,000 inquiries, and some weeks later sales growth was running at 10–14 percent a month with first-year projected sales at $6.7 million.

Meanwhile, Stouffers Lean Cuisine, a line of frozen food, suddenly boosted its market share by more than 30 percent in the $500 million frozen-entree food market, catching the entire industry by surprise.

In 1978 the Clorox Company had reached $1 billion in sales but profits were unimpressive, and shortly after that half of the $1 billion revenue disappeared when a key division was sold. Yet only six years later Clorox again hit $1 billion in sales, but this time profits were double those of 1978.

What do these three vastly different types of companies in totally different industries have in common other than success? The answer is the marketing plan, in each case a marketing plan that played a major role in enabling the company to reach the success that surprised competitors and business associates alike.

A MARKETING PLAN IS ESSENTIAL FOR EVERY BUSINESS OPERATION

A marketing plan is essential for every business operation and for efficient and effective marketing of any product or service, even for marketing within a company. Seeking success for any project without the use of a marketing plan is like trying to navigate a ship through incredibly stormy waters while under torpedo attack and with neither a map nor a clear idea of where you are going. It requires time to develop a marketing plan, but it is time well spent and will save you time overall. The marketing plan will allow you to visualize clearly both where you are going and what you want to accomplish along the way. At the same time, a marketing plan details the very important steps required to get you from where you are to where you want to be. An added benefit is that in compiling and developing the marketing plan, you will have thought through how long it will take to accomplish each step and what resources in money, time, and effort will be needed in order to do this. Without a marketing plan, you will not even know whether you have reached your objectives.

WHAT A MARKETING PLAN WILL DO FOR YOU

A properly developed marketing plan can accomplish a lot for a relatively small amount of focused effort. The benefits of a marketing plan include all of the following:

It will act as a road map.
It will assist in management control and implementation of strategy.

It will inform new participants of their roles in implementing the plan and reaching your objectives.

It will assist in helping to obtain resources for implementation.

It will stimulate thinking and the better use of limited resources.

It will help in the organization and assignment of responsibilities, tasks, and timing.

It will help you become aware of problems, opportunities, and threats in the future.

Let's look at each of these benefits in turn.

Act as a Road Map

Perhaps the basic purpose of the marketing plan is to act as a road map and tell you how to get from the beginning of the plan to your objectives and goals. Like a road map, the plan describes the environment in which you are likely to find yourself along the way. A road map might describe the geographical terrain as well as the type and classification of the various road arteries, times, distances, and available stops for emergencies, gasoline, food, repair, or lodging. In the same fashion the marketing plan will describe the environment of the marketplace including your competitors, politics, laws, regulations, economic and business conditions, state of technology, forecast demand, social and cultural factors, demographics of the target market, as well as the company's available resources.

Assist in Management Control and Implementation of Strategy

As the driver of a motor vehicle proceeds along a route using a road map, a detour may be necessary because of unplanned circumstances. Perhaps there is road maintenance or severe weather that makes the most direct route or the planned route impossible to negotiate. In this same way your strategy tells you the route that you must take and describes it on your road map along with the expected environment. But as you proceed various problems may occur. In fact, unlike a trip that you planned by car, it is virtually certain that almost nothing will go exactly as originally planned. Yet, because you have anticipated potential changes in your environment which may require detours and have planned for these detours, the marketing plan will allow you to spot and redirect your activities toward alternate paths in order to arrive at your objective with minimum difficulty. You will be able to see clearly the difference between what is happening during the implementation of your strategy and what you had planned to happen. This will give you control of the situation and allow you to take the corrective action necessary to put your project back on track and to keep it on track to reach your final objective.

Informing New Participants in the Plan of Their Roles and Functions

Successful implementation of a strategy requires integration of many actions, usually by many different people and departments both inside and outside the organization. Timing is frequently critical. And it is most important that all concerned individuals understand what their responsibilities are as well as how their tasks or actions fit into the overall strategy. Having a marketing plan enables you to describe the big picture in detail. It allows everyone to see how their actions coordinate with the actions of others. New people may be assigned to activities involving your plan. They, too, can be brought immediately up-to-date regarding their responsibilities and actions and how to adapt to the work of others. Thus the marketing plan is a document that can be used to inform all participants of your objectives and how these objectives will be accomplished: by whom, with what, and when.

Acquiring Resources for Implementation

Resources are always limited. This is true whether you are an individual entrepreneur attempting to obtain resources outside the company or you are working in a large corporation and seeking resources for your particular project. In either of these situations a marketing plan plays an important part in persuading those who have the authority to allocate money, people, and other assets to your project. And with resources scarce, you must convince these individuals that you are going to use capital, goods, and labor in the most effective and efficient manner and that your objectives are not only achievable but that, despite competition and other potential threats, you will ultimately achieve victory. Therefore your marketing plan is also a sales vehicle. Even more than a sales tool, the marketing plan demonstrates your control over the project from start to finish. It demonstrates that you can visualize the ultimate objective and that you know what you must do at every point—this includes actions, costs, and alternatives. Because you have mastered the project on paper, you're already halfway there, and those with the authority to grant or lend you the resources to proceed will also be more likely to recognize your potential.

Stimulate Thinking and Make Better Use of Resources

Resources are always limited. Successful strategy will help you to make the most of what you have to build on your strengths and minimize your weaknesses, and to obtain a differential advantage over your competition at the decisive point. This leads to success. As you do the research for your marketing plan and analyze your strategic alternatives your thinking will be stimulated. As the plan unfolds you will change and modify it as new ideas are generated. Eventually you will reach the optimum: a well-organized, well-integrated plan that will make efficient use of the resources available and will assist you to anticipate every eventuality that can help or hinder your progress.

Assignment of Responsibilities, Tasks, and Timing

It is a fact that no strategy will ever be better than those who implement it. Therefore timing and the assignment of responsibilities are crucial. A marketing plan clearly outlines these responsibilities; there is no question where they lie. It is also important that all action be scheduled to maximize the impact of the strategy of the overall plan while taking full advantage of the environment that is expected to exist at the time of its execution. By hard thinking during development this integration will preclude suboptimization. In *suboptimization* one small unit or element of the plan is optimized to the detriment of the entire project. Let's say that you have been working on a marketing plan for a new computer component from its conception to its establishment in the marketplace. If the technical details alone are optimized, the funds allocated for development may be so great that suboptimization will occur and no funds will remain for marketing strategy. Technically, you have an excellent product but no funds with which to market it. Therefore because of suboptimization the product fails. Yet a less technical solution might have been fully acceptable at a lower cost. Funds would then have been at hand to carry out the marketing plan. In other words, if done correctly a marketing plan will guarantee that every task will be assigned to someone responsible for performing it in the correct sequence and that all elements and strategies will be coordinated synergistically to maximize their effect and ensure the completion of the project with the resources available.

Awareness of Problems, Opportunities, and Threats

Intuitively, even without a marketing plan, you may recognize some of the problems, opportunities, and threats that may occur as you work toward your objective. Your marketing plan will not only document those of which you are aware but will help you to identify others that may appear during its preparation. It will enable you to think strategically and to consider what must be done about opportunities, problems, and threats that lie in the future. Without question, the more development and analysis that you do as your plan is prepared, the more you will understand their nature and what can be done about them. They must never be ignored; instead your marketing plan must be constructed and modified to take maximum advantage of the opportunities, solve the problems, and avoid the threats.

GETTING IN A COMPETITIVE POSITION BEFORE YOU START

Overall you will be put in a better competitive position even before you begin to execute your plan. You will have systematically thought it through from start to finish. You will already know where the future may lead. On paper, you will have coordinated all efforts to attain a specific objective. You will have developed performance standards for controlling objectives and goals and you will have sharpened your strategy and tactics to a much greater extent than would otherwise have been possible. You will be much better prepared than any of your competitors for sudden developments and you will have anticipated those that are potential and will know instantly what to do when they occur. Finally, more than any competitor, you will have a vivid sense of what is going to happen and how to make it happen. Your competitors are going to react, but you will have already acted in anticipation.

TYPES OF MARKETING PLANS

Marketing plans tend to fall into a number of categories for a number of purposes. The two basic types are the new product and annual marketing plans.

New Product Plan

The new product plan is prepared for a product, service, product line, or brand that has not yet been introduced by the firm. It is wise to develop a complete new product plan even before the project has been initiated. Granted that the information at this stage may be sketchy. Still it is far better to start your thinking as early as possible before any major resources have been committed. In this way alternatives can be compared and analyzed and you will have a general idea of the overall costs and timing of competitive projects. Naturally the marketing plan for a new product will have many more unknowns than the annual marketing plan, because customarily you will have little or no feedback from the marketplace and the product or service may have no track record with your firm. This last point is an important one to consider. It is not unusual for products that have achieved successful sales performance with one firm to fall far short of these goals in another. This is frequently due to certain strengths of the first firm that the second firm cannot duplicate. With a new product plan it is sometimes necessary to make assumptions based on similar products or services that the company has marketed or that have been introduced by other companies. But don't forget. If you use information based on other companies' experiences, you must assess your ability to duplicate their performance. Other sources of information may be necessary to modify data from other companies' experiences. This will be discussed later in this book. A marketing plan for a new product or service may also include development of the product from scratch. Of course if the product already exists, its technical development as a part of your plan is not needed.

Annual Marketing Plans

Annual marketing plans are for those products, projects, services, and brands that are already established in the company's product line. Periodically, preferably once a year, this planning must be formally reviewed. Of course the plan may be adjusted and modified in the interim as changes occur in the environment or in the company. But the review and annual creation of a new marketing plan for the coming year help to identify emerging problems, opportunities, and threats that may be missed during the day-to-day operations and fire fighting associated with the management of an ongoing product or service. Again, however, notice that the plan is for the future; it's how you will get from your present position to some other at a later time. Therefore there will still be unknowns, for which information must be forecast, researched, or, in some cases, assumed. Although annual marketing plans are usually prepared for only one year, it is of course possible to plan for several years and to modify the plan annually. On the other hand, product plans generally cover the entire life of the project from initiation to its establishment in the marketplace. *Establishment* means that the product is beyond the introductory stage and is growing at a predetermined specified rate.

SUMMARY

In this chapter we have discussed the importance of the marketing plan in satisfying objectives in the most efficient manner possible. We have noted the main benefits of a marketing plan:

Acting as a road map

Assisting in management control and implementing strategy

Informing new participants in the plan of their roles and functions

Obtaining resources for implementation

Stimulating thinking and making better use of resources

Assigning responsibilities and tasks and setting time

Being aware of problems, opportunities, and threats

Knowledge of the preparation of a marketing plan is not the option of a successful manager of marketing activities. It is a requirement. But beyond that it is an effective and valuable tool that will enable you to work on a daily basis to accomplish the objectives that you have set for the particular project which you are going to market.

2

DEVELOPING THE MARKETING PLAN

A good marketing plan needs a great deal of information gathered from many sources and then used it to develop marketing strategy and tactics to reach a specific set of objectives and goals. Accordingly the process is not necessarily difficult but it does require organization. This is especially true if you are not developing this plan by yourself but are depending on others within or outside your organization to assist you or to accomplish parts of the plan. Therefore it is important before you start to "plan for planning." The time spent will pay dividends later. Not only will you save that time, but you will avoid making mistakes that could cost time *and* money.

To prepare for planning you must look first at the total job you are going to do and then organize the work so that everything is done in an efficient manner and nothing is left out. If you do this correctly, every element of your plan will come together in a timely fashion. This means that you won't be completing any task too early and then waiting for some other task to be finished before you can continue. It also means that no member of your planning task force will be overworked or underworked. To accomplish this you must study the structure of the marketing plan and all of its elements. Next you must organize your major planning tasks by using a marketing-plan action-development schedule. This will give an overview of the entire marketing planning process, including who is going to do what and when each task is scheduled for completion.

THE STRUCTURE OF THE MARKETING PLAN

Every marketing plan should have a structure to ensure that no important information is left out and that this information is presented in a logical manner. A marketing plan outline is shown in Figure 2-1. In going through it, you can pick out the requirements and the information that must be obtained to complete your plan. Let's examine each section of this marketing plan structure in more detail.

The Executive Summary

The first part of the marketing plan structure or outline is the executive summary, which is a synopsis or abstract of the entire plan. It includes a description of the product or service, the differential advantage of your product or service over that of your competitors, the investment needed, and the anticipated results, all of which can be expressed as a return on investment, sales, profits, market share, or in any one of the ways discussed in Chapter 8.

The executive summary is especially important if your marketing plan is going to be used to help you to obtain the resources for implementation. Top management executives are busy. There may well be more than just your marketing plan on which they must make funding decisions. Sometimes several competing marketing plans are submitted simultaneously, and only one is given the green light. If you submit your marketing plan to a venture capitalist, there will be many competing plans. Therefore it is hard to minimize its importance. The executive summary is a summary of the entire plan, running from a few paragraphs to a few pages in length. From it a busy executive can get a quick idea whether to spend time on the project without reading the entire plan. Therefore, no matter how good the main body of your plan, your executive summary must be

I. Executive Summary
Overview of entire plan, including a description of the product or service, the differential advantage, the required investment, and anticipated sales and profits.

II. Table of Contents

III. Introduction
What is the product or service? Describe it in detail and explain how it fits into the market.

IV. Situational Analysis
A. The Situational Environs
   1. Demand and demand trends. (What is the forecast demand for the product: is it growing or declining? Who is the decision maker? The purchase agent? How, when, where, what, and why do they buy?)
   2. Social and cultural factors.
   3. Demographics.
   4. Economic and business conditions for this product at this time and in the geographical area selected.
   5. State of technology for this class of product. Is it high-tech state-of-the-art? Are newer products succeeding older ones frequently (short life cycle)? In short, how is technology affecting this product or service?
   6. Politics. Are politics (current or otherwise) in any way affecting the situation for marketing this product?
   7. Laws and regulations. (What laws or regulations are applicable here?)

B. The Neutral Environs
   1. Financial environment. (How does the availability or unavailability of funds affect the situation?)
   2. Government environment. (Is current legislative action in state, federal, or local government likely to affect marketing of this product or service?)
   3. Media environment. (What's happening in the media? Does current publicity favor this project?)
   4. Special interest environment. (Aside from direct competitors, are any influential groups likely to affect your plans?)

C. The Competitor Environs
   1. Describe your main competitors, their products, plans, experience, know-how, financial, human, and capital resources, suppliers, and strategy. Do they enjoy the favor with their customers? If so, why? What marketing channels do the competitors use? What are their strengths and weaknesses

D. The Company Environs
   1. Describe your products, experience, know-how, financial, human, and capital resources, and suppliers. Do you enjoy the favor of your customers? If so, why? What are your strengths and weaknesses?

V. The Target Market
Describe your target market segment in detail by using demographics, psychographics, geographics, life-style, or whatever segmentation is appropriate. Why is this your target market? How large is it?

FIGURE 2-1. Marketing plan outline.

13

VI. **Problems and Opportunities**
State or restate each opportunity and indicate why it is, in fact, an opportunity.
State or restate every problem. Indicate what you intend to do about each of them.
Clearly state the differential competitive advantage.

VII. **Marketing Objectives and Goals**
State precisely the marketing objectives and goals in terms of sales volume, market
share, return on investment, or other objectives or goals for your marketing plan and
the time needed to achieve each of them.

VIII. **Marketing Strategy—**
Consider alternatives for the overall strategy; for example, for a new market penetration a marketer can enter first, early, or late, penetrate vertically or horizontally, and
exploit three different niche strategies.
If the marketing strategy is at the grand strategy or strategic marketing management
level, a market attractiveness/business capability matrix and product life cycle analysis
should also be made.

IX. **Marketing Tactics***
State how you will implement the marketing strategy(s) chosen in terms of the product, price, promotion, distribution, and other tactical or environmental variables.

X. **Implementation and Control**
Calculate the break-even point and make a break-even chart for your project. Compute sales projections and cash flows on a monthly basis for a three-year period. Determine start-up costs and a monthly budget, along with the required tasks.

XI. **Summary**
Summarize advantages, costs, and profits and restate the differential advantage that
your plan offers over the competition and why the plan will succeed.

XII. **Appendices**
Include all supporting information that you consider relevant.

FIGURE 2-1. Continued

*Note under the marketing strategy and tactics sections how your main competitors are likely to respond
when you take the action planned and what you will then do to avoid the threats and take advantage of
the opportunities.

---

well thought out and succinct. It must demonstrate that you know
what you're talking about and that your proposal has potential and
a reasonable likelihood of success. If not, the executive judging your
plan will probably read no further.

Usually the executive summary is one of the last elements to be
prepared. This is because it is impossible to summarize accurately
until you complete every other part. But even though you save it for

last remember that it will come at the beginning of the plan's documentation and must persuade the reader to read further.

Contents

A contents table sounds rather mundane and you may feel that it is unnecessary. You might be especially inclined to discard the idea if your marketing plan is short. But, let me tell you, a contents table is necessary, whether your marketing plan is only a few pages or a hundred pages long. It is required, never optional, because of a psychological factor that affects those who will evaluate your marketing plan for approval or disapproval. If you are using it to acquire money or other resources to implement it, the contents table is important because many individuals from many functional disciplines will be sitting on the review board. Some may be experts in the technical area; they will be interested primarily in the technical details of your product or service. Others will be financial experts; they will want to examine your break-even analysis, the financial ratios you have calculated, and other financial information. In fact, every expert tends to look first at his or her own area. Now, if you submit a contents table, this will be fairly easy to do. The reader will scan the list of subjects and turn in a few seconds to the correct page. But if you fail in this regard the evaluator of your plan will have to search for the information. If you are lucky, it will be found readily anyway, but the problem is you won't always be lucky. When many plans must be reviewed, the evaluator may spend only a few minutes or even a few seconds in the search. If the information can't be found, it may be concluded that it is not there. This not only raises questions of completeness but may also give the competitive edge to a marketing plan done by someone else who has made the information easy to find.

The need for a contents table is especially critical when your plan is being submitted to venture capitalists. Venture capitalists put up large sums of money to businesses that already have a track record and have a marketing plan, sometimes called a business plan, for future growth, but in many cases, especially in smaller companies and with start-ups and new products, marketing and business plans are identical. When you are trying to obtain resources from a venture capitalist, or any investor, the two plans are synonymous. Either the business plan must have a heavy marketing emphasis or the marketing plan must include complete financial, manufacturing, and technical data.

Typically, funds are available for investment in less than 1 percent of the plans that are submitted. One venture capitalist I know said that he receives more than 100 marketing plans every month, each of which contains a minimum of 30 pages and some exceed 100. Under the circumstances do you think that anyone could actually go over all of them in great detail? Of course not. Accordingly this venture capitalist looks first at the executive summary, and if it appears to be interesting spot-checks the contents for critical information. Only if interest is maintained by this initial check is the plan read in more detail. Other plans, in which the critical information could not be easily found are given no further attention. In this initial screening most of the plans are dropped, leaving only a few for a more detailed reading and a final decision. So don't forget this mundane tool, and be certain that the contents table is an accurate list of all the important topics in your marketing plan.

Introduction

The introduction is the explanation of the details of your project. Unlike the executive summary, it is not an overview of the project. Its purpose is to describe your product or service so that any reader, whether familiar with your industry or not, will understand exactly what it is you are proposing. The introduction can be a fairly large section. After reading it the evaluator should understand what the product or service is and what you propose to do with it.

Situational Analysis

The situational analysis contains a vast amount of information and, as the term indicates, is an analysis of the situation that you are facing with the proposed product or service. Sometimes referred to as *environmental scanning,* the situational analysis is divided into four categories that I call the environs of the marketplace: situational environs, neutral environs, competitor environs, and company environs. Let's look at each in turn.

Situational Environs. Situational environs include demand and demand trends for your product or service by the potential customers you have targeted. Is this demand growing, is it declining, or has it leveled off? Who are the decision makers regarding purchase of the product and who are the purchase agents? Sometimes the decision maker and purchase agent are the same, but often they are not; for example, one member of a family may be the decision maker with regard to purchasing a certain product, say a brand of beer. But the individual who actually makes the purchase may be another family member. How, when, where, what, and why do these potential customers purchase? What are the social and cultural factors, the demographics, including educational backgrounds, and income, and the economic conditions during the period covered by the marketing plan? Is business good or is it bad? Actually, fortunes can be made in a good or bad business environment, but we must document exactly what these conditions are. What is the state of technology for this class of product? Is your product high-tech state-of-the-art? Are newer products frequently succeeding older ones, thus indicating a short product life cycle? In short, how is technology affecting the product or service and the marketing for this product or service? Are politics, current or otherwise, in any way affecting the marketing of this product? What potential dangers or threats do the politics in the situation portend? Or do the politics provide opportunities? What laws or regulations are relevant to the marketing of this product or service?

Neutral Environs. Neutral environs include the financial element. How does the availability or unavailability of funds affect the situation? What about government? Is legislation on the state, federal, or local level likely to affect the marketing of the product or service? What's happening in the media? Does current publicity favor your project or does it make any difference? Special interest groups are examined. Aside from direct competitors, are any influential groups (e.g., consumer organizations) likely to affect your plans for marketing this product or service?

Competitor Environs. Competitor environs include those elements that are competing against you. They are important because they are the only elements of the environment that will intentionally act against your interests. In this section of the situational analysis describe in detail your main competitors, the products they offer, their plans, experience, know-how, financial, human, and capital resources, suppliers, and, most important of all, their current and future strategies. Also note whether they enjoy favor with their customers and why. Describe and analyze your competitors' strengths and weaknesses, what marketing channels they use, and anything else that you feel is relevant to the marketing situation as it will exist when you implement your project.

Company Environs. Company environs describe your situation in the company and the resources that you have available. Describe your current products, experience, and know-how, financial, human, and capital resources, suppliers, and other factors as you did for competitor environs. Do you enjoy favor with your customers and why? Summarize your strengths and weaknesses as they apply to your project.

The Target Market

The target market is the next major section in your plan documentation. Describe exactly who your customers are and what, where, when, why, how, how much, and how frequently they buy. You may think that everyone is a candidate for your product or your service. In a sense this may be true, but some segments of the total market are far more likely candidates than others. If you attempt to serve them all, you cannot satisfy those that are most likely to buy as well as you should. Furthermore, you will dissipate your resources by trying to reach them all: for example, if you pick the most likely target market, you can devote the maximum amount of money to advertising your product or service in a message that your most likely customers can best understand. In fact the basic concept of strategy is to concentrate your resources at the decisive point. In marketing this point is the most important target market. You should also indicate why the target market you have selected is a better candidate for purchase than others. Also include the size of each market.

How will you define your target markets? First in terms of (1) demographics (i.e., such vital statistics as age, income, and education); (2) geographics (i.e., their location); (3) psychographics (i.e., how they think); and (4) life-style (i.e., their activities, interests, and opinions).

Knowing your customers is as important as knowing yourself (the company environs), your competitors (the competitor environs), and the other environs that you have analyzed.

Problems and Opportunities

The problems and opportunities section is really a summary that emphasizes the main points you have already covered in preceding sections. As you put your plan together, developed your situational analysis, and described your target market, you probably covered implicitly the problems and opportunities inherent in your situation. But here you should restate them explicitly and list them one by one, grouped first by opportunities, then by problems. Indicate why each is an opportunity or a problem. Also indicate how you intend to take advantage of each opportunity and what you intend to do about each problem. Many marketing planners do well in showing how they will take advantage of the opportunities, but they do not explain adequately what they will do about the problems. To get full benefit from your plan you must not only foresee the potential problems and opportunities but also decide what they mean to the actions you must take when your plan is implemented. Not only will this help you during implementation but it will impress those who will decide whether to allocate resources for your particular project. It will give you a decided edge over the others who are submitting plans but have not taken the time or trouble to consider the potential problems or opportunities that have been identified.

Marketing Objectives and Goals

Marketing objectives are those you intend to achieve with the help of your marketing plan. You have already prepared your reader on your earlier analysis of the target market. In this section you must spell out in detail exactly what you intend to accomplish in terms of overall sales, market share, return on investment, or any other goal that you consider important.

Two cautionary notes are in order. First, it is important that you document your objectives and goals precisely. It is not enough to say that you wish "to establish our product in the market." That is only the overall objective. You should also say, for example, that you intend to have 10 percent of the total market within a year. (Note how your goals more precisely describe your objective.) The second cautionary note is to ensure that your objectives or goals do not conflict; for example, your ability to capture a market share may be at odds with a per-unit profitability objective because the market share may be tied in with a lower price and a lower price will mean lower profitability on a per-unit basis. Therefore recheck your objectives and goals to avoid conflict.

Marketing Strategy

In this section you will want to describe what is to be done to reach your objectives and goals. Your strategy may be one of differentiating your product from that of its competitors, of segmenting your total market in preparation for attack, of positioning it in relation to other products, and carving out and defending a certain niche. Marketing strategy is a what-to-do section.

One important part of the marketing strategy section that is frequently left out and that you're *not* going to leave out, is what your main competitors are likely to do when you implement your planned strategy, and what you will do to take advantage of the opportunities created, solve potential problems, and avoid serious threats.

Marketing Tactics

Just as strategy tells you what you must do to reach your objectives, tactics tell you how you will carry out your strategy. In military terms strategy is what is done before arrival on the battlefield. What is done on the battlefield is tactics. You are going to list every action required to implement each of the strategies described in the preceding section and you are going to indicate the timing of these actions. These tactical actions are described in terms of what is called the marketing mix, strategic variables, or the *4 Ps* of marketing. Note that although they are known as *strategic variables,* these variables are really tactical. The 4 Ps are product, price, promotion, and place. We discuss them in detail in Chapter 6.

Implementation and Control

In the implementation and control section you are going to calculate the break-even point and forecast other important information to help control the project once it has been implemented. You are also going to compute sales projections and cash flow on a monthly basis for a three-year period and calculate start-up costs in a monthly budget. After implementation you can use this information to keep the project on track. Thus, if the budget is exceeded you will know where to cut back or to reallocate resources. If sales aren't what they should be, you will know where to turn your attention to realize an improvement.

Summary

In the summary you discuss advantages, costs, and profits and clearly state the differential advantage, once again, that your plan for this product or service offers the competition. The differential or competitive advantage is what you have that your competitors lack. Basically it says why your plan will succeed.

The summary completes your marketing plan outline. You now have a general idea of the information that is required. As you go through this book, forms will be provided to assist in completing every section of the marketing plan that we've talked about in this chapter. As you complete these forms you will automatically be completing your marketing plan.

Figure 2-2 is a sample marketing plan action development schedule that will assist you in planning to plan. Your schedule should be adjusted to your particular situation. It lists the actions that must be taken and shows you where to start and how long each action should take to complete. The horizontal bar begins when the action is to be

Weeks After Initiation

Task	1	2	3	4	5	6	7	8	9	10	11	12
Secondary research into demographics, situational factors				↑								
Market research regarding potential demand					↑							
Audit of competitors' and company environs						↑						
Investigation of neutral environs						↑						
Establishment of objective, goals, and overall strategy							↑					
Development and specification of tactics; additional marketing research as required										↑		
Development and calculation of implementation and control information											↑	
Writing and development of marketing plan document												↑

FIGURE 2-2. Sample marketing plan action development schedule.

Task	1	2	3	4	5	6	7	8	9	10	11	12

FIGURE 2-3. Blank marketing plan action development schedule.

initiated and is shaded when it is to be completed. An adjusted date is provided by a dashed line; thus as you proceed you can use the action schedule to adjust dates when certain information is not immediately forthcoming and the schedule must be modified. In this way you can develop and coordinate a planning process that fits you and your organization and any deadlines you might have for completing your plan. If more than one individual is working on the plan, their names can be written in the space provided to indicate who is responsible for every action. A blank development schedule is provided in Figure 2-3 for your use in planning to plan.

KEEPING YOUR MATERIAL ORGANIZED

It is very important to keep your material together to guard against loss and for updating as new data are received. A loose-leaf notebook is a helpful tool for these purposes. Each section can be marked off— executive summary, introduction, situational analysis, target market, problems and opportunities, marketing objectives and goals, marketing strategy, marketing tactics, control, and summary. As additional information is received in its rough form it can be added to the appropriate section. Place the blank form that is provided in this book in the front of each section. When all are filled out with the supporting material, you will have your marketing plan ready for implementation.

SUMMARY

In this chapter you have prepared yourself by planning to plan. You have examined the structure that will be used for developing your marketing plan, the information required in each of its sections, and the forms for its preparation. Finally, you have determined how to keep your material organized in a simple way by using a loose-leaf notebook.

3

THE SITUATIONAL ANALYSIS AND ENVIRONMENTAL SCANNING

In this chapter you are going to decide what information you need for the introductory and situational analysis sections of your marketing plan and where you can obtain this information.

THE INTRODUCTION

In the introduction you must state what the product or service is, describe it in detail, and note why there is demand for it in the marketplace. To do this accurately and completely you need information that goes beyond product or service attributes and benefits. Every product passes through a life cycle just as if it were a living thing. The classic product life cycle is shown in Figure 3-1. Note that its stages are introduction, growth, maturity, and decline. Note also that both sales and profits are plotted as a curve that changes shape from stage to stage. Because of this changing shape, you will want to know in what stage of the product life cycle your product or service occurs.

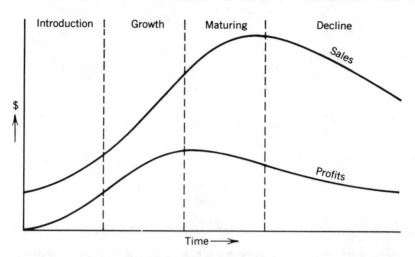

FIGURE 3-1. Classic product life cycle.

The shape of the curve will have important strategic implications which are discussed in Chapter 5. For now, notice that the sales and profit curves differ; for example, note that profits peak in the growth stage, whereas sales continue to rise and peak in the maturity stage.

Your first step is to decide whether your product is in the introductory, growth, maturity, or decline stage. If you have a product that has never been used by anyone before, perhaps something in genetic engineering, this product would be in the introductory stage. Perhaps your product is a new piece of peripheral computer equipment that might be in the growth stage of its product life cycle. This could be confirmed if the product had already been on the market for some time but sales are still growing. A product that has spent time in the marketplace and for which sales may still be growing but profits are not is probably in the maturity stage. A typical product might be music recorded on a cassette tape. Finally, your product or service may be in the decline stage; for example, a cigarette lighter might be said to be at the end of its product life cycle. It is usually unwise to introduce a new product that is approaching the end of its life. In certain circumstances, however, this might be a wise marketing move such as under circumstances where your new product would immediately capture most of the shrinking market. You should also examine complementary products, which are those that do not directly compete with your product but in some way comple-ment it or are used with it; for example, if your new product is a computer, a complementary product could be a computer disk, pe-ripheral equipment, or furniture built especially for computers. If your new product is a soft drink, complementary products could be the bottle, the bottle cap, or the package.

You should then investigate substitute products; that is, products that are substitutes for the product you are introducing. In many cases competing products that are direct substitutes for yours are already on the market. But if your product represents a technolog-ical breakthrough, you may have indirect competition from substi-tute products. When the Wright Brothers built the first airplane, no other airplanes existed. Therefore there was only indirect competi-tion from substitute products that consisted of other means of short-range transportation.

Now you are ready to describe your product or service: its size, weight, color, shape, the material of which it is made, its function, what it does, and its benefits to potential users.

THE SITUATIONAL ANALYSIS

The situational analysis is an extensive portion of the marketing plan and an important one, as noted in Chapter 2. On the basis of the situational analysis, you will develop an optimal strategy that you can use to reach your goals and objectives. To make a situational analysis you must answer questions about the environment you are facing. (See Figure 3-2.) Let's go over each element in this form individually.

Target Market

Under the target market section the first environmental question has to do with location. You will want to describe this location and its special climatic and geographical features. Is it a hot, humid envi-ronment? A cold, dry one? A desert? Mountainous area? Ocean front? Suburban? Urban? Or what? Every climatic or topographical feature should be noted.

Target Market

Geographical location _____

Special climate or topography _____

_____

Consumer buyers

Cultural, ethnic, religious, or racial groups _____

_____

_____

Social class(es) _____

Reference groups(s) _____

Basic demographics: Sex _____ Age range _____

Education _____ Income _____

Household size and description _____

_____

Stage of family life cycle _____

Family work status: Husband _____ Wife _____

Occupation (husband and wife) _____

Decision maker _____ Purchase agent _____

Risk perception: Functional _____ Psychological _____

Physical _____ Social _____ Financial _____

Income for each family member _____

Disposable income _____

FIGURE 3-2. Situational analysis: Environmental questions for the marketing plan. (Copyright © 1985 by Dr. William A. Cohen. Note: This form is based on an earlier form designed by Dr. Benny Barak, then, of Baruch College.)

Additional descriptions, classifications, and traits of target market _____

_____

_____

Target market wants and needs I. _____

2. _____ 3. _____

4. _____ 5. _____

Product general description _____

_____

Frequency of usage _____ Traits _____

_____

Marketing factor sensitivity _____

_____

_____

Size of target market _____

Growth trends _____

Media Habits

	Hours/Week	Category
Television	_____	_____
Radio	_____	_____
Magazines	_____	_____
Newspapers	_____	_____

FIGURE 3-2. continued

Industrial Buyers

Decision makers _____

_____

_____

_____

Primary motivation of each decision maker _____

_____

_____

_____

_____

Amount of money budgeted for purchase _____

_____

_____

Purchase history _____

_____

_____

_____

_____

Additional descriptions, classifications, and traits of target market _____

_____

_____

FIGURE 3-2. Continued

Target market wants and needs 1. _____

2. _____ 3. _____

4. _____ 5. _____

Product general description _____

_____

Frequency of usage _____ Traits _____

Marketing factor sensitivity _____

_____

_____

Size of target market _____

Growth trends _____

Media Habits

	Hours/Week	Category
Television	_____	_____
Radio	_____	_____
Magazines	_____	_____
Newspapers	_____	_____
	Number/year	
Trade shows	_____	_____
Conferences	_____	_____

FIGURE 3-2. Continued

Competition

Competitor	Products	Market Share	Strategy
_____	_____	_____	_____
	_____	_____	_____
	_____	_____	_____
	_____	_____	_____
_____	_____	_____	_____
	_____	_____	_____
	_____	_____	_____
	_____	_____	_____
_____	_____	_____	_____
	_____	_____	_____
	_____	_____	_____
	_____	_____	_____
_____	_____	_____	_____
	_____	_____	_____
	_____	_____	_____
	_____	_____	_____

Resources of the Firm

Strengths: 1. _____

2. _____

3. _____

4. _____

5. _____

FIGURE 3-2. Continued

Weaknesses: 1. _____

2. _____

3. _____

4. _____

5. _____

Technological Environment

_____

_____

_____

Economic Environment

_____

_____

_____

Political Environment

_____

_____

_____

Legal and Regulatory Environment

_____

_____

_____

FIGURE 3-2. Continued

Social and Cultural Environment

_____

_____

_____

Other Important Environmental Aspects

_____

_____

_____

_____

_____

Problems/Threats

1. _____

2. _____

3. _____

4. _____

5. _____

Opportunities

1. _____

2. _____

3. _____

4. _____

5. _____

FIGURE 3-2. Continued

Now the buyer can actually be categorized into consumers and industrial buyers. Industrial buyers use your product or service to produce some other product or service. An industrial buyer would include the U.S. government, plastics for a manufacturer, or light bulbs for a department store. Let's look at consumers first.

Cultural, Ethnic, Religious, and Racial Groups. It is important not only to note the groups that are potential targets for the product or service you are going to provide but also the size and characteristics of each. Years ago marketers thought that they could maximize their profits by mass marketing; that is, by selling the identical product to everyone. Extensive research and experimentation discovered that it was far more profitable to segment the market according to certain common characteristics and to concentrate on marketing to particular segments. This is consistent with the marketing concept of focusing on the customers rather than on the product. By focusing on certain characteristics you can satisfy the needs; for example, it would be difficult to succeed as a marketer by selling food products that consisted mainly of pork to Jewish or Moslem groups. Certain ethnic groups prefer certain types of product. Have you ever heard of peanut butter soup? In West Africa it is a delicacy. Orientals eat tofu or fermented soybean extract, and sushi (raw fish) is popular fare in Japan. Some Chinese groups drink soybean milk, whereas goat's milk or cow's milk may be the choice in other regions. In all areas these preferences are important and can spell the difference between success or failure. Cultural, ethnic, religious, and racial segmentation of the market is only the tip of the iceberg. As you will see, there are many other ways to segment—all of which may help you to satisfy your potential customers and make your product or service a success.

Social Classes. The next environmental question has to do with social classes. The basic divisions are upper, middle, and lower, but you can categorize them more precisely as lower-lower, upper-lower, lower-middle, upper-middle, and upper class. Social classes are important as segments because people behave differently even though, in some cases, their income levels may be the same. Years ago a survey was conducted of three social groups, all making the identical incomes. At the upper end were young attorneys just graduating from law school. What money they had was invested in homes in prestigious neighborhoods. Large homes in a prestigious neighborhood cannot be found for a modest amount. Therefore they tended to be very small homes. Next, the researcher called on owners of small businesses (e.g., grocery stores) who made the same amount of money as the young attorneys. But do you think the same kind of home was purchased? Not at all. These businessmen bought much larger homes but in a neighborhood that was not quite as prestigious. Finally, the researcher examined groups in the lower class. Certain workers had been employed for years by large companies and were making the same salaries as businessmen and lawyers. For this group, however, a home was not an important consideration at all. It might be small and unpretentious in a less affluent neighborhood, but what was important were other items like the automobile and television set. Both were more expensive than those purchased by the attorneys or the businessmen. If this research were conducted today, however, the findings might be different. Yet some kind of variation in buyer behavior among the social classes is still likely. Therefore this segmentation is important and the identification of the segments, which may constitute your target market, is required.

Reference Groups. Reference groups are those you turn to for information. They are especially important in the case of an information blackout. Let's say that you are a member of a trade association that recommends a certain product. When other information is scarce or unavailable, this recommendation can be extremely influential in persuading others to use a product. A reference group can also be a small number of trusted friends. Thus it is unimportant whether the reference group is large or small—only that you look to it for advice in making purchase decisions.

Demographics. The situational analysis question form now asks you to investigate certain fundamental attributes of your potential customers known as demographics. Of what sex is your target market? Are you trying to sell to both male and female or male or female only? What is the primary age range? What education do your prospects enjoy? Most products appeal primarily to certain demographic segments that can be defined by answering these questions. If your product is an encyclopedia, would it appeal primarily to college or noncollege graduates? In most cases the answer would probably be college graduates. Similarly, certain other types of product or service appeal to individuals with certain levels of education. Look at income. How much money is your prospect making? Can you sell a Rolls-Royce to someone whose annual income is less than $10,000 a year? Unless there is independent wealth, probably not.

Household size is also important. How many people are in the household? Is it headed by a single parent? Male or female? Guardians? How many children are in the family and what are their ages? Like a product, a family has also been described as having a life cycle, but the descriptive terms are different from those of the product life cycle. The family life cycle has been divided in nine stages:

1. The bachelor not living with parents
2. A newly married couple; young with no children
3. A full nest; the youngest child under six
4. A full nest; the youngest child six or older
5. A full nest; an older married couple with dependent children
6. An empty nest; no children at home; head of family in the labor force
7. An empty nest; family head retired
8. A solitary survivor in the labor force
9. A solitary survivor retired

Family Work Status and Occupations. If husband and wife are employed, both occupations should be listed. Also note whether one or both are retired or on welfare.

Decision Maker and Purchase Agent. Note the spaces on the form for the decision maker and the purchase agent. The decision maker is the one who actually decides to buy the product; the purchase agent buys it. Thus a husband may prefer a certain brand of beer but it may be his wife who actually buys this brand. In business-to-business sales a buyer may purchase a certain type of stationery but it may have been the office manager who decided what to buy. Consider also those who have influence on the decision maker and purchase agent. Children are subjected to a considerable amount of television advertising for many products such as toys and breakfast cereals. But children may act neither as decision maker nor purchase agent. Still their influence on other family members is so great that the advertising millions invested in reaching them is considered well spent.

Company demographics such as annual sales and number of employees also provide information that contributes to a precise identification of the market.

Risk Perception. Risk perception concerns the chance taken in buying a product, and certainly any new product has a certain amount associated with it that the buyer must accept. Functional risk refers to its dependability; that is, whether it will work. The psychological risks refer to the possibility that the buyer may be disappointed or feel cheated or in some other way be affected if the product proves to be less than expected. Physical risk has to do with damage to the user. Social risk is the one taken if the buyer feels open to ostracism or ridicule for using the product or service. Finally, there is financial risk, the risk of money lost in buying a product that may be undesirable. In all cases note that the risk is a perceived one and may or may not actually exist. An outstanding product may be considered by the potential buyer as a high risk and a less worthy product perceived as a low risk.

Income for Each Family Member. In this section of the form additional income that may come from other members of the family is documented. This income may be important because the total may alter drastically what your prospect can afford and is therefore, likely to buy.

Disposable Income. Disposable income is the amount left over after the bills for basic necessities such as food and shelter have been paid. Money left over is disposable income; for example, for entertainment, a vacation, or luxuries like expensive clothes. Disposable income will vary, depending on geographical, cultural, ethnic, religious, or racial considerations.

Additional Descriptions, Classifications, and Traits of the Target Market. This space in the form allows you to describe further your potential buyers in any terms that have been omitted here and that are peculiar to the particular market you are targeting.

Target Market Wants and Needs. Wants and needs are both important. Although a need (such as food) is stronger than a want, most people are in the business of satisfying wants rather than needs. Satisfying both can be profitable if it can be done efficiently. An important illustration of wants and needs comes from Professor Maslow at the University of Chicago. His theory of human motivation involves a hierarchy of needs, beginning with basic physiological needs and progressing successively to safety or security, the need for love, for esteem or self-respect, and self-actualization. Also at a high level, but not fitting with the others, are two more classes: aesthetic needs and the need to know and understand. There might be some overlap between them but Professor Maslow's basic theory is that if one need is satisfied, the next higher need must also be satisfied, and so on. To understand the value of these needs as a motivator in buying and its progression from one level to the next, consider the very lowest—a physiological need like breathing. If someone suddenly began to choke you and you could no longer breathe, your interest in anything else, including purchasing a product no matter how attractive, would immediately have ceased. Your immediate need would have been for oxygen! But once you had regained the ability to breathe, you might then have been interested in the next level—safety or security. Again, would you really be interested in buying an automobile if you didn't know where your next meal was coming from? So we can see how needs are important to the motivation of customers to buy the products or services offered to them. No matter how good our product or service is, if some other major lower level need of your potential customers has not been satisfied, they may not be interested. In this section of the situational analysis form (Figure 3-2) you must identify specific target wants and needs that you intend to satisfy with the product or service you offer.

Product Description. The general description here is really an abbreviated version of the more detailed material given in the introduction to the marketing plan—with certain additional items noted. First, frequency of use; how frequently will the customer use your product or service? Also, its traits; what are the main traits or attributes of your product or service? They may include price, size, quality, packaging, and service. Finally you will want to rank the market factor sensitivity; that is, how sensitive are your customers to the traits of your product or service, from the most important to the least?

Size of the Target Market. Here the total potential of the target market segments that you're going after is stated. How large is each segment? Precise figures are called for.

Growth Trends. Growth trends describe what is happening to your target market. Is it growing? Is it declining? Has it leveled off? Profits can be made under each of these conditions but each will call for different marketing actions; therefore it is important to know where you are.

Media Habits

Media habits is a major classification on the form. It is significant because if you know the habits of your prospects, whether they are individual consumers or business or professional people, you will understand how to reach your target market most effectively. The basic media to be considered are television, radio, newspapers, and magazines. It would be helpful to know how many hours a week are devoted to each category by your prospective customers.

Industrial Buyers

For industrial buyers you must consider first the decision makers. Sometimes these decision makers will include engineers and their supervisors, purchase agents, and test and quality assurance groups, each of whom will have different motivations. The primary motivation of each decision maker involved in a purchase should be determined and noted on the form.

The Amount of Money Available or Budgeted for the Purchase. It is important to obtain an estimate of the amount of money available for the particular purchase for which the marketing plan is being developed. This is necessary because significant differences in the amount charged lessen the chances of success in marketing the product and at the very least must be explained; for example, if a group is accustomed to paying $25 per unit in quantities of 1000 a year, $25,000 will have been budgeted. If a greater amount is to be charged, the decision makers are going to ask why because an increase in the budget will be required. Even a lower price must be explained lest it be viewed as representing a change to a lower quality.

Purchase History. The purchase history of the same or similar products will reveal buying patterns relating to the time of year in which the product was purchased and the quantities ordered.

Additional Industrial Buyer Information. Additional industrial buyer information is similar to that of consumer buyer information, as indicated on the form; the exception is media information about trade-show and conference attendance.

Competition

Competition is a critical element because it is an intelligent environmental factor that will definitely act against you in many circumstances, especially when you are targeting a stagnant or even declining market. Therefore the more you know about your competition, the better. You should study your competitors, the products they are offering, the share of the market they control, and the strategies they are following. All of this information can be used as you plan your optimal strategy that will help you to win out by giving your market better service.

Resources of the Firm

Resources of the firm should be indicated in terms of strengths and weaknesses. No organization is strong in every way. Perhaps you are strong technically, like many firms in the Silicon Valley, or perhaps you have a lot of marketing know-how or financial resources. What you have a lot of and excel in are your strengths, which may be in the form of money, capital goods, buildings, machinery, contacts with customers, or simply good old-fashioned know-how. At the same time, those resources you lack become your weaknesses, and you must be careful to note what they are.

Technological Environment

The technological environment is the technological situation you are facing. Sometimes technology changes and expands rapidly; for example, in a single year in the early seventies hand-held calculators declined in price by more than 80 percent, whereas their beneficial features actually increased. The technological environment may not be relevant to your particular situation. If it is relevant, write down exactly what the situation is.

Economic Environment

The economic environment involves the economy and business conditions that you will face as you enter the proposed market. It is true that fortunes can be made in recessions and depressions, during inflations, and in periods of economic well-being. However, the products and services with which you are most likely to be successful in these economic conditions are varied. Therefore an analysis of the economic and business conditions that you are likely to encounter would be well worth the time.

Political Environment

The political environment must be examined because of the potential effect that politics may have on your project. There are certain countries to which the U.S. government will not permit you to export, just as there are certain products from certain countries that cannot be imported. In recent months Japanese imports and illegal sales of military equipment to Iran have been in the news. They clearly affect marketing of certain products, and few marketers can ignore the political environment with impunity.

Legal and Regulatory Environment

The legal and regulatory environment is always critical. One small company invested more than $100,000 in its development of a new police helmet, which was thought to be somewhat bullet-protective before it discovered that because of product liability and other laws and regulations the product could not be sold at a profit. An entrepreneur invested thousands of dollars in a new wine cooler on the assumption that the alcoholic beverage tax would be the same whether or not he used another firm's wine to mix with his fruit juice. It wasn't and the difference in tax made his product unprofitable. Be forewarned. Note the impact of this environment before you invest.

Social and Cultural Environment

Fifty years ago wearing a bikini on a public beach would have been cause for arrest. Sushi or raw fish has been a popular product in Japan for hundreds of years. Yet only a few years ago sushi bars probably would have been unsuccessful in the United States. Today, sushi has become extremely popular. Timing of your entry into a market may be the dominant factor and it is therefore necessary to define the social and cultural environment for your product or service at the time of planned introduction.

Other Important Environmental Aspects

In this section other important environmental aspects that are peculiar to your product or service should be listed and analyzed.

Problems and Opportunities

The problems and opportunities section of the form is really a summary of all that has gone before. You should review the entire environmental situation and list every problem and opportunity that you can anticipate. Naturally there may be more or less than five problems and five opportunities, so don't be restricted simply because the form allows space only for that number.

Many marketing planners who have no trouble recognizing their opportunities hesitate to discuss their problems. This is a mistake. First, it is important to identify the problems clearly to give yourself the opportunity to avoid them once you have begun to develop your strategy. Second, if you have failed to include them and have listed only your opportunities, readers of your plan will suspect that you left them out intentionally or were not smart enough to acknowledge them. They would be more impressed if you described how you proposed to overcome them.

SOURCES OF INFORMATION FOR COMPLETING THE ENVIRONMENTAL QUESTIONS FORM

To answer environmental questions you must do a great deal of research. It can be primary or secondary. Primary research entails interviews, business surveys, and a personal search for the answers. In secondary research you consult other sources. Secondary research is generally preferable because it is already available. It should be examined before you spend the time and money to do primary research. What are some secondary research sources?

1. *Chambers of Commerce.* Chambers of Commerce have all sorts of demographic information about geographical areas in which you may be interested, including income, education, businesses and their size, and sales volume.

2. *Trade Associations.* Trade associations also have information regarding the background of their members and their industries.

3. *Trade Magazines and Journals.* Trade journals and magazines frequently survey their readership. They also contain articles of in-

terest to you that describe competitive companies, products, strategies, and markets.

4. *The Small Business Administration.* The U.S. Small Business Administration was set up to help small business. Whether you own a small business or are a marketing planner in a large company, the studies sponsored can be extremely valuable to anyone doing research in the situational analysis of a marketing plan. The many printed aids supplied include statistics, maps, national market analyses, national directories for use in marketing, basic library reference sources, information on various types of business, including industry average investments and cost, and factors to consider in locating a shopping center.

5. *Data Bases.* Data bases are electronic collections of relevant data based on trade journals, newspapers, and many other public or private sources of information. They are accessed by computer and companies sell the computer time to search the data bases they have available.

6. *Earlier Studies.* Earlier marketing studies are sometimes made available to interested companies or individuals. These studies may have cost $40,000 or more when done as primary research. As a consequence, their results are not sold cheaply, although in effect you are sharing the cost with other companies that purchase the results with you. Several thousand dollars for a short report is not atypical. Nevertheless, if the alternative is to do the entire primary research project yourself, it may be far cheaper to pay the price.

7. *The U.S. Industrial Outlook.* Every year the U.S. government publishes a document known as the *U.S. Industrial Outlook,* which contains detailed information on the prospects of more than 350 manufacturing and service industries.

8. *The Statistical Abstract of the United States.* This abstract is also an annual publication of the U.S. government. It contains a wealth of detailed statistical data having to do with everything from health to food consumption, to population, public school finances, individual income tax returns, mortgage debt, science and engineering, student

numbers, and motor vehicle travel. It is published by the U.S. Department of Commerce, Bureau of the Census.

9. *The U.S. Department of Commerce.* If you are interested in export, the U.S. Department of Commerce has numerous sources of information, including amounts exported to foreign countries in the preceding year, major consumers of certain items, and detailed information on doing business in countries around the world. You can find the office of your local U.S. Department of Commerce listed under U.S. government in your telephone book.

10. *The U.S. Government in General.* The U.S. government has so many sources of information that it is impossible to list them all here. But so much information is available, and so much of it is free, that you would be well advised to see what can be obtained from federal government sources. One recommended source that will give you access to this information is *Information U.S.A.* by Matthew Lesko (Viking, 1983). Another excellent source is the *Entrepreneur and Small Business Problem-Solver* by William A. Cohen (Wiley, 1983). An additional listing of secondary-source information is contained in Appendix B of this book.

PRIMARY RESEARCH

In some cases you must do primary research yourself. It is best to minimize the cost as much as possible by thorough planning. Three basic methods of gathering primary data are face-to-face interviewing and mail and telephone surveying. Each has its advantages and disadvantages; for example, in face-to-face interviewing more detailed information can usually be obtained and the interviewer can use verbal feedback and read body language or facial expressions to probe for answers. But face-to-face interviewing can be costly in time and money. Mail surveys are perhaps the quickest but most impersonal method. Their disadvantages are low return rate and lack of feedback. The telephone is an excellent means of surveying the country in the shortest time. Telephone calls, however, can also be expensive and will provide no visual feedback to your questions.

SUMMARY

In this chapter we explored the environmental questions, the answers to which are necessary to complete the situational analysis of your marketing plan. We have also recorded some of the sources of this information. The information will not be available by the time the marketing planning must be done, in which case you must make the best assumptions possible, based on the information you have already acquired. It is important, however, to state clearly the assumptions that have been made to prevent others from accepting them as completely factual.

Having done the research and situational analysis required and knowing what your product or service is facing in the marketplace, you are now ready to establish goals and objectives.

4

ESTABLISHING GOALS AND OBJECTIVES

"Would you tell me, please, which way I ought to go from here?" asked Alice.
"That depends a good deal on where you want to get to," said the cat.
"I don't much care where," said Alice.
"Then it doesn't matter which way you go," said the cat.
Lewis Carroll, Alice's Adventures in Wonderland

You can't get *there* unless you know where *there* is. This chapter deals with establishing goals and objectives. Without them, you haven't got a marketing plan—you have a collection of facts and unrelated ideas.

ESTABLISHING OBJECTIVES

Your objectives answer the question: What are you trying to achieve? The following objectives are typical:

To establish a product, product line, or brand in the marketplace

To rejuvenate a failing product

To entrench and protect a market under attack by competitors

To introduce a new product

To harvest a product that is in the declining stage of its life cycle

To introduce a locally successful product nationally or overseas

To achieve maximum return on investment with a product or product line

Normally, the statement of the objective should focus on a single task but it is possible to have more than one objective or to specify additional conditions as long as they do not conflict with each other; for example, if your objective is to introduce a new product, you might add: "To dominate the market while achieving maximum sales."

In the same vein your objective might be worded: "To rejuvenate a failing product while maintaining high profitability and with minimum investment."

But in establishing more than one objective, or a main objective with additional conditions, care must be taken that the objectives do not conflict. It may be desirable to maximize the market share that you have been able to capture for a new product and at the same time achieve maximum profitability, but the two may not be achievable simultaneously. Capturing a maximum market share may require a penetration pricing strategy, and the low price and lower margins may result in something far less than maximum profitability. In fact, you may be lucky to reach a break-even point. Therefore, when you establish your objectives and you add conditions to them, be certain that there is no conflict and that achievement of one will not make it impossible to achieve another.

You should spend some time making sure that your statement is worded as precisely and correctly as possible and that all important conditions have been incorporated. Even after you have finished with it, however, it will not be complete until you have specified a time by which the objective must be achieved. Ask yourself the question, "By what time?" for every objective that you establish. Let's say that you want to introduce a new product, dominate the market, and build maximum sales. "By what time?" Three months? Six months?

Nine months? A year? Longer than that? If one of your objectives is to harvest a product that is in the decline stage of its product life cycle, how much time will you have? If you are going to introduce a nationally successful product overseas, how long will it take before this introduction can be said to have been made?

Psychologists, time management experts, business researchers, and practitioners all tell us that recording a time frame is extremely important. It will give you a target on which to focus and guide that will tell you whether you're on schedule. Most important, it provides a date toward which everyone concerned with the marketing plan can aim. In 1960 John Kennedy set an objective for the United States. He said, "We're going to have a man on the moon by 1970." Note that he didn't just say, "We're going to put a man on the moon sometime." He said, "We're going to put a man on the moon by 1970." In actuality this goal was achieved in 1969. The fact that President Kennedy specified a date played no small part in this early achievement.

Professor George A. Steiner, a man famed for his expertise in strategic planning, recommends 10 criteria to help in developing objectives. Use them as guidelines to ensure that your objectives, whatever they are, will benefit the firm's overall mission:

Suitability. Your objectives must support the enterprise's basic purposes and help to move the company in that direction.

Measurability Over Time. Objectives should state clearly what is expected to happen and when so that you can measure them as you proceed.

Feasibility. Your objectives must be feasible. If they cannot be fulfilled, they motivate no one. Be certain that they are realistic and practical even if they are not easy and require considerable effort.

Acceptability. The objectives you set must be acceptable to the people in your organization or to those who may allocate resources to implement your marketing plan. If your objectives are not acceptable, you will not receive the necessary funds. If someone besides yourself is working on the marketing plan and the objectives are not acceptable, you cannot expect to receive the same cooperation.

Flexibility. Your objectives should be modifiable in the event of unforeseen contingencies and environmental changes. This does not mean that they should not be fixed, only that, if necessary, they can be adapted to environmental changes.

Motivation. Objectives should motivate those who must work to reach them. If your objectives are too easy or so difficult that they are impossible to achieve, they will not be motivating. It does help, however, to have difficult but achievable, precisely defined objectives to challenge those who work to reach them.

Understandability. Your objectives should be stated in clear, simple language that can be understood by all. If they are not clear, they may be misunderstood and some individuals may unintentionally be working against them. You may also alienate those who allocate resources and capital. In fact, your plan may be stopped midway through execution simply because your objectives were not clear to everyone.

Commitment. When objectives are set, especially by more than one person, it must be made certain that everyone working on the development, planning, selling, and execution of the marketing plan is committed to those objectives.

People Participation. Professor Steiner points out that the best results are obtained when those who are responsible for achieving the objectives take some part in setting them. Thus it's important to consult with all who might participate in any way with the execution of the plan. If other staff members are committed to your objectives from the start, you will have much less trouble keeping them on track throughout the implementation of your plan.

Linkage. Naturally the objectives should be linked with the basic purposes of your organization, but they must also be linked with the objectives of other collateral organizations in your firm. They must be consistent with and meet top management objectives. It's no good, for example, to set objectives which involve high sales if this runs counter to top management's overall phi-

losophy at the time of securing market share. Therefore, ensure that the objectives you set are linked to other aspects within
and without your organization which may be important.[1]

After you have decided on the time frame for achieving your objectives, indicate it on the form in Figure 4-1.

GOALS

Goals are the specifics of the objectives. Let's look at one of them
again: "Introduce a new product and dominate the market while
achieving maximum sales." Time to achieve: one year.

Now the question is: Does *introduction* mean to distribute it among
500 major retail outlets or at only one? Is maximum sales $100,000
in six months and then $1 million in one year? What are the figures
that demonstrate introduction? What exactly do the words in your
objectives mean? How about *dominating* the market? Is dominating
the market having a market share of 100, 90, or 50 percent? When
the market is fragmented, you may dominate the market by taking
a 25 percent share (or less). Note that objectives can be broken down
into smaller intermediate units within the overall time period specified. These shorter term objectives are also goals. Thus maximum
sales may be defined at the end of the period indicated (one year) as
well as at shorter intervals, say six months. The same can be done to
define *dominating the market.*

Let's look at another example: "Rejuvenate a failing product with
minimum investment while maintaining high profitability."

First, what does *rejuvenate* mean? In this case let's say that it means
increasing sales by 30 percent over the preceding year. How about
minimum investment? Let's say that your minimum investment is
$100,000. And *high profitability?* Well, profitability usually has to do
with the margin; that is, your costs compared with the selling price
that was set. Let's say that the definition of high profitability is a
margin of 60 percent.

---

[1] George A. Steiner. *Strategic Planning.* New York: Free Press, 1979, pp. 164–168.

Objectives	Time to achieve
1. _____	_____
2 _____	_____
3. _____	_____
4. _____	_____
5. _____	_____

Goals	Time to achieve
1. _____	_____
2. _____	_____
3. _____	_____
4. _____	_____
5. _____	_____

Statement of differential advantage:

_____

_____

_____

_____

_____

_____

_____

FIGURE 4-1. Objectives, goals, differential advantage statement. (Copyright © 1985 by Dr. William A. Cohen.)

Again, you must consider the time for achieving these goals. You may want to indicate quarterly sales increases over the preceding year with a total sales increase of 30 percent at the end of the coming year. Both final and the intermediate figures are goals.

You can now complete the goals section in Figure 4-1. Specifying your goals and writing them down has a sound psychological basis. It allows you to concentrate your efforts on achieving what is really important in order to obtain the objectives that were set earlier.

Specificity also affects vision. Vision has to do with the future as the leader or manager sees the outcome of the project. Warren Bennis and Burt Nanus, both of the University of Southern California, completed a major study of leaders and strategies for taking charge in a variety of situations and organizations, which they discuss in their book *Leaders* (Harper & Row, 1985). One of the things they discovered was that groups were far more likely to follow leaders and were much more enthusiastic about doing so when the leaders set specific objectives and goals.

Finally, when goals and objectives are made specific, it is much easier to avoid conflict between individuals and groups that must assist in carrying out the tasks to reach them. Furthermore, because the target has been identified, not only is conflict avoided but, with good leadership, individuals will work together to coordinate their efforts in a synergistic way far more effective than if their actions were simply to achieve movement in a general direction toward a less specific goal.

THE CONCEPT OF COMPETITIVE OR DIFFERENTIAL ADVANTAGE

In all cases you must direct your efforts toward satisfying the customer and toward achieving a competitive or differential advantage over our competitors. Thus organizations that produce and market similar or identical products or services are continually competing to improve their services. As they get better and better at what they do, the customer wins by getting better products at lower prices. It is extremely important that in your marketing plan you think about, develop, and promote this differential advantage that you have over actual and potential competitors. If you have no competitive advantage you cannot win. After all, regardless of your goals or objectives—whether you are seeking to introduce a new product into the marketplace or rejuvenate an old product—why should your customers help you by buying your product if it is identical to a competitor's product with which they are already satisfied? Therefore the key question is, "Why should anyone buy from us as opposed to one or more of our competitors?"

Although your objectives and goals focus on what *you* want, the differential competitive advantage must eventually focus in an advantage for the customer. You must think this through to determine how the two are linked—the competitive advantage that you see and the eventual benefit that the customer receives because of it; for example, over the last 15 years Japanese cars have been seen as a benefit to the customer termed as "quality at an affordable price." This quality was made possible, perhaps, by a combination of the Japanese work ethic and low-cost labor. Assuming this to be correct, the Japanese work ethic, or at least its application in building cars, and the labor rate could be considered as competitive disadvantages to American automobile manufacturers. This is not to say that American manufacturers may not also have competitive differential advantages that will eventually result in benefits to customers that may exceed those currently offered by Japanese companies. As a matter of fact, that is exactly what American manufacturers have been doing in recent years—capitalizing on their own differential advantages. The point to be recognized here is the linkage between the competitive differential advantage and benefits to the customer and that it may develop from a variety of situations.

A competitive differential advantage could be the ability to buy in quantity from special sources not enjoyed by others. The resulting benefit to the customer: low price. You may have a great number of PhDs in your research and development department; The resulting benefit to the customer: state-of-the-art technology. You may have a restaurant for which you have employed the best chef in your entire geographical area. The resulting benefit to the customer: the best gourmet food. Knowledge can also be a competitive differential advantage that will result in customer benefits; for example, marketing know-how translates into better satisfied customer needs.

Many attributes that apply to objectives and goals must also apply to differential advantages. Make sure that the competitive advantage you are going to work with has the following characteristics:

It must be real. Wishes will not make it so. Some retail stores claim that their prices are lower than those of all their competitors. Sometimes even a cursory inspection will prove this to be untrue or that they are lower only in certain circumstances. Thus their advantage will not be translated into a benefit for the customer.

It must be important to the customer. Note that I say to the customer and not to you. A good friend of mine, Freeman Gosden, Jr., who is president of Smith/Hemmings/Gosden, the largest direct-response agency on the West Coast and a division of the major advertising agency of Foote, Cone, Belding, says, "It's not what you want to sell, but what your customer wants to buy." This principle is directly applicable to the competitive advantage. It's not the competitive advantage that you seek but rather the benefits as the customer sees them. A major supplier of U.S. Air Force helmets once thought about getting into the motorcycle helmet market. As this company saw it, it could make a better protective motorcycle helmet than its competitors because of its experience with pilot helmets. This it did. These more protective helmets, however, were priced at approximately 30 percent more than the preceding top-of-the-line motorcycle helmets. This pricing was not arbitrary, merely based on higher manufacturing costs. If that was not enough, this expensive helmet was 15 percent heavier than competitive models, despite all of which the company felt it had a competitive edge because of the greater protection. Within a year this manufacturer had acquired this wisdom for half a million dollars when the product failed in the marketplace. When the perception of competitive differential advantage varies between supplier and customer, the customer always wins.

Lee Iacocca says that in 1956, when he was employed by the Ford Motor Company, Ford decided that safety was of primary interest to the consumer and emphasized it in all the advertising of its 1956 models. Ford's sales plummeted and the competition won on all fronts. Quickly realizing that he lacked a competitive differential advantage, Iacocca hit on what was really the main issue—ability to purchase. The year 1956 was one of mild recession. Therefore Iacocca instituted a policy in his district by which customers could purchase new cars for only $20 down and $56 a month. This made it easier to buy Fords than competitive cars. Iacocca hit on the correct differential advantage, as perceived by his potential customers, and his district soon went from last place to first in sales.[2]

Must be specific. Whatever the competitive differential advantage is, it must be specific, just as objectives and goals must be specific. It is not enough to say, "We're the best." The question is, the best what? And why? To the customer nonspecificity translates into mere puffery and is not a competitive differential advantage.

Must be promotable. Whatever the competitive differential advantage is, it must be promotable to the customer. The Edsel was a great failure in the marketplace and is frequently cited as a prime example of poor marketing. Yet Ford did extensive market research to determine what the customer wanted before introducing the Edsel line. This research indicated that power was an important competitive differential advantage. The Edsel was designed to be one of the most powerful cars, ever built, for the price. Unfortunately in the same year that the Edsel was introduced a new government regulation limited automobile advertisers from promoting the high horsepower of engines. As a result this competitive differential advantage, although it existed and may have been desired by the customer, could not be promoted by advertising. If you are planning on a specific differential advantage, it is essential that your customer know it; otherwise it might as well not exist.

Now return to Figure 4-1 and enter your statement of differential advantage in the space provided on the form. What is it that you have that others haven't and how does it translate into benefits to your potential customers?

[2] Lee Iacocca. *Iacocca.* New York: Bantam, 1984, p. 39.

SUMMARY

In this chapter we have examined objectives and goals—objectives being what you are trying to achieve and goals, the specifics of your objectives. In both cases it is very important to indicate the time frame within which these objectives and goals should fall. Remember, there is a sound psychological basis for both specificity and time frame that will help you to organize your efforts. Although your objectives and goals are what you want—as the supplier of the product or service—and that's fine, you must also be aware of what is wanted by your potential customers. Thus you must build and emphasize a competitive differential advantage, something unique that you will have but your competition will not. Otherwise your customers won't buy. Finally the competitive differential advantage must translate into benefits and satisfaction perceived by your customers, not by yourself. If you can provide these three things correctly, you will be well on your way to achieving what you intend in your marketing plan and be ready to develop strategy and tactics to reach your objectives and goals and to demonstrate your competitive advantage.

5

DEVELOPING MARKETING STRATEGY

The word *strategy* stems from the Greek *strategos,* which means the art of the general. In fact, many of the concepts that we use in marketing strategy evolved from early use in military strategy. The very top level of strategy is frequently called grand strategy and it entails many other elements besides that of military force, including economic power and diplomacy. At the next level down is military strategy itself. Military strategy involves all actions taken by military forces up to the point of reaching the battlefield. Finally, according to the military concept of strategy, we have tactics. Tactics are those actions taken on the battlefield once combat has been enjoined. In all cases there are objectives—national objectives achieved by grand strategy, military objectives achieved by military strategy, and operational objectives on the battlefield, the product of tactics.

THE STRATEGY PYRAMID

A similar concept of strategy can be observed in marketing, in what I call the strategic pyramid (See Figure 5-1). At the very highest level

FIGURE 5-1. The strategic pyramid.

of the pyramid is strategic marketing management which seeks to achieve those objectives set by a firm for the entire organization. What businesses, product lines, or products to pursue or drop would be a decision made at the top levels of the company.

One level down would be marketing strategy, the strategy you would follow to implement what you had decided to do in strategic marketing management; for example, let us say that at the corporate or top organizational level a decision had been made to exploit the capability that your company has for manufacturing certain types of product. This would be a decision for the strategic marketing management. Moving one level down to the marketing strategy level, how might this be accomplished? Penetrating new markets might be one way. Expanding the share of the market that you already have for this product might be another. If you selected the option for new market penetration, you might consider a niche strategy or a vertical versus horizontal strategy and an entry strategy of being first, early, or late in the market. If you decide on a strategy of market share expansion, you might choose product differentiation versus market segmentation and a limited share expansion versus a general share expansion.

The lowest level in your strategic pyramid is marketing tactics, the actions that you take to implement the marketing strategy decided on at the preceding level. To do this you manipulate certain marketing variables having to do with the product, price, promotion, and distribution. Let us say, for example, that the marketing strategy you have decided on is market share expansion and, specifically, you have decided to concentrate your resources on only a specific segment of the market. This may involve optimizing your product for that market and would be a product tactic. It may involve a certain price, higher or lower than what is currently being asked, to satisfy this specific segment. It may involve advertising—a part of promotion—in certain media, and it could involve certain distribution channels. Because resources are always limited, you usually cannot do all of these; therefore you allocate your resources, including your money, time, personnel, facilities, capital goods, and equipment, where they can have the most effect. The resulting tactical mix, known as a marketing mix, is what finally implements the decision that started at the very top of the corporate ladder.

Now let's look at the details of making these strategy decisions.

STRATEGIC MARKETING MANAGEMENT

To make the decisions that are necessary for developing strategy at the level of strategic marketing management and then, ultimately, to incorporate them into your marketing plan you will need a structured method of controlling the overall situation that faces the highest level of organization. Two different devices will be needed. Both concern products, product lines, or product-line groups. The first is a four-cell matrix that represents business strength and market attractiveness in which you will locate products, product groups, or product lines. The second structure is a product life cycle that shows the business, product line, or product grouping in one of four phases—introduction, growth, maturity, or decline. Let's look at the four-cell matrix first.

The Four-Cell Matrix for Decision Making in Strategic Marketing Management

The first step in using the four-cell matrix is to decide whether you are going to work with individual products, product lines, product line groups, or even an entire business. If you have only a few products, you will plot their individual product positions in the matrix. If you have more products that can be delineated and categorized into various product lines, these lines can be used as your unit for plotting. If, however, you are employed by a large manufacturer of many products and product lines, special groups must be made. The idea is to form a group with a distinct focus for which a strategic plan can be developed. Whether a single product, product line, or group of products or product lines, they are called strategic product units (SPUs). The objective in establishing SPUs is to avoid having to analyze and develop separate marketing plans for products that can and should be grouped and analyzed together. Therefore look for similarities in customers served, product lines under a single manager, or products having identical competitors. Once you have your SPUs established you must calculate the values of the SPUs for both business strength and market attractiveness.

Calculation of SPU Value for Business Strength. The first step in calculating the SPU value for business strength is to list the criteria important to the SPU being analyzed; for example, typical business strength criteria that may be relevant include current market share, SPU growth rate, sales effectiveness, the proprietary nature of product, price competitiveness, advertising or promotion effectiveness, facilities' location or newness, productivity, experienced curve effects, value added, raw materials cost, image, product quality, technological advantages, engineering know-how, personnel resources, product synergies, profitability, return on investment, and distribution. The question is, which of these is relevant to you in your situation?

Once you've established which criteria of business strengths are relevant, establish relative importance weightings. These weightings must total unity, or 1.00. Let's consider a simple example. Let's say that only four business strength criteria are considered important to you. You will say that these are engineering know-how, size of your organization, organizational image, and productivity. Now, the question is, what is the relative importance of each of these four business strength criteria? You'll make the assumption, after some thought, that you feel that the most important is engineering know-how and that it is worth 40 percent of the total importance assigned. Next in importance is organizational image, worth 30 percent. You'll say that the size of your organization and productivity are worth 15 percent for each. The addition of 40, 30, 15, and 15 percent equals unity, or 100 percent. These weightings will be used to rate all of your products, or SPUs, on a point assignment system: (1) very weak; (2) weak; (3) fair; (4) strong; and (5) very strong. Let's say for the specific SPU that you are analyzing you award a point rating of 5 for engineering know-how, 4 for organizational image, 2 for size of the organization, and 3 for productivity. You must now multiply the point rating for this particular SPU by the weightings you have established for all SPUs (Figure 5-2) to arrive at a weighted rank for business strength of 3.95.

Repeat this process for every SPU you are analyzing on the business strength computation sheet (Figure 5-3). Use a separate sheet for each product to calculate the rated rank of business strength.

✓ *Market Attractiveness.* Next you are going to plot market attractiveness along the horizontal axis of your matrix. Typical market attractiveness criteria include size of the market segment, growth of the market segment, market pricing, customer's financial condition, cyclibility of demand, vulnerability to inflation and depression, strength of the need for the product, government regulation, availability of raw materials, energy impact, ease of entry, life-cycle position, competitive structure, product liability, political considerations, and distribution structure.

	Weight × *Rating*
Engineering know-how	.40 × 5 pts = 2.00
Size of the organization	.15 × 2 pts = 0.30
Organizational image	.30 × 4 pts = 1.20
Productivity	.15 × 3 pts = 0.45
	Total = 3.95

FIGURE 5-2. Calculation of SPU value for business strength.

SPU # _____ Date _____

Business Strength Criteria	Weights	× Rankings	= Weighted Rank
	1.00	× Rank	=

FIGURE 5-3. Business strength computation sheet. (Copyright © 1983 by Dr. William A. Cohen.)

Let's assume that only four marketing attractiveness criteria are considered important, with relative importances as assigned:

Size of market	.30
Growth of market	.30
Ease of entry	.25
Life-cycle position	.15
Total	1.00

Note that once again the relative importance of all the market attractiveness criteria must equal unity, or 1.00.

Again, you must rate each market attractiveness criterion for the SPU being analyzed on a scale of (1) very unattractive; (2) unattractive; (3) fair; (4) attractive; and (5) very attractive.

Let's assume that you assigned the following ratings: size of market, 4; growth of market, 4; ease of entry, 1; and life-cycle position, 5.

You then calculate the rated rank for each market attractiveness criterion and add it to find the total (Figure 5-4). Note that the total value is 3.40. Now we repeat the process for other SPUs by using Figure 5-5.

You are now in a position to plot the location of your SPU on the matrix (Figure 5-6). Note that in this matrix business strength increases from bottom to top and market attractiveness from right to left and that the SPU is located at coordinates business strength, 3.95 and market attractiveness, 3.40.

You can illustrate the amount of current sales for this SPU by the size of the circle illustrated and can indicate the percentage of the market share that this SPU represents with a shaded portion of the circle.

	Weight × *Rating*
Size of market	.30 × 4 pts = 1.20
Growth of market	.30 × 4 pts = 1.20
East of entry	.25 × 1 pts = 0.25
Life cycle position	.15 × 5 pts = 0.75
	Total = 3.40

FIGURE 5-4. Calculation of SPU value for market attractiveness.

SPU # _____ Date _____

Market Attractiveness Criteria	Weights	× Rankings	= Weighted Rank
	1.00	× Rank	=

FIGURE 5-5. Market attractiveness computation sheet. (Copyright © 1983 by Dr. William A. Cohen.)

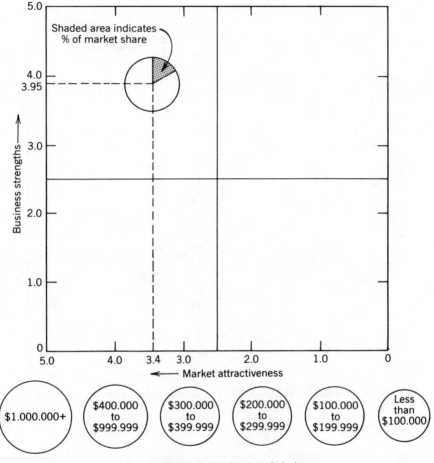

FIGURE 5-6. Matrix showing sales, size of market, and location of SPU: business strength versus market attractiveness.

You can plot other SPUs in the same manner (see Figure 5–7). Each is calculated and compared against the criteria for business strength and market attractiveness, using the same relative importance. Only the ratings for each market attractiveness or business strength criterion differ which result in different positions for each SPU.

The location of the SPU in the matrix suggests a number of strategic moves. Those in the upper left quadrant imply investment

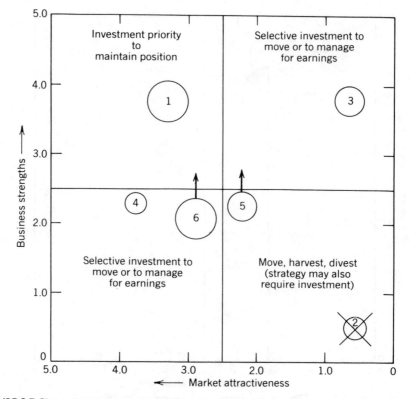

FIGURE 5-7. Planning strategic moves of SPUs on four-cell multifactor analysis matrix. Strategic alternatives: (1) maintain position, (2) move, (3) drop.

priority in order to maintain this position: SPUs located in this quadrant are known as *stars;* SPUs that fall in the upper right-hand quadrant of the matrix imply selective investment to make the SPU a star or to manage this particular SPU for earnings; SPUs that fall in this quadrant of the matrix are typically known as *question marks* or *problem children.* The lower left quadrant of the matrix contains SPUs in which you must apply selective investment to move to star status or, again, to manage for earnings. These SPUs are known as *cash cows.* Finally you have SPUs known as *dogs* located in the lower right-hand quadrant of the matrix. They must be moved, harvested, or divested because the market is not attractive, nor have you the strengths to reap primary benefits from this market.

PRODUCT LIFE CYCLE ANALYSIS

Each product has a cycle of life that contains different stages: introduction, growth, maturity, and decline. During each stage the product exhibits characteristics and performance that favor the use of different strategies. Close attention to the product life cycle is important for two reasons when planning your strategies. First there is an overall trend for products to proceed more rapidly through the product life cycle. The mechanical watch was invented hundreds of years ago and over the centuries proceeded very slowly through its life cycle. Yet over the last 15 years electronic watches have exhibited life cycles that are measured in months, not years. In fact, in the market today, electronic watches that once sold for $100 now sell for less than $10.

The other major reason that the product life cycle must be closely analyzed is to maintain a product life cycle product mix; that is, it would be unwise for an established organization to have a portfolio of products all of which were in the maturity or decline stage of the product life cycle. At the same time, it would probably be unwise unless unavoidable for all products to be in the introduction stage because the considerable expense of product introduction would ensure a heavy negative cash flow. Therefore it is important for an organization to know in what stage of the product life cycle all of its products exist.

The Introductory Stage

In the introductory stage of the product life cycle the organization experiences high costs due to marketing; the fact that manufacturing is generally involved in short production runs of highly skilled labor content and an overcapacity also leads to high production costs. Furthermore, buyers have not yet been persuaded to purchase the product on a regular basis. In fact many buyers may be unaware of the product at all. Generally, the only good news in the introductory stage of a new product is that competitors are few or nonexistent. Profits, or course, are negligible. The basic strategy during this stage is generally to establish market share and to persuade early buyers to adopt the product.

Growth

In the growth stage the situation begins to change. The product has established itself and is successful. Sales are continuing to increase. As a result, other companies are attracted and new competitors may be rapidly entering the market with their own products. Marketing costs are still high but manufacturing costs are reduced somewhat, and there is an undercapacity because of a shift toward mass production. Although distribution channels may have been limited in the introductory stage simply because of a limited number of resources, in the growth stage distribution tends to become intensive and multiple channels are used. All other things considered, profits tend to reach peak levels during this stage because of the increased demand and the fact that most companies take advantage of this demand with high pricing. Strategies followed during the growth stage are new market penetration and market share expansion. Tactical support of these strategies are product improvement, development of new channels of distribution, and a manipulation of price and quality.

Maturity

The product in the maturity stage has changed its situation again. Although many competitors are left over from the growth stage, they are now competing for smaller and smaller market shares. As a result the competition heats up and what is known as a shake-out begins to occur. Less efficient competitors go under or withdraw from the market. Buyers who have been purchasing the product exhibit repeat buying, and although sales continue to increase during this stage profits begin to fall. Manufacturing costs are much lower during this stage, but the increased competition for a smaller market share ultimately results in falling prices. This stage encourages a strategy of entrenchment, yet a search for new markets is still possible. Typical tactical decisions include reducing some channels to improve profit margins, a low-price tactic against weaker competitors, and increasing emphasis on promotion.

Decline

In the decline stage, as in the introductory stage, there are again few competitors. Buyers who are purchasing the product are now sophisticated and much more selective. Production again has problems because there will be an overcapacity caused by reduced demand, although marketing expenditures will probably be reduced. In this stage not only profits but sales are declining and at some point will force a liquidation of inventory. The most logical strategy for the decline stage is some form of withdrawal, although entrenchment may also be followed in selective markets over the short term. Tactics in support of this strategy include reduction of distribution channels to those that are still profitable, low prices, and selective but quick spurts of promotion when rapid liquidation is needed. Perhaps the major factor of which the astute marketer must be aware is a product's decline stage, for whether immediate liquidation or a slow milking and harvesting of all possible benefits over a period of time is needed, the marketing manager must now be prepared for ultimate product removal.

LOCATING THE PRODUCT IN ITS PRODUCT LIFE CYCLE

Before an analysis of strategy implications can be performed, the product must be located in its life cycle. This is somewhat difficult to accomplish for several reasons. First, although the general shape of the product life cycle shown in Figure 3-1 is true in many cases, it is not true in all. As a matter of fact many other shapes for product life cycle have been calculated, such as those shown in Figure 5-8. Thus, before you can find out what position the product has taken in its life cycle, you must know what the life cycle shape looks like. First, you look at what has happened to the product so far. For this purpose use Figure 5-9, which includes sales, profits, margin, market share, and prices for varying periods over the product's life so far. You will wish to know whether your sales are high, low, or average or very high or very low. The same is true for profits, margins, and

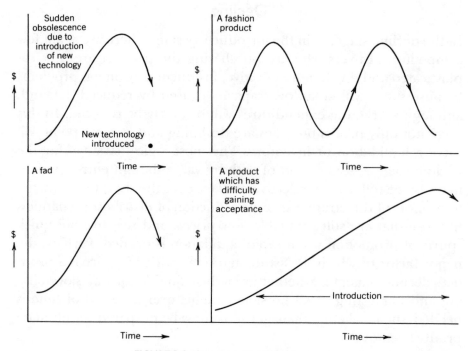

FIGURE 5-8. Various product life cycle shapes.

the other elements. You will also want to look at the trends and characterize them as declining steeply, declining, on a plateau, ascending, or ascending steeply.

Next, you will use Figure 5-10 to analyze the recent trends in competitors' product share and their strengths. These can be characterized as very weak, weak, medium, strong, or very strong.

Now you will take a closer look at recent trends in competitive product quality, performance characteristics, shifts in distribution channels, and their relative advantages. You will note this information in Figure 5-11.

Finally you will accomplish an analysis of your competitors' short-term tactics in Figure 5-12, noting not only its actions but the probable meaning of each.

You will now leave the analysis of the product and its competition and scan the historical information on product life cycles of similar

Product _____ Date _____

	Period 1	Period 2	Period 3	Period 4	Trend
Sales					
Profits					
Margins					
Market share					
Prices					

Complete matrix with following information:

Very low or very small

Low or small

Average

High or large

Very high or very large

Characterize trends as:

Declining steeply   →

Declining   ↗

Plateau   ↑

Ascending   ↖

Ascending steeply   ←

FIGURE 5-9. Historical trend analysis matrix. (Copyright © 1983 by Dr. William A. Cohen.)

Your Product _____ Date _____

Strength code: VW = very weak   M = medium   VS = very strong
                 W   = weak   S = strong

Competitor	Market Share	Strength	Products

FIGURE 5-10. Recent trends of competitor's products, share, and strength. (Copyright © 1983 by Dr. William A. Cohen.)

Your Product _____ Date _____

Company	Product	Quality and Performance Characteristics	Shifts in Distribution Channels	Relative Advantages of Each Competitive Product

FIGURE 5-11. Recent trends in competitive products. (Copyright © 1983 by Dr. William A. Cohen.)

or related products. What you want to do is take a product that is similar to the one you are analyzing and determine what happened to it over a period of time: its introduction, growth, maturity, and decline. These data will include the number and strength of competitors, profits, pricing, strategies used, and the length of time in each stage. For this purpose use Figure 5-13.

With this information turn to Figure 5-14, a matrix that contains sales and profits on a vertical axis and time in years or months on the horizontal axis. Sketch a rough sales curve and a rough profit curve for the similar or related product you have just analyzed.

Your next step is to project sales of your current product over the next three to five years, based on information from the first part of your analysis of your own and competing products. You will use Figure 5-15 to estimate sales, total direct costs, indirect costs, pretax

Your Product _____ Date _____

Competitor	Actions	Probable Meaning of Action	Check Most Likely

FIGURE 5-12. Analysis of competitors' short-term tactics. (Copyright © 1983 by Dr. William A. Cohen.)

Product _____ Similar or Related Product _____

Product stage	Introduction	Growth	Maturity	Decline
Competition				
Profits				
Sales (units)				
Pricing				
Strategy Used				
Length of Time in Each Stage				

FIGURE 5-13. Developing life cycle of similar or related product. (Copyright © 1983 by Dr. William A. Cohen.)

profits, and a profit ratio—which is the estimate of total direct costs to pretax profits.

By comparing this information with the historical product information that you have already documented, you can make an estimate of the profitable years that remain for your product. Now you are in a position to plot your product in its product life cycle.

First, make the assumption that the historical curve that you plotted for a similar or related product is applicable and that you will use the information you have analyzed for your product and its competing products, along with the sales and profits projections, to determine in what stage of the product life cycle your product will fall (Figure 5-16).

DEVELOPING STRATEGIES FOR PRODUCTS IN EACH STAGE OF THE PRODUCT LIFE CYCLE

To develop strategies for products in each stage of the product life cycle you must consider industry obsolescence trends, the pace of new product introduction, the average lengths of product life cycles of all the products that are in your product line, growth and profit

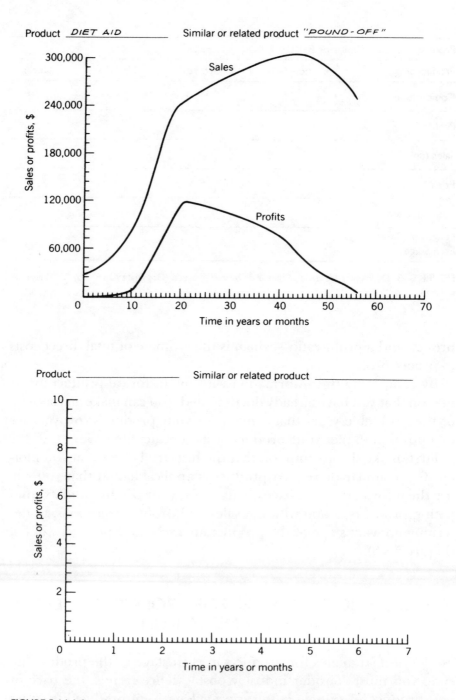

Product __DIET AID__   Similar or related product __"POUND-OFF"__

Product _____   Similar or related product _____

FIGURE 5-14. Life cycle curve of similar or related product. Sketch a rough sales curve and a rough profit curve for a similar or related product. (Copyright © 1983 by Dr. William A. Cohen.)

Product _____ Date _____					
Year	1	2	3	4	5
Estimated sales					
Estimated total direct costs					
Estimated indirect costs					
Estimated pretax profits					
Profit ratio (est. total direct costs to pretax profits)					

FIGURE 5-15. Sales and profit projections. (Copyright © 1983 by Dr. William A. Cohen.)

Product _ECONOMY INSURANCE POLICY_ Date: _OCTOBER 3, 1986_

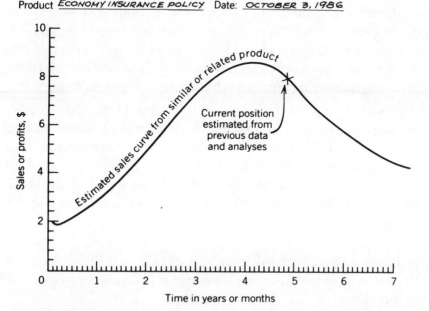

FIGURE 5-16. Position in product life cycle curve. (Copyright © 1983 by Dr. William A. Cohen.)

objectives, and the general situation you are facing because of the present stage of the product's life cycle. Use the alternative marketing strategies discussed in the next section. However, before you leave the product life cycle per se you must understand that changes will sometimes occur in the product life cycle that will alter its anticipated shape. This may be true for a number of reasons:

A need may disappear. Demand for the buggy whip is close to zero today not because the buggy whip itself was replaced but because the buggy was replaced by the automobile. Thus there was no longer a need for the product. In the same vein the iron lung, once essential to the breathing of many polio victims, no longer is in the same demand simply because the disease has been eradicated.

A better, cheaper, or more convenient product may be developed to fill a need. All engineers once carried a device known as a slide rule, which was a mechanical unit used for making mathematical and other scientific calculations. When the electronic calculator was introduced in the early 1970s, it replaced hundreds of thousands of slide rules overnight.

A competitive product may, by superior marketing strategy, suddenly gain an advantage. Adam Osbourne's second generation of computers failed and suddenly had its product life cycle terminated not because of technological inferiority but by IBM's superior marketing strategy when it introduced its famous PC.

Intentional change in the shape of the curve by product repositioning, innovation, or extension. Arm and Hammer baking soda was once used only as an additive for home cooking, but as the product went into the decline stage its life was extended by its use as an odor absorbent in refrigerators. In the same way the DC-10 became an advanced cargo tanker for the Air Force.

Any of these occurrences will cause the anticipated life-cycle curve to change and a new marketing plan and marketing strategy must be developed.

ALTERNATIVE STRATEGIES FOR THE MARKETING PLAN

The major alternative strategies that you might pursue are new market penetration, market share expansion, entrenchment, and withdrawal.

New Market Penetration

There are four classes of new market penetration strategy which may be pursued simultaneously, although they need not be. They involve entry, niche, dimension, and positioning. Let's look at each in turn.

Entry. In new market penetration you can be first, early, or late. A company that chooses a strategy of being first is the first to benefit from its learning curve; that is, as it gains experience in manufacturing and marketing of the product it is using for new market penetration its cost goes down. Thus, as competitors attempt to enter the market, the company that was there first has a cost advantage that can be passed on to the customer in the form of a lower price or used against the competition in the form of additional financial resources for promotional tactics, channels of distribution, and other ways of increasing the effectiveness as well as the efficiency of its strategies or tactics. Those customers who have been persuaded to buy the first product on the market and whose needs have been satisfied will be reluctant to switch due to built-in inertia. Finally the firm that enters first has a certain momentum. Firms that enter subsequently must catch up. Thus the first firm has an advantage. It can continue to innovate to maintain a slight lead over its competition. The first firm into a market also has an edge in dominating that market. Yet being first is not without its risks. As pointed out by Peter F. Drucker in his book *Innovation and Entrepreneurship,* to reap the benefits of being first requires an extreme concentration of effort on a clear-cut goal. And once a firm is successful in entering the marketplace first it must expend considerable effort to maintain leadership or everything that has been invested will be lost to one of the later-entering competitors. Being first does not automatically ensure victory. This firm must react and react strongly to later-entering competitors to maintain its lead.

A second possibility is that of entering the market early but not first. This early entry may be intentional or unintentional. Perhaps the firm intended to be first but was edged out by another firm. When this happens, the firm that is edged out may suffer all of the disadvantages of being first but reap none of the advantages. Early rather than first entry can be advantageous if the firm has sufficient resources to fight the firm ahead of it. It has somewhat reduced risk because risk in demand, technological obsolescence, and other areas of business have been absorbed by the first entry. Some knowledge will be gained of what works and what does not, again paid for by the firm that enters first. Finally, coincident with lower risk, much of the opportunity in the marketplace still exists. It is not a case of a product being in the mature stage of its life cycle, with many competitors fighting for reduced shares, or even of the later growth stages, with many competitors entering the market, but rather in the very early stage of its introduction. The major disadvantages of being early but not first are that barriers to entry due to the first entry must be overcome and that market opportunity may be somewhat reduced. IBM overcame these disadvantages and captured a good share of the market for personal computers even though Apple got there first.

Finally, we have a late entry. A late entry implies entering the market after it is already established and other competitors are already there. Yet there are some advantages, for example, the fact that earlier entrants are probably committed to their previous investments but late entrants can include the latest technological improvements without penalty. The Japanese entered the American car market with brand new plants and manufacturing processes that competed against older, established American competitors who were tied to their obsolescent capital equipment and facilities. Late entrants may also be able to achieve greater economies of scale because all entrants have a better idea of the actual size and demand of the market and can produce optimal facilities. Late-entry firms may also be able to get better terms from suppliers, employees, or even customers because earlier entrants may be locked into negotiations or fixed ways of doing business. Late entrants will enjoy reduced costs of research and development because they have been borne by earlier competitors. Finally the late entrant can attack a perceived soft spot in the market, whereas a defending firm may have to defend everywhere. Nevertheless, a late entrant has some obvious disadvantages. At this stage several competitors have become established in the market and the opportunities are probably perceptibly reduced.

Niche. A niche strategy simply means finding a distinguishable market segment, identifiable by size, need, and objective, and seeking to concentrate all resources on fulfilling the needs of this particular niche and no other. This strategy can work because a niche must be such that it is not worthwhile to the larger competitor to spend its resources to defend it. This is a real advantage because the organization that practices a niching strategy may be smaller, yet be a king in its niche. It becomes a "big frog" in its particular pond. Peter Drucker has identified three separate niching strategies: the toll-gate, the specialty skill, and the specialty market.

A company attempting to dominate a particular niche with the toll-gate strategy seeks to establish itself to the extent that potential buyers cannot do without its product. This means that the product must be essential, that the risk of not using it must be greater than the cost of the product, and that the market must be eliminated so that whoever controls the niche preempts others from entrance. One maker of a small valve needed in all oxygen masks for fliers had strong patents protecting it. As a result many companies manufactured oxygen masks but all had to use that particular valve. The niche was such that it was not worthwhile for other companies to attempt its manufacture. The specialty skill strategy can be used when a company has a particular skill that is lacking in other organizations. A management consultant who has acquired a particular skill in locating venture capital through his contacts, knowledge, or other expertise usually has developed a particular niche that others cannot enter.

Then there is the specialty market strategy, which is somewhat akin to the specialty skill but, unlike one that is unique, it requires a particular market that is also unique. Adam Osbourne was initially successful with his portable business computer because he was able to carve out a specialty market for it and expanded his company's sales from zero to $150 million in one year. Peter Drucker notes that the danger is that the specialty market will become a larger market and more attractive to larger competitors. This, in fact, is what happened to Osbourne and encouraged manufacturers like IBM to develop strategies that overcame his lead.

Dimension. Another alternative for new market penetration is vertical versus horizontal expansion. Vertical penetration involves combining under single ownership of two or more stages of the production or marketing processes. Thus a farm that formerly sold its chickens to a food processor in turn buys a processor and sells prepared chickens to a retail store. In a sense vertical integration can be a type of niching. It also has the advantage of a narrow focus that can make marketing activities easier and more effective by the concentration of resources in a certain class of market. There may also be advantages in the economy of scale of combined operations; for example, lower transaction costs, a greater supply of raw materials, and greater profits. But vertical market penetration also has its disadvantages. There is a potential loss of specialization due to different management requirements for different types of operation in the vertical integration. Capital investment requirements and higher fixed costs are definitely increased. In addition, the methods of management, marketing, and production of vertical markets, say, raising chickens versus processing them, can be different and the skills learned in one may not be applicable to the other. Thus instead of an overall net reduced cost there may be an overall increase in costs.

Horizontal expansion means expansion into new markets. The risk here is that the new markets may not be well understood, even though the supplier has a good handle on the product and its processing and marketing. Horizontal expansion may have an additional advantage in greater potential for sales than in vertical integration. It is a workable strategy in those markets that are untapped by the product or service offered by the firm. It is more difficult, however, when competitors are already established in those markets in which penetration is sought.

Both vertical and horizontal new market penetration require an investment in resources. Therefore an assessment of the investment and the potential payoff, as well as the risks and uncertainties, must be considered before a decision can be made.

Positioning. Positioning refers to the position of the product in relation to those of competing products in the minds of the customers. The position of your product is always important. The position occupied by Rolls-Royce is different from Volkswagen's. A Brooks Brothers suit does not occupy the same position as a suit purchased at K-Mart. But there are more subtle differences than these extremes. As a result it is always important to have a particular position in mind and to strive to achieve it with your other marketing strategy objectives. Sometimes the positioning of the product can be the center of gravity in the whole situation and it should receive emphasis equal to those of entry, niche, and dimension strategy.

Market Share Expansion

There are two basic market share expansion strategies. One is product differentiation versus market segmentation, the other, limited versus general expansion.

Product Differentiation versus Market Segmentation. Product differentiation and market segmentation are frequently used as alternatives. Basically, product differentiation promotes product differences to the target market, whereas market segmentation is a strategy that recognizes that the market is such that not all of its buyers are identical nor a single mass of look-alike and act-alike prospects, but rather consists of various submarkets with common characteristics that can be classified according to these characteristics into unique segments. Each segment can therefore be considered individually.

Although product differentiation and market segmentation can be employed simultaneously, they are usually applied in sequence in response to changing market conditions. This is due in part to the fact that successful market differentiation results in giving the marketer a horizontal share of a broad and generalized market, whereas successful market segmentation tends to produce greater sales to the market segment that has been selected. Both involve coordinating the market with the product offered: first, market segmentation by finding the correct market for the product, then product differentiation by attempting to change the product to distinguish it from other products that are competing against it, and ultimately to find the correct product for the market served.

Varying conditions tend to call for one strategy or the other; for example, one marketing scientist, R. William Kotruba, developed a strategy selection chart (Figure 5-17) that illustrates the alternatives that must be considered. Consider the size of the market. If the market segment served is already small, additional segmentation may not

Use product differentiation												Use market segmentation
Emphasis on Promoting Product Differences	**Strategy Selection Factors**											**Emphasis on Satisfying Market Variations**
Narrow	Size of market											Broad
							Ⓐ			Ⓑ		
	1	2	3	4	5	6	7	8	9	10		
High	Consumer sensitivity to product differences											Low
			Ⓑ				Ⓐ					
	1	2	3	4	5	6	7	8	9	10		
Introduction	Stage of product life cycle											Saturation
							Ⓐ			Ⓑ		
	1	2	3	4	5	6	7	8	9	10		
Commodity	Type of product											Distinct
	Ⓑ								Ⓐ			
	1	2	3	4	5	6	7	8	9	10		
Few	Number of competitors											Many
		Ⓑ					Ⓐ					
	1	2	3	4	5	6	7	8	9	10		
Product differentiation	Typical competitor strategies											Market segmentation
			Ⓑ	Ⓐ								
	1	2	3	4	5	6	7	8	9	10		

FIGURE 5-17. Strategy selection chart, Ⓐ—home computers; Ⓑ—salt. Adapted from R. William Kotruba, "The Strategy Selection Chart," *Journal of Marketing*, (July 1966), p. 25.

be possible because the financial potential is insufficiently attractive. In some cases the consumer or buyer may be insensitive to product differences. This would also argue for a market segmentation strategy. The stage of a product life cycle may also have an effect. As noted earlier, a new-product priority is to become established in a market segment as large as possible. This would argue against a market segmentation strategy and for product differentiation. The type of product may also be important. Oil, butter, salt, and gasoline are commodity products, which means that if these products are differentiated the variation will stand out and can be readily promoted to potential customers. The number of competitors can also be important. With many competitors in the marketplace it is far more difficult to differentiate the product. Thus market segmentation strategy may be called for. Of course, we must also consider competitive strategies. If many competitors are using the strategy of market segmentation, it will be difficult to counter with a product differentiation strategy because attempting to sell to all segments simultaneously means becoming all things to all people, a difficult proposition. Your best choice may be to adopt a market segmentation of your own and to select your target market, along with your competitors, carefully. On the other hand, if many of your competitors are using a product differentiation strategy, you probably could counter with a market segmentation strategy.

Limited versus General Expansion. Depending on resources, objectives, and the competition, a firm can also initiate a limited or a general market share expansion. More than 100 years ago Confederate general Nathan Forrest Bedford said that strategy was a matter of getting there "furstest with the mostest." Thus a new product intended for introduction on a national basis had better pursue a market share expansion that is general rather than alert its competitors to its intentions and give them the opportunity to preempt with a general market share expansion of their own. On the other hand, sometimes limited resources force a company to adopt a limited market share expansion strategy, or perhaps a limited market share expansion into certain areas or segments of the market, simply because a general expansion is not possible due to the strength of the competition.

Entrenchment

Entrenchment means digging in. It is not a withdrawal strategy, neither is it one of new market penetration or market share expansion. Entrenchment may be necessary when a product is in its mature or even somewhat declining stage of the life cycle. In any case, the market is no longer expanding. Two different entrenchment are possible: repositioning and direct confrontation.

Repositioning. Repositioning means changing the position of your product in the mind of the buyer in relation to competitive products. Repositioning strategy means that you will no longer position the product where it was before but will put it somewhere else. Some years ago a successful men's after-shave was called Hai Karate. After several years of success the market contracted. There was a general shake-out, after which few competitors were left. Hai Karate was positioned first as a brand of after-shave whose image was better than the old standbys like Old Spice, Aqua Velva, and Mennen but less than the prestige brands like English Leather. When the market collapsed, marketing strategy options included withdrawal and entrenchment. One alternative for entrenchment was to reposition. The product could be repositioned as a cheap brand with a lower image than that of the old brands or as a prestige brand. In this case the brand survived by being repositioned against Old Spice and other similar brands. Did you know that Marlboro, the macho man's cigarette, was once a woman's cigarette and that Parliament, repositioned as a cigarette for white and blue collar workers, was once a prestige cigarette, the Rolls-Royce of its product category? The advantage of repositioning is finding a position in which competition is less or can be overcome more easily. The disadvantage is the cost of repositioning, which includes promotion to make the consumer aware of the new position of the brand in relation to its competitors and possibly repackaging and establishing new distribution channels.

Direct Confrontation. Direct confrontation means that you're going to fight it out toe-to-toe against the competition. Obviously this should never be attempted unless you are certain you are going to win, and it must mean that you have superior resources or the know-how to use your resources better than the competitors you are confronting. Reentrenchment by a direct confrontation is really a power strategy. If you lack power that exceeds that of your competition, then you shouldn't attempt it.

Withdrawal

Withdrawal means that you are going to leave the marketplace with this particular product or service. The only question is when and how. The mildest type of withdrawal is risk reduction, in which you don't withdraw the entire product or service from all geographical areas, but merely try to limit the risk of loss of profits. Going up the scale, you may consider harvesting. Harvesting implies an eventual total withdrawal but at a planned rate. You will harvest this particular product for maximum profits even as you are withdrawing from the marketplace. Finally there is liquidation or sell-out. In liquidation you are leaving the marketplace now. This strategy is adopted when there are no advantages to harvesting over a period of time and an immediate use can be found for the resources that you gained by getting out of the marketplace at once. Repositioning can also be a part of this strategy.

Certain alternative marketing strategies tend to be more effective at different stages of the product life cycle. This is shown in Figures 5-18. A summary of the alternative strategies is contained in Figure 5-19.

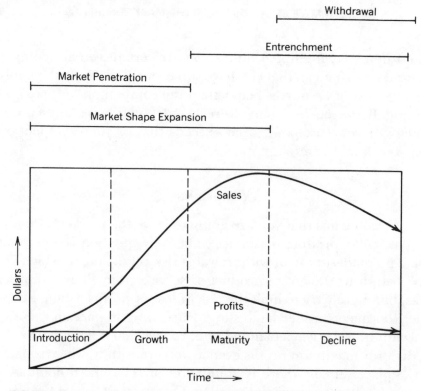

FIGURE 5-18. The product life cycle with alternative marketing strategies implied at each stage.

I. New Market Penetration
  A. Entry
    1. First
    2. Early
    3. Late
  B. Niche
    1. Toll gate
    2. Specialty skill
    3. Specialty market
  C. Dimension
    1. Vertical
    2. Horizontal
  D. Positioning

II. Market Share Expansion
  A. Product differentation versus
    market segmentation
  B. Limited versus general
    expansion
  C. Repositioning

III. Entrenchment
  A. Direct confrontation
  B. Repositioning

IV. Withdrawal
  A. Harvesting
  B. Risk reduction
  C. Liquidation
  D. Repositioning

FIGURE 5-19. Marketing strategies.

SUMMARY

In this chapter you've seen the three different levels of strategy, that is, strategic marketing management, marketing strategy, and marketing tactics, and examined ways of developing strategies by the use of a four-cell matrix that measures factors having to do with business capabilities, and marketing attractiveness, and product life cycle. You have also considered alternative strategies: new market penetration, market share expansion, entrenchment, and withdrawal. In preparing your market plan, it would be helpful to indicate exactly what strategies are planned to meet the goals and objectives set. You will implement strategies with the tactics that are discussed in Chapter 6.

6

DEVELOPING MARKETING TACTICS

Tactics tell you how you will implement the strategy you have developed. Two basic methods are used in implementing marketing tactics. The first incorporates those marketing variables that you can control. The second makes use of the marketplace environs. Let's look at each in turn.

MANIPULATING THE CONTROLLABLE VARIABLES

The controllable variables have been conceptualized under four generalized headings, each beginning with the letter P, by Professor E. Jerome McCarthy. These are product, price, promotion, and place. Because of this classification system, these four categories of controllable variables are known as the four Ps of marketing.

Product

There are three basic things that can be done with any product. It can be introduced into the marketplace, it can be modified or changed, and it can be withdrawn. Each can be a workable marketing tactic under different conditions. A product may be introduced into the market to support a strategy of new market penetration, but a tactic of product withdrawal may also support the same strategy because the resources that were once used to market the product and is now being discontinued can be put to use elsewhere to help the marketing effort. A product may also be changed or modified to alter the shape of the product's life cycle. When a product has been effectively rejuvenated in this fashion, various benefits accrue, including retention of goodwill and product awareness that were associated with the product as it formerly existed. As a consequence, promotional costs for introducing and familiarizing the consumer with a brand new product are unnecessary.

In addition, other actions can be taken that will also affect your ability to implement a marketing strategy. These actions include decisions related to product quality, branding, and packaging. Research has shown that product quality not only affects the image and the price that can be charged but also business profitability. This does not necessarily mean that the highest quality product is desired by customers in all instances. Rather it does mean that various segments associated with any market will attract customers for high-quality products and for those at the low end of the scale. Both can be extremely profitable. Some marketers, however, tend to equate low-quality products with profitability simply because the production costs are generally lower. This is incorrect. The good marketing tactician must observe the complete picture. When the United States sank into depression in 1929, cigar smokers bemoaned their fate with the proclamation, "What this country needs is a good 5-cent cigar." Yet a company selling premium cigars was started in the middle of that period and grew into a multimillion dollar company that still exists to this day with a product that sells at many times the price.

Branded products sell for much more than products that are not branded. You've heard of Chiquita bananas and Sunkist oranges and Dole pineapples. But have you heard of Tom Ahtoes? Tom Ahtoes sell at about 30 percent per pound more than unbranded tomatoes. Yet higher profit margins are only one reason for branding a product. Another is image and identification. Once a product's name has been planted in the mind of the consumer, it can be as important as any functional aspect of the product.

In general, there are four branding possibilities: (1) A company can use a new brand with a product or service in a category that is completely new to the company. (2) A company can introduce a new brand in a category in which the firm is already selling products. (3) A company can use a line-extension tactic in which the company's brand name is used to cover a new product as well as others already in the product line. (4) A firm can adopt a franchise extension in which a brand name familiar to the consumer is applied to products in a category that the firm has never marketed. A new get-well card in Hallmark's line of greeting cards or a new flavor for ice cream are examples of line extension, whereas franchise extension may include Ivory shampoo and conditioner developed from Ivory soap.

There are advantages and disadvantages to each of these tactics. A brand-line extension attempts to capitalize on some of the company's valuable assets in the form of goodwill, brand name, and brand awareness. The expectation is that a synergistic effect will help to promote the old and new products under the same label. On the other hand, there are disadvantages to brand extension in some situations. An inexpensive Cadillac may increase sales over the short run for individuals who wish to own a big car but do not wish to pay a lot of money for it. Over the long run this tactic may cause the loss of buyers in Cadillac's traditional market segment of more affluent consumers because Cadillac would no longer clearly represent a high-priced brand but something else. In the extreme, using a brand name for everything like Cadillac greeting cards or Cadillac gasoline may destroy the name and provide the new product with little gain.

Packaging is important to protect the product, to help promote it, and to make it stand out when displayed among many other products. Last year more than 5000 new items appeared on grocery shelves and many experts have shown that simple repackaging can increase brand identification and awareness significantly.

Price

Three basic pricing tactics may be followed in introducing a new product: penetration pricing, meet-the-competition pricing, and price skimming. Penetration pricing involves entering the market with a low price that will capture as large a share of the market as possible. The lower price is emphasized as a major differential advantage over the competition. Once the product is well established in the marketplace, the price may be raised to be level with or even higher than the competition; for example, when the Datsun-Nissan was introduced to the United States as a sports car in the early seventies, it carried a low price compared with similar sports cars. Then, as the market responded and the car became an established brand, the price was slowly raised. At the present time it maintains a position on the high end of the price scale for its class.

Meet-the-competition pricing involves introducing a product or service at about the same level as that of its competitors. If this particular tactic is used, you must differentiate in some other way; that is, by increased product quality and service, bundling many benefits together to increase the value of the overall product (e.g., an entertainment system that contains a television, radio, FM stereo, and record case all in one console), and charging approximately the price that would accrue if these components were ordered separately. Otherwise there is no reason for a consumer to switch from a competitive product or service.

Price skimming involves a new, relatively high priced product. Skimming is frequently done when this particular product or service is a first in the marketplace. Thus computers, when introduced, frequently bore a high price not only because of the cost of components and assembling but also because competition was almost nonexistent. As competitors enter the market the price is usually reduced to meet a lower competitive level or to make it more difficult for the competition to enter. In the meantime, however, additional financial resources have been accumulated because of the higher profit margin, and these resources can be used to fight the competition on some other front, say, with promotion or additional distribution channels. The price can also be raised, however. Marketing genius Joe Cossman introduced a plastic-hose, lawn-sprinkling system that consists of a single flexible plastic tube with many holes in it. Although highly innovative, this product was easy to copy and manufacture and could not be protected by patent. Cossman recognized that, although he dominated the first selling season as first in the market, competition in the following year would be heavy and at a lower price. Cossman's tactics were unique. He raised his recommended selling price and decreased the wholesale price to the retailer. Because of the larger margins offered to the middlemen, Cossman actually maintained a market share through a second year by charging the consumer a higher price.

Other Tactical Pricing Considerations. Other pricing considerations include promotional versus baseline pricing; that is, a lower price to promote the product versus a standard price. Promotional pricing can increase sales. Care must be taken, however, that the two (baseline and promotional prices) don't become confused in the minds of your buyers. Otherwise it will be difficult to sell at the baseline price once the promotional period has ended.

Various psychological pricing tactics are also useful and must be considered. Have you ever wondered why the odd numbers such as $3.99 and $6.98 are used in selling products rather than $4.00 and $7.00? Psychologists have discovered that $3.99 is frequently seen as $3.00 rather than $4.00, and $6.98 as $6.00 rather than $7.00. There are other important psychological considerations. On the low end, say in the $1.00 to $2.00 range, a 10 percent difference may be perceived as significant by a potential buyer or prospect and as a result may make a difference in sales. However, if the product sells for much more, say, $30.00 to $40.00, a 10 percent difference, although larger than the absolute price difference at a lower range, may not make any impact at all. The price difference is simply not perceived by the prospect as significant.

Markdowns must be examined in the same light. An important key here is that the premarkdown price is perceived as a real value for the product. A markdown will increase sales and the baseline price can be restored more easily.

You must also consider discount pricing. Most buyers expect that the greater the quantity purchased, the lower the price. This expectation is so pervasive that if you do not discount on larger quantities you must have valid reasons that are acceptable to the buyer.

Finally you must never forget the psychological aspect of pricing's effect on image. A high price denotes an expensive image and a low price, a cheap image. The same is true of quality. Thus many buyers,

if no contrary information is available, will spend a higher amount
for a product, feeling that this increases the chances of their getting
a higher quality product for their money.

Place

Place has to do with channel and distribution tactics to support the
strategy selected. There are six basic channel alternatives to be considered by the marketing manager: (1) direct or indirect channels;
(2) single or multiple channels; (3) length of channel; (4) type of
intermediary; (5) number of distributors at each level; and (6) which
intermediaries to use.

A direct channel implies selling directly to the ultimate consumer.
This may be important for some products (e.g., perishables or specialty products that require a great deal of explanation and demonstration). The limited resources of a smaller firm, however, may
prohibit the use of a direct channel, especially when a large number
of customers are widely scattered. The use of indirect channels includes employment of retailers, wholesalers, and industrial supply
houses and manufacturer's representatives and agents. The fact that
your profit margin on each item is far lower when sold through these
intermediaries may be outweighed by the fact that you can reach
many more customers than would otherwise be the case. Thus your
overall profit would be much greater than if you did not use them.

The choice of multiple channels means working more than one
simultaneously. Because an additional channel would seem to involve
more outlets for sales and more chance for selling, you may wonder
why multiple channels are not always selected. There are several
reasons. First, additional channels cost more money, which may not
be available to you. Thus, not infrequently, small companies will start
with a single channel and expand to a greater number as more resources build up; for example, a company may distribute locally and
later nationally as more financial resources are acquired. Interchannel rivalry is another reason for not always using multiple channels.
Let's say you sell to conventional retail outlets. These outlets will not
be enthusiastic about your selling to other channels, particularly discount houses. Similarly, a mail-order house won't want to see its
product in retail stores and vice versa. The importance of these

points is that if you choose to operate with multiple channels, despite interchannel rivalry, one or more of them may not push your product or service aggressively. In fact, some channels will refuse to handle your product at all if rival channels are used.

The length of the channel is based on the number of intermediaries along a single line of distribution. You don't have to sell to a retailer. You can sell to a wholesale distributor who, in turn, sells to a retailer. But your channel could be even longer. Perhaps you will employ an agent or sell to a jobber who sells to a wholesaler. There is no single answer to the length of a channel. Factors to be considered are your own strength as a manufacturer, average order size, concentration of customers geographically, seasonality of sales, geographical distance from producer to market, and the perishability of the product.

Types of intermediary are another question. A wholesaler may be desirable when greater distribution is required over a larger area. When this is unnecessary, retailers may be preferred. A small company with limited resources may choose to work with manufacturer's representatives or agents who do not take title to the goods even though their profitability would be far greater with a sales force of their own. Why? To recruit, train, and maintain a sales force takes a lot of money and a lot of other resources and many small companies lack them. Also, established manufacturers and agents who take a percentage of the sales price may also have the contacts and know-how to sell the product better than you could in the near term.

A decision regarding the required number of distributors at each level of distribution is also important. More distributors at each level are needed when the unit value is low, the product is purchased frequently, technical complexity of the product is high, service requirements and inventory investment are high, product differentiation is significant, the total market potential is high, geographic concentration is low, the manufacturer's current market share is high, competition is intense, and the effect on the customer's production process due to lack of availability is significant.

The selection of specific intermediaries does not depend only on their track records. There are other factors, such as the market segment served, how well the intermediary knows and understands this market, how you and the intermediary fit together in policy, strategy,

and image, and whether the manufacturer and distributor understand the roles they play in marketing the product.

Place tactics also require decisions in regard to physical distribution of the product: what physical distribution services are needed,
how they should be provided, and what resources are required.
Warehousing, packaging for transportation, form of transportation,
and distribution points should be noted and the tactical implication
of one action over another, weighed.

Promotion

Promotion is further divided into categories of face-to-face selling,
sales promotion, advertising, and publicity. Face-to-face selling requires decisions about establishing your own sales force versus using
the services of an agent to sell for you. This decision can be especially
important in the early stages of a firm's growth, when limited resources may argue against investing large sums to develop a sales
force. The advantages of personal selling over other promotional
methods include (1) more flexibility, in that the salesperson can tailor
the sales presentation to fit a customer's needs, behavior, and motives
in special situations; (2) immediate feedback from the customer,
which will allow a presentation to be adjusted to target special demands; (3) instant receipts or sales; (4) additional services to be ren-
dered at the time of the sales call; and (5) flexible time to make the
sale. In developing tactics for face-to-face selling, decisions must be
made regarding recruitment, compensation, and training, of a sales
force, the allocation of exclusive or nonexclusive sales territories,
and, perhaps most important, motivation of the salesperson to maximum performance.

Use of Sales Promotion Tactics. Sales promotion is one of the hottest
areas of the promotional tactic variable. It is currently in excess of a
$60 billion annual investment. Its importance is clear when you con-
sider that a single display at the front of a store can increase a product's sales 600 percent. Sales promotion techniques can entail
sampling, coupons, trade allowances, price quantity promotion, pre-
miums, contests and sweepstakes, refund offers, bonus packs, stamp
and continuity plans, point-of-purchase displays, and participation

in trade shows. Naturally, each of these options has a cost associated with it. Therefore testing is essential to determine the most beneficial, given a particular product or service and situation. It is doubtful that any firm would be strong enough financially to employ all of these techniques simultaneously or even most of them. Therefore resources should be concentrated where they will have the greatest payback in implementing the strategy selected. Sales promotion tactics are especially useful for new product introduction and during periods of high competition, when additional stimulation is necessary to increase sales.

Advertising and Publicity Tactics. Advertising and publicity tactics must be employed because, no matter how good the product or service, there will be no sales if the potential buyer or prospect has never heard of it and therefore cannot buy. Thus the main objective is to make the product or service known to the market and to present it in its most favorable light in comparison with competitive products. Some marketers think that advertising and publicity works automatically and should be used in every marketing situation. This simply is not true. For one thing, it can be extremely expensive, and no company has unlimited resources to spend on advertising everywhere simultaneously. In some cases advertising may be only marginally beneficial or may not work at all. Cigarette advertising on television and radio came to an end on January 2, 1971, after many manufacturers claimed that the end of the cigarette industry in the United States was at hand. Yet sales actually increased. The forced move from radio and television uncovered the amazing fact that printed advertising was actually far more effective and that some advertising on TV and radio was actually reducing sales.

Publicity is sometimes touted as free advertising, with the added advantage of greater credibility because promotion seems to come from a third party. But publicity costs money. Even a simple release involves preparation and mailing costs. Several years ago the promotion of a science fiction book, *Battlefield Earth,* by L. Ron Hubbard, cost a staggering $750,000. Therefore, although it definitely makes sense to consider a publicity campaign in addition to advertising, it is not free advertising.

One final point about this tactical variable. Keep in mind that advertising can never force a consumer to buy products or services that are not really wanted or are believed to have low value. This is not only because various governmental and nongovernmental regulatory agencies forbid misleading and inaccurate advertising, but also because the product or service must live up to its advertising or publicity claims or the customer will not buy it again. Raising the expectations of the consumer by too much hype may cause products to be returned or ignored in the future, even though it has met all the claims in its advertising.

Five key issues will determine whether your use of advertising and publicity will be successful:

Where to spend
How much to spend
When to spend
What to say
How to measure results

The answers to these questions depend on your overall advertising and publicity objectives, your target market, and the broad alternatives for reaching the advertising objective on which you have decided. These alternative objectives are to stimulate primary demand for the product or service; to introduce unknown or new advantages or attributes; to alter the assessed importance of an existing product or service attribute; to alter the perception of a product or service; or to change the perception of competing products.

In advertising, *media* refers to TV, radio, print, or whatever carries your message; *vehicle* is the TV channel and spot, magazine, or newspaper. In every case you must not only outline the cost of advertising in the media and vehicles chosen but also the expected benefits. These benefits should be quantified by sales increase or market share achieved in a specific time period. In other words, an acceptable publicity or advertising objective would be to sell 500,000 units in three months or to capture one percent of the market in six months. Only in this way can you reconcile costs and benefits or determine whether results have met your expectations in your advertising and publicity tactical campaign.

USE OF THE MARKETPLACE ENVIRONS

For many years the use of the environs for marketing tactics were largely ignored. Of course, it was recognized that demand, social and cultural factors, state of the technology, and politics and laws could be influenced. In general, however, it was felt that it was far easier and less demanding of resources to attempt to manipulate the variables of product, price, promotion, and place. More recently the possibility of changing the context in which the organization operates, in terms of constraints on the marketing function and limits on the marketing organization, has been investigated. It was found that these conditions can be used effectively and less expensively than was imagined.

Thus environmental marketing tactics should also be considered. Examples are a company engaging in a private legal battle with a competitor on the grounds of deceptive advertising, or efforts to lobby for a particular political action before Congress to ensure a more favorable business environment or to limit competition. Two marketing scientists, Carl P. Zeithaml and Valarie A. Zeithaml, have done a great deal of work in this field and have prepared a framework of environmental management tactics which they published in the Spring 1984 issue of the *Journal of Marketing*. Their division of these tactics into independent, cooperative, and strategic subcategories is shown in Figure 6-1.

TACTICAL QUESTIONS FOR THE MARKETING PLAN

Figure 6-2 contains questions in each of the areas discussed in this chapter—product, price, promotion, and place—as well as in the use of the marketing environs to develop tactics.

Environmental Management Tactic	Definition	Examples
	Independent Tactics	
Competitive aggression	Focal organization exploits a distinctive competence or improves internal efficiency of resources for competitive advantage.	Product differentiation. Aggressive pricing. Comparative advertising.
Competitive pacification	Independent action to improve relations with competitors.	Helping competitors find raw materials. Advertising campaigns which promote entire industry. Price umbrellas.
Public relations	Establishing and maintaining favorable images in the minds of those making up the environment.	Corporate advertising campaigns.
Voluntary action	Voluntary management of and commitment to various interest groups, causes, and social problems.	McGraw-Hill's efforts to prevent sexist stereotypes. 3M's energy conservation program.
Dependence development	Creating or modifying relationships such that external groups become dependent on the focal organization.	Raising switching costs for suppliers. Production of critical defense-related commodities. Providing vital information to regulators.
Legal action	Company engages in private legal battle with competitor on antitrust, deceptive advertising, or other grounds.	Private antitrust suits brought against competitors.
Political action	Efforts to influence elected representatives to create a more favorable business environment or limit competition.	Corporate constituency programs. Issue advertising. Direct lobbying.
Smoothing	Attempting to resolve irregular demand.	Telephone company's lower weekend rates. Inexpensive airline fares on off-peak times.
Demarketing	Attempts to discourage customers in general or a certain class of customers in particular, on either a temporary or a permanent basis.	Shorter hours of operation by gasoline service stations.

FIGURE 6-1. A framework of environmental management strategies. From "Environmental Management: Revising the Markets Perspective," by Carl P. Zeithaml and Valerie A. Zeithaml, *Journal of Marketing* (Spring 1984), pp. 50–57. Used with permission.

Cooperative Tactics

Implicit cooperation	Patterned, predictable, and coordinated behaviors.	Price leadership.
Contracting	Negotiation of an agreement between the organization and another group to exchange goods, services, information, patterns, etc.	Contractual vertical and horizontal marketing systems.
Co-optation	Process of absorbing new elements into the leadership or policymaking structure of an organization as a means of averting threats to its stability of existence.	Consumer representatives, women, and bankers on boards of directors.
Coalition	Two or more groups coalesce and act jointly with respect to some set of issues for some period of time.	Industry association. Political initiatives of the Business Roundtable and the U.S. Chamber of Commerce.

Strategic Maneuvering

Domain selection	Entering industries or markets with limited competition or regulation coupled with ample suppliers and customers; entering high growth markets.	IBM's entry into the personal computer market. Miller Brewing Company's entry into the light beer market.
Diversification	Investing in different types of businesses, manufacturing different types of products, vertical integration, or geographic expansion to reduce dependence on single product, service, market, or technology.	Marriott's investment in different forms of restaurants. General Electric's wide product mix.
Merger and acquisition	Combining two or more firms into a single enterprise; gaining possession of an ongoing enterprise.	Merger between Pan American and National Airlines. Phillip Morris's acquisition of Miller Beer.

FIGURE 6-1. Continued

Product

Product description _____

_____

_____

Life cycle stage _____

Characteristics of stage _____

_____

_____

_____

_____

Complementary products   1. _____   2. _____

3. _____   4. _____   5. _____

Substitute products   1. _____   2. _____

3. _____   4. _____   5. _____

Package: Message _____

Size _____ Shape _____ Color _____

Function _____ Material _____

Brand: Name _____

Type of branding _____

Forecast sales volume _____

Forecast production volume _____

_____

Basic product strategy _____

FIGURE 6-2. Tactical questions for the marketing plan. (Copyright © 1985 by Dr. William A. Cohen. Note: This form is based on an earlier form designed by Dr. Benny Barak, then, of Baruch College.)

Price

Objectives 1. _____ 2. _____

3. _____ 4. _____

Basic per unit cost of acquisition _____

Other relevant costs _____

_____

_____

Discount policy _____

_____

Pricing strategy _____

_____

Unit pricing _____

_____

_____

Forecast revenue _____

Forecast profit _____

Distribution

Channels to be used and timing _____

_____

_____

_____

Alternative strategies: Push/pull _____

Intensive/selective/exclusive _____

FIGURE 6-2. continued

Promotion

Positioning _____

_____

Advertising: Objectives 1. _____

2. _____ 3. _____

Campaign theme _____

_____

Copy theme _____

_____

_____

_____

Graphics and layout _____

_____

_____

_____

Media plan	Description	Length/size	Freq/dates	Cost
Newspapers	_____	_____	_____	_____
	_____	_____	_____	_____
	_____	_____	_____	_____
Magazines	_____	_____	_____	_____
	_____	_____	_____	_____
	_____	_____	_____	_____

FIGURE 6-2. continued

Media plan	Description	Length/size	Freq/dates	Cost
Television	_____	_____	_____	_____
	_____	_____	_____	_____
	_____	_____	_____	_____
Radio	_____	_____	_____	_____
	_____	_____	_____	_____
	_____	_____	_____	_____
Other	_____	_____	_____	_____
	_____	_____	_____	_____
	_____	_____	_____	_____

Budget for advertising _____

Publicity: Objectives 1. _____ 2. _____

3. _____ 4. _____

Action/cost/timing

Description of action	Timing	Cost
_____	_____	_____
_____	_____	_____
_____	_____	_____
_____	_____	_____
_____	_____	_____
_____	_____	_____

FIGURE 6-2. continued

Description of action	Timing	Cost
_____	_____	_____
_____	_____	_____
_____	_____	_____

Budget for publicity _____

Personal selling: Objectives: 1. _____

2. _____ 3. _____

Sales force size and type _____

_____

Sales territories _____

_____

_____

Method of compensation _____

_____

_____

Budget for personal selling _____

Sales promotion: Objectives 1. _____

2. _____ 3. _____

Methods and costs
Method	Timing	Cost
_____	_____	_____
_____	_____	_____
_____	_____	_____

FIGURE 6-2. continued

Method	Timing	Cost
_____	_____	_____
_____	_____	_____
_____	_____	_____
_____	_____	_____

Budget for sales promotion _____

Summary of overall goals/costs/time to achieve of project

Goals 1. _____ 2. _____

3. _____ 4. _____

Overall cost _____ Timing _____

_____

_____

_____

_____

FIGURE 6-2. continued

SUMMARY

In this chapter you have learned how to develop marketing tactics to implement the strategies that were selected in Chapter 5. You have also seen that the implementation of marketing tactics has to do with manipulation of product, price, promotion, and place—the four Ps of marketing—as well as use of the marketing environs. In Chapter 7 you will learn how to determine the total potential available in any given market, and to forecast sales, given the strategy and tactics that have been selected.

7

FORECASTING FOR YOUR
MARKETING PLAN

Forecasting predicts the future. To a significant extent it is done by analyzing the past. Of course, this does not necessarily mean that whatever happened in the past will continue to happen in the future, but here the process of forecasting must begin. By forecasting you will be able to establish in your marketing plan more accurate goals and objectives and the strategies and tactics for reaching these objectives. In fact, forecasting will help you to do all of the following:

Determine markets for your products

Plan corporate strategy

Develop sales quotas

Determine whether salespeople are needed and how many

Decide on distribution channels

Price products or services

Analyze products and product potential in different markets

Decide on product features

Determine profit and sales potential for products

Determine advertising and sales promotion budgets

Determine the potential benefits of various elements of marketing
tactics

Thus sales forecasting involves decisions made in all sections of
your marketing plan. As you will see as you proceed, forecasting
involves some guesswork and a great deal of managerial judgment.
Nevertheless, even guesswork becomes far more valuable when supported by facts and careful analysis. If you had simply pulled facts
out of thin air and constructed your marketing plan on them as a
foundation rather than using a logical methodology and research
integrated with good marketing judgment, even your basic assumptions would likely be as wrong as right. Succeeding under these
conditions would be largely a matter of luck. In the following paragraphs you will learn exactly how to optimize your hunches and
increase your chances of success.

THE DIFFERENCE BETWEEN MARKET AND SALES POTENTIAL AND SALES FORECAST

Market potential, sales potential, and *sales forecast* mean different things
in forecasting. *Market potential* refers to the total potential sales for a
product or service or any group of products being considered for a
certain geographical area over a specific period. Market potential
relates to the total capacity of the market to absorb everything that
an entire industry may produce, whether airline travel, light-bulb
manufacturers, or business books.

Sales potential is the ability of the market to absorb or purchase the
output of a single company in that industry, presumably yours.
Thus, if you are manufacturing motorcycle helmets, you might talk
about a total market potential of $700 million a year, whereas the
ability of the market to purchase that output might be only $50 mil-
lion.

The term *sales forecast* refers to the actual sales you predicted that
your firm will realize in this market in a single year. In turning to
your motorcycle helmet example, perhaps your sales forecast will be

only $20 million, even though the market potential is $700 million for the entire industry and $50 million for your company. Why the difference? Why can't you reach the full market potential in sales? Sales potential may not exceed market potential because of your production capacity. You can produce only $50 million in helmets, not $700 million. There may be many reasons for not trying to achieve 100 percent of the sales potential of which you are capable. One may have to do with limited resources. Perhaps reaching the entire market would require more money than you have available for your marketing campaign, or the margin of return on your investment may be responsible. To achieve 100 percent of anything requires consideration of the law of diminishing returns, which means that the marginal cost of each additional percentage point becomes greater and greater as you try to achieve your potential. Therefore it may be wiser to stop at 90, 80, or even 70 percent of your sales potential because the significantly higher costs of achieving those final percentage points to get to 100 percent make the goal less desirable. There may be far better uses for your resources because the return on each dollar you invest elsewhere may be greater. Finally there may be some factor in the marketplace that will prohibit you from achieving 100 percent; for example, a strong competitor or an unexpected change in an environment. Perhaps the law that requires cyclists to wear helmets is suddenly repealed.

Now the question is how do you find your market and sales potentials and sales forecast for any product, line of products, or your entire company?

FINDING MARKET POTENTIAL

Sometimes it is possible to find the market potential for any specific product already in published form in research done by someone else. It could be the U.S. government, a trade association, or an industrial magazine. At other times it is necessary to derive the market potential for your products by using a chain of information or *chain ratio* which involves connecting many bits of related facts to arrive at the total you are looking for. Some years ago, I wanted to explore the market potential for bulletproof vests or body armor used by foreign military forces for an export project. Because at that time only a few countries used this equipment, this number had to be determined by a chain ratio method. First, the number of units of body armor used by U.S. military forces was calculated from a government publication known as the *Commerce Business Daily*. An average number of body armor units per year was derived from military orders published in it. The size of the U.S. Army in that period and the number of ground troops most likely to use the units were also published in U.S. government sources. From these facts; that is, the total annual sales of body armor to the U.S. Army and the average size of the ground forces during the same period, a ratio of body armor units per soldier could be developed. Next I consulted the *Almanac of World Military Power,* which listed the strength of army ground forces for all countries. Because the body armor was an export military item, the sale of which was controlled by the U.S. government, not every country was a candidate. Therefore only those candidates likely to be approved by the U.S. government were included in the data summary. These figures were totaled and a worldwide total of candidates for the product was calculated. Next, the ratio of body armor units per soldier developed earlier from U.S. data was utilized. The result was a total market potential of military body armor for export from the United States to foreign armies. Note that this was not the sales potential for the sale of body armor by any single company for this market, nor was it a forecast of what body armor would be sold. It was the total market potential.

Let's look at another example. Let's say that a dance studio wishes to know the market potential for dance students in its geographical area. The first step would be to note the total population in the area served by the studio. If the area has a 5-mile circumference, then you will want to know its population. These population figures can be obtained from the Census Surveys of the Department of Commerce. Sometimes your local Chamber of Commerce may have this information or surveys may have been done by local or state governments. Once you have the population, the next step is to arrive at the per-capital expenditure for dancing lessons. Again, government surveys may be helpful or perhaps the industry or associations of dance studios may be able to provide this information. You might also look for trade magazines having to do with professional dance instruction. Naturally you must be sure that the geographical information furnished corresponds closely with the geographical area you are examining because the per-capita expenditure can differ greatly, depending on the region of the country, its culture and climate, and the feelings and interests of its people. If you multiply the population in the 5-mile area by the per-capita expenditure for dance lessons, you will end up with a total annual expenditure.

The market potential for any product or class of product or service can be determined by doing a little thinking about the relevant information you need and then linking it to obtain the final answer.

The Index Method of Calculating Market Potential

An alternate way of calculating market potential is by the use of indices that have already been constructed by someone else from basic economic data; for example, *Sales and Marketing* publishes a survey of buying power indices in July and October each year for consumer markets and in April for industrial and commercial markets. The commercial indices developed by combining estimates of population, income, and retail sales result in a positive indicator of consumer data demand according to regions of the U.S. Bureau of the Census by state, by its organized system of metro areas by counties, or even by cities with populations of 40,000 or more. It is important to recognize that this buying power index, or BPI, is not an absolute one. It therefore must be multiplied by national sales figures to obtain the market potential for any local area. Let's say that you sell a certain brand of national television but only in the local area in your own city store. From the manufacturer you learn that 10 million units are sold every year. Now you want to calculate the market potential for your city which, you assume, is the city of Bakersfield, California, as shown in Figure 7-1. Take the BPI of .1916 listed and multiply it by 10 million. The answer is a market potential of 1,916,000 for the city of Bakersfield, California.

You can also use the index method of calculating market potential for a new product. To do so you would first decide on the demographic, economic, and distribution factors that are important to your product according to the segmentation in the survey of buying power in *Sales and Marketing* or to the instructions furnished with

CALIFORNIA

CAL. ■■■ ESTIMATES			POPULATION—12/31/83						RETAIL SALES BY STORE GROUP 1983				
METRO AREA County City	Total Population (Thousands)	% Of U.S.	Median Age of Pop.	% of Population by Age Group				Households (Thousands)	Total Retail Sales ($000)	Food ($000)	Eating & Drinking Places ($000)	General Mdse. ($000)	Furniture/ Furnish./ Appliance ($000)	Automotive ($000)	Drug ($000)
				18–24 Years	25–34 Years	35–49 Years	50 & Over								
ANAHEIM - SANTA ANA	2,129.4	.9041	30.8	13.6	18.7	20.2	22.0	780.6	13,972,616	2,958,436	1,566,344	1,979,738	673,843	2,107,252	374,620
Orange	2,129.4	.9041	30.8	13.6	18.7	20.2	22.0	780.6	13,972,616	2,958,436	1,566,344	1,979,738	673,843	2,107,252	374,620
• Anaheim	236.6	.1005	30.2	15.0	19.4	18.5	22.2	88.8	1,356,810	289,508	195,112	113,378	110,508	173,300	40,091
Buena Park	67.2	.0285	29.5	15.0	17.4	20.3	20.2	23.1	583,257	140,801	41,002	146,045	18,440	99,835	19,571
Costa Mesa	88.4	.0375	30.4	17.3	22.8	18.2	21.4	36.0	1,479,281	114,986	103,770	436,613	82,210	313,132	8,642
Cypress	44.9	.0191	30.2	12.8	14.7	26.0	16.9	14.5	209,660	85,013	31,172	13,068	6,738	15,138	5,855
Fountain Valley	55.4	.0235	30.4	10.4	15.2	27.9	15.1	16.7	296,437	87,719	25,332	56,413	23,613	5,883	10,242
Fullerton	109.9	.0467	30.9	16.2	18.7	18.5	23.9	42.1	701,368	108,352	87,747	155,267	23,728	128,366	26,524
Garden Grove	129.3	.0549	30.2	14.1	18.1	19.0	22.3	45.4	616,405	192,780	79,021	30,266	22,147	125,638	25,449
Huntington Beach	186.6	.0792	30.0	13.8	20.3	22.0	18.0	69.0	1,172,626	300,185	107,217	137,507	45,107	175,424	32,882
Irvine	74.3	.0315	29.9	12.0	23.9	24.1	13.6	26.4	348,009	97,126	61,218	3,676	5,268	56,416	6,845
La Habra	48.0	.0204	31.1	14.6	17.3	18.2	25.1	18.1	306,183	45,613	26,948	33,873	14,760	107,770	6,445
Newport Beach	68.3	.0290	37.2	13.1	17.8	22.1	31.4	31.3	777,298	120,059	171,947	79,956	17,443	178,416	17,245
Orange	99.9	.0424	30.6	13.6	18.2	20.3	21.6	35.7	919,441	98,882	61,079	180,324	48,469	128,507	12,996
• Santa Ana	223.2	.0948	27.6	15.5	21.0	15.9	18.6	72.5	1,547,475	269,169	161,360	144,875	67,835	246,977	56,111
Westminster	74.8	.0318	30.8	12.8	17.2	21.0	21.7	26.3	904,847	132,701	64,338	242,185	85,047	116,107	7,974
SUBURBAN TOTAL	1,669.6	.7088	31.4	13.2	18.4	21.0	22.4	619.3	11,068,331	2,399,759	1,209,872	1,721,485	495,500	1,686,975	278,418
BAKERSFIELD	443.4	.1883	29.8	12.5	17.3	17.2	23.7	156.8	2,444,657	693,275	250,345	211,605	89,729	334,365	100,935
Kern	443.4	.1883	29.8	12.5	17.3	17.2	23.7	156.8	2,444,657	693,275	250,345	211,605	89,729	334,365	100,935
• Bakersfield	121.3	.0515	29.3	13.6	20.3	16.7	21.8	46.3	1,384,641	345,796	131,787	175,084	68,947	233,686	76,597
SUBURBAN TOTAL	322.1	.1368	30.0	12.1	16.3	17.4	24.4	110.5	1,060,016	347,479	118,558	36,521	20,782	100,679	24,338

CAL. ■■■ ESTIMATES	EFFECTIVE BUYING INCOME 1983						
METRO AREA County City	Total EBI ($000)	Median Hsld. EBI	% of Hslds. by EBI Group: (A) $10,000–$19,999 (B) $20,000–$34,999 (C) $35,000–$49,999 (D) $50,000 & Over				Buying Power Index
			A	B	C	D	
ANAHEIM - SANTA ANA	28,206,195	32,715	16.6	28.3	23.8	21.8	1.1396
Orange	28,206,195	32,715	16.6	28.3	23.8	21.8	1.1396
• Anaheim	2,850,531	28,886	19.7	31.0	21.9	16.1	.1156
Buena Park	787,169	32,391	15.8	31.4	26.2	17.7	.0374
Costa Mesa	1,139,635	28,329	20.1	31.7	20.3	16.0	.0694
Cypress	581,740	38,967	10.6	25.2	29.8	28.6	.0216
Fountain Valley	709,070	41,548	9.3	22.6	32.0	32.6	.0274
Fullerton	1,515,198	31,274	17.5	28.8	21.7	21.4	.0596
Garden Grove	1,489,831	31,053	17.3	31.2	25.2	16.2	.0586
Huntington Beach	2,554,557	34,533	14.7	28.3	25.5	23.6	.1003
Irvine	1,213,880	43,393	7.8	23.2	28.9	36.7	.0412
La Habra	591,949	30,209	17.9	31.5	24.0	16.1	.0245
Newport Beach	1,489,592	38,587	13.5	22.8	18.5	36.1	.0574
Orange	1,245,329	32,058	17.5	27.9	24.3	20.0	.0585
• Santa Ana	2,086,824	26,409	21.8	33.2	21.1	10.2	.1029
Westminster	911,506	33,361	15.8	28.7	27.0	19.4	.0488
SUBURBAN TOTAL	23,268,840	34,140	15.5	27.5	24.4	23.9	.9211

CAL. ■■■ ESTIMATES	EFFECTIVE BUYING INCOME 1983						
METRO AREA County City	Total EBI ($000)	Median Hsld. EBI	% of Hslds. by EBI Group: (A) $10,000–$19,999 (B) $20,000–$34,999 (C) $35,000–$49,999 (D) $50,000 & Over				Buying Power Index
			A	B	C	D	
BAKERSFIELD	4,294,002	23,628	24.2	30.3	17.5	10.1	.1916
Kern	4,294,002	23,628	24.2	30.3	17.5	10.1	.1916
• Bakersfield	1,357,537	26,249	21.1	30.3	20.2	12.1	.0745
SUBURBAN TOTAL	2,936,465	22,638	25.4	30.4	16.4	9.2	.1171
CHICO	1,404,070	17,930	30.2	28.1	10.9	5.4	.0617
Butte	1,404,070	17,930	30.2	28.1	10.9	5.4	.0617
• Chico	235,052	15,119	27.9	25.2	8.4	4.6	.0151
SUBURBAN TOTAL	1,169,018	18,487	30.6	28.9	11.4	5.6	.0466
FRESNO	5,351,877	22,689	25.3	29.8	16.3	10.0	.2318
Fresno	5,351,877	22,689	25.3	29.8	16.3	10.0	.2318
• Fresno	2,452,246	21,204	25.9	29.0	15.9	7.9	.1172
SUBURBAN TOTAL	2,899,631	24,145	24.5	30.8	16.8	12.0	.1146
LOS ANGELES - LONG BEACH	84,749,032	25,280	22.0	28.5	17.9	14.4	3.5274
Los Angeles	84,749,032	25,280	22.0	28.5	17.9	14.4	3.5274
Alhambra	715,447	23,529	24.9	32.0	17.1	9.3	.0323
Arcadia	725,480	34,862	16.2	24.2	21.2	28.6	.0334
Baldwin Park	361,573	23,775	22.8	38.2	16.1	5.6	.0157

FIGURE 7-1. California. Source: *Sales and Marketing Management*, (July 23, 1984).

whatever index you are working. Perhaps you are an automobile dealer and have a franchise for a certain brand of sports car. Demographically, you decide that your target market is in the 25 to 34 age group and that, economically, your target market must make between $35,000 and $49,999 a year. You assume that your dealership is in the Anaheim/Santa Ana region of California. In Figure 7-1 this would be group C. You would select the automotive distribution category from Figure 7-1—Retail Sales by Store Group. Now you must assign a relative weighting among the three factors to equal

100 percent, which will tell you the relative importance of each factor in targeting your market with your new product. In this case you will assume that the weighting of demographics is 20 percent of your total, 30 percent of the economic group, and 50 percent of the distribution. Note that 20, 30, and 50 equal 100 percent and that you consider distribution more than twice as important as demographics—50 versus 20 percent. Calculation of your special BPI therefore equals $.2 \times X$ percent plus $.3 \times Y$ percent, plus $.5 \times Z$ percent.

At this point you are missing the values for X, Y, and Z. Let's find them: X, or the demographic factor, equals the market population aged 25 to 34 divided by the total U.S. population. Because you're looking at the Anaheim/Santa Ana area in Figure 7-1, the population 25 to 34 is given as 18.7 percent. Now multiply this number by the total population for the geographical area of 2,129,400 and divide by the total U.S. population for this segment of 40,541,000 (Figure 7-2). This gives you the value for X, which is .0098.

To calculate Y, or the economic group C that you selected for those earning $35,000 to $49,999 a year, the number of these individuals in the Anaheim/Santa Ana area is listed as 23.8 percent in Figure 7-1. Multiply this amount by the number of households in the area of 780,600 and divide by the total number of U.S. households in this income bracket or 14,511,800 (Figure 7-2). This equals .0128 and is, of course, your value for Y.

Finally, to calculate Z, you go to automotive distribution. Sales of automobiles listed for the Anaheim/Santa Ana area (2,107,252,000) are divided by the national figures in Figure 7-2 (203,052,245,000). This equals .0104 and is the value for Z.

Now, you have the values to put into your equation so let's do it: BPI = $.2 \times .0098 + .3 \times .0128 + .5 \times .0104$, equals .011. The BPI of .011 can be used as a relative indicator to compare the potential buying power of the market you have targeted for your product. You can repeat this sequence for each market targeted. Remember that the total U.S. BPI equals 100.000.

You now calculate sales potential by how much of this market potential belongs to your firm. With no competition perhaps it's all yours. But, again, you must consider your capacity for handling a given number of automobiles. Once you have a sales potential figure you can turn to forecasting.

1983 REGIONAL AND STATE SUMMARIES OF POPULATION

REGION / State	12/31/83 Total Population (Thousands)	% Of U.S.	Median Age of Population	Population by Age Group					12/31/83 Households (Thousands)	% Of U.S.
				0-17 Years (Thousands)	18-24 Years (Thousands)	25-34 Years (Thousands)	35-49 Years (Thousands)	50 & Over (Thousands)		
TOTAL UNITED STATES	235,524.3	100.0000	31.4	62,237.9	29,721.4	40,541.0	41,865.9	61,158.1	85,691.5	100.0000

1983 REGIONAL AND STATE SUMMARIES OF EFFECTIVE BUYING INCOME

REGION / State	1983 Total EBI ($000)	% Of U.S.	Per Capita EBI	Average Household EBI	*Median Household EBI	Households by Effective Buying Income Group				
						Under $10,000 (Thousands)	$10,000-$19,999 (Thousands)	$20,000-$34,999 (Thousands)	$35,000-$49,999 (Thousands)	$50,000 & Over (Thousands)
TOTAL UNITED STATES	2,329,209,922	100.0000	9,889	27,181	23,420	16,122.5	20,114.1	26,257.5	14,511.8	8,685.6

1983 REGIONAL AND STATE SUMMARIES OF RETAIL SALES

REGION / State	1983 Total Retail Sales ($000)	% Of U.S.	Per Household Retail Sales	Retail Sales by Store Group						Sales/Advertising Indexes		
				Food ($000)	Eating & Drinking Places ($000)	General Merchandise ($000)	Furniture/Home Furnish./Appliance ($000)	Automotive ($000)	Drug ($000)	Sales Activity	Buying Power	Quality
TOTAL UNITED STATES	1,186,387,251	100.0000	13,845	278,427,387	118,934,921	147,353,807	52,188,469	203,052,245	39,123,696	100	100.0000	100

FIGURE 7-2. Regional and state summaries of population; regional and state summaries of effective buying income; regional and state summaries of retail sales. Source: *Sales and Marketing Management Magazine*.

BOTTOM-UP AND TOP-DOWN SALES FORECASTING

There are two basic ways to forecast sales: the bottom-up and top-down methods. With the bottom-up method the sequence is to break up the market into segments and calculate separately the demand for each segment. You simply sum the segments for the total sales forecast. Typical ways of doing this are by sales force composites, industry surveys, and intention-to-buy surveys. Each of these is examined shortly.

To accomplish top-down forecasting the sales potential for the entire market is estimated, sales quotas are developed, and a sales forecast is constructed. Typical methods used in top-down surveys are executive judgment, trend projections, a moving average, regression, exponential smoothing, and leading indicators. Let's look at each of these forecasting methods.

Executive Judgment

Executive judgment is known by a variety of names like *jury of executive opinion, managerial judgment,* or *gut feeling.* With this method you just ask executives who have the expertise. This could be many individuals or one single person who may be responsible for the program. This method of forecasting is fairly easy to use, but it is not without its dangers. After all, experts on anything have differing opinions. To overcome individual bias, in fact to provide interchange and reassessment by experts during the survey, some fairly sophisticated methods of exercising executive judgment have evolved. Perhaps the most sophisticated is known as Delphi. Experts are asked their opinions on various questions relating to forecasting events or facts in the future. This survey methodology, however, does not stop with a single round of information gathering. After completion of an expert opinion survey an analysis of the results is conducted to include the range of answers, average, and possibly why the respondents answered the way they did. The summary results of this analysis are given to the experts who responded to the survey during the first round. A second round is then conducted and the same questions are asked. This process may be repeated several times, and a group consensus converges to result in the final forecast. Because this "voting" for sales potential is conducted in secret, it eliminates many psychological factors inherent in a roundtable discussion or consensus building that might block a legitimate input, like relative power in the group of experts. Accordingly, the Delphi method has been a useful and accurate method of using executive judgment in forecasting.

Sales Force Composite

A sales force composite can be obtained by assigning each of your salespeople the duty of forecasting sales potential for a particular territory. These territorial estimates are then summed to arrive at an overall forecast. The dangers in obtaining a forecast this way are based on the possibility that customers may not be entirely truthful in giving information to the salesperson and that the salesperson may overstate or understate the area's potential. Why would a salesperson do this? Perhaps fear of being assigned sales quotas that are difficult to reach may cause the potential to be understated. On the other hand, the salesperson may overstate the potential to prevent the area from being eliminated.

Trend Projections

A trend projection in its simplest form is an analysis of what has already happened, extended into the future. Thus recorded observations of sales over the preceding three years may reveal that they have increased on an average of 10 percent every year. A simple trend projection would assume that sales will increase by 10 percent for the coming year as well. A moving average is a more sophisticated trend projection. With this approach the assumption is made that the future will be an average of past performance rather than a simple linear projection. This minimizes the danger of a random event or element that could create a major impact on the forecast and cause it to be in error; for example, if sales two years ago were $100,000 and last year, $300,000, and you projected the trend into the future by percentage, you would estimate $900,000 for next year. If you estimated in absolute terms of increase in sales; that is, an increase of $200,000 each year, you would estimate $500,000 next year; but if you took a moving average—the average of $100,000 and $300,000 for two years is $200,000—you would forecast $200,000 for the coming year. Thus the moving average equation is simply summing up the sales in a number of periods and dividing by that number.

Industry Survey

In the industry survey method you will survey companies that make up the industry for a particular product or service. A survey may include users or manufacturers or both. The industry method clearly has some of the characteristics of the bottom-up method, rather than the top-down, and some of the advantages and disadvantages of executive opinion and sales force composites. Representatives of companies may, for example, answer inaccurately or companies may be focused on production rather than sales and simply not be aware of the sales for their product.

Regression-Type Analyses

A regression analysis may be linear or it could have to do with multiple regression. With linear regression relationships between sales and a single independent variable are developed to forecast sales data. With multiple regression relationships between sales and a number of independent variables are used. Computer programs are written to assist the marketer in this respect. Sales predictions are made by estimating the values for independent variables and incorporating them into the multiple regression equation. Thus, if a relationship could be found among various independent variables, say units of computers sold, number of males between the ages of 36 and 55, average family income, rate of inflation, and per-capita years of education, a multiple regression equation based on this information can be developed to predict sales for the coming year.

Intention-to-Buy Survey

The intention-to-buy survey is done before the introduction of a new product or new service or for the purchase of any product or service for some period in the future. The main problem with these surveys is that individuals may not always give accurate information regarding their intention to buy products or services in the future. This may be due to an inadequate explanation, a misunderstanding on the part of the respondent, or to other psychological factors, such as the individual's unwillingness to offend or a desire to respond in a way that is socially acceptable. Face-to-face surveys regarding sexually explicit reading matter frequently indicate almost no intent to purchase. Yet, if *Playboy* magazine is used as an example, this is a multimillion dollar business with a large number of readers and subscribers in the general population.

Exponential Smoothing

Exponential smoothing is a timed series approach similar to the moving average method of trend analysis. Instead of a constant set of weights for the observations, however, an exponentially increasing set of weights is used to give the more recent values more weight than the older values. This is exponential smoothing in its most basic form. More sophisticated models include adjustments for factors like trend and seasonal patterns. Again forecasting methods based on exponential smoothing or incorporating it are available in various computer programs.

Leading Indicators

Leading indicators are used in economics to predict recessions and recoveries and, in fact, are the key issues found to have forecasting value by the National Bureau of Economic Research. Typical leading indicators reported by this bureau include the prices of 500 common stocks, new orders for durable goods, index of net business formation, corporate profits after taxes, industrial material prices, and changing consumer installment credit. The problem of sales forecasting with these leading indicators is in relating them to specific products or services. When relationships are found a multiregression model can be constructed, as explained earlier. In fact, leading indicators are incorporated into some computer programs available for forecasting.

Which Method to Use

Some methods are more popular in forecasting than others. A survey of 175 firms conducted some time ago indicated that the jury of executive opinion and sales force composite were the two most popular. This is shown in Figure 7-3. Another study, which confirms that the executive opinion method is still the most popular, found that the two quantitative methods—time series smoothing and regressional analysis—were in second and third place, respectively, with sales force composite following.

Consideration of a sales forecasting method for your particular situation and for your marketing plan should not be based merely on popularity of the method but on situational factors that affect you. These factors include the resources that you have available, the time available, accuracy required, your estimation of the accuracy that can be attained by different methods given to your sales force, your customers, the individuals surveyed, and the cost of the forecast. Thus your judgment in choosing a sales forecasting method, or a combination of methods, is of extreme importance. Alvin Toffler, author of *Future Shock* and *The Third Wave,* probably said it best: "You can use all the quantitative data you can get, but you still have to distrust it and use your own intelligence and judgment."

Method	Regular Use (%)	Occasional Use (%)	Never Used (%)
Jury of executive opinion	52	16	5
Sales force composite	48	15	9
Trend projections	28	16	12
Moving average	24	15	15
Industry survey	22	20	16
Regression	17	13	24
Intention-to-buy survey	15	17	23
Exponential smoothing	13	13	26
Leading indicators	12	16	24

FIGURE 7-3. Utilization of sales forecasting methods by 175 firms. Adapted from Douglas J. Dalrymple, "Sales Forecasting Methods and Accuracy," *Business Horizons, 18* (December 1975), p. 71.

FORECASTING COST AND OTHER IMPORTANT INFORMATION

Forecasting sales alone is insufficient when developing financial information for your marketing plan. You must also forecast the costs involved, their timing, and when they occur in relation to sales. This is done with a project development schedule, a break-even analysis, a balance sheet, a projected profit and loss statement, and cash-flow projections. Let's look at each in turn.

The Project Development Schedule

The project development schedule shown in Figure 7-4 lists every task necessary to implement the project and the money spent during each period. These periods can be months or, in the case of the example indicated, weeks. A further elaboration of the project development schedule can be made with projects in which many different individuals are involved; that is, the expenditures by each individual by time period can also be included on the project development schedule. The project development schedule can be extremely useful in helping to monitor and control the project once it has been implemented.

The Break-Even Analysis

A break-even analysis is used for evaluating relationships among sales revenues, fixed costs, and variable costs. The break-even point is the point at which the number of units sold covers all costs of developing, producing, and selling the product. Prior to this point, you will be losing money, but beyond it you will make money. It is an excellent means for helping you forecast both the success of the product and what you need to succeed before the project is actually initiated because it will tell you the following:

How many units you must sell in order to start making money.

How much profit you will make at any given level of sales.

Months After Project Initiation

Task	1	2	3	4	5	6	7	8	9	10	11	12
Manufacture of units for test manufacturing	$5000											
Initial advertisement in test area	$10,000	$10,000	$10,000									
Shipment of units in test market area	$300	$200										
Analysis of test		$500	$700	$200								
Manufacture of units—1st year				$5000	$10,000	$10,000	$10,000	$10,000				
Phase I advertising and publicity				$10,000	$30,000	$30,000	$15,000					
Shipment of units					$1,000	$1,000	$1,000	$1,000	$500			
Phase II advertising								$10,000	$10,000	$5000	$5000	$5000

FIGURE 7-4. Project development schedule.

How changing your price will affect profitability.

How cost increases or reductions at different levels of sales will affect profitability.

To accomplish a break-even analysis, you must first separate the cost associated with your project into two categories: fixed costs and variable costs.

Fixed costs are those expenses associated with the project that you would have to pay whether you sold one unit or 10,000 units or, for that matter, whether you sold any units at all. If it were necessary to rent a building to implement your project and the owner of the building charged you $50,000 for the period of the project, then this would be a fixed cost for that period. You would have to pay the $50,000 whether you sold no units or millions of units. Research and development costs for a project or a product would also be considered fixed costs. This money would have to be expended whether you sold any of the product or not.

Variable costs are those that vary directly with the number of units that you sell. If it costs you $1.80 to manufacture one unit, and you make the assumption that you will sell all units that you manufacture, then $1.80 is considered a variable cost. If postage for mailing your product to a customer is $1.00, then $1.00 is also a variable cost. If you sell 10 units, then your postage is 10 times $1.00, or $10.00. If you sell 100 units, your total variable costs for postage would be 100 times $1.00, or $100.00. It is sometimes difficult to decide whether to consider costs as fixed or variable, and there may not be a single correct answer. The secret, again, is the use of judgment, along with the advice of financial or accounting experts if they are available. As a general guideline, if there is a direct relationship between cost and number of units sold, consider the cost as variable. If you cannot find such a relationship, consider the cost fixed. The total cost of your project will always equal the sum of the fixed costs plus the variable costs.

Consider the following example for an item that you are going to sell for $10.00. How much profit would you make if you sold 1,000 units?

Fixed Costs

Utility expense at $100 per month for 36 months	$3600
Telephone at $200 per year for three years	600
Product development costs	1000
Rental expense	2500
Total fixed costs	$7700

Variable Costs

Cost of product	$1.00 per unit
Cost of postage and packaging	.50 per unit
Cost of advertising	3.00 per unit
Total variable costs	$4.50 per unit

To calculate the break-even point, start with an equation for profit. Total profit equals the number of units sold times the price at which we are selling them, less the number of units sold multiplied by the total variable cost, less the total fixed cost. If P stands for profit, and p for price, and U equals the number of units sold, V equals variable costs, and F equals fixed costs, then our equation becomes

$$P = (U \times p) - (U \times V) - F$$

You can simplify this to

$$P = U(p - V) - F$$

Substituting the values given in your example, you have

$$P = \$1000(\$10 - \$4.50) - \$7700 =$$
$$\$5500 - \$7700 = -\$2200$$

The significance of the minus is that instead of making a profit at the particular number of units you have estimated; that is, 1000 units, you have lost money—$2200 to be exact. If you wanted to know how many units you must sell in order to make money, or at least at what point you will stop losing money; that is, the break-even point, you can again use the equation for profit:

$$P = U(p - V) - F.$$

Since profit at the break-even point is by definition zero, you can transpose terms and let $P = 0$. Then the break-even point equals F divided by $p - V$.

Because you know that $F = \$7700$ and $p = \$10.00$ and $V = \$4.50$, then the break-even point must equal $\$7700$ divided by $\$10.00 - \$4.50$, or 1400 units.

This means that if you don't change price or reduce expenses in any way you must sell 1400 units of the product before you can start making money. You can calculate this graphically by using the chart in Figure 7-5. A break-even chart has an advantage over using the break-even equation in that it shows you the relationship between profits and sales volume graphically. It is therefore easier for you to see how cost and other factors affect the results.

Even though there are advantages to break-even analysis, keep in mind that there are some limitations. First, break-even analysis shows profit at various levels of sales but does not show the return for our investment. Because there are always alternative uses for a firm's financial resources, it is impossible to compare return on investment solely on the basis of break-even analysis. Yet return on investment, or ROI, is one of the major factors that we must consider. For this type of comparison you must use one of the financial ratio analyses in Chapter 8. Also, break-even analyses do not allow you to examine the cash flow. It is generally accepted that one appropriate way to compare investment or capital budgeting alternatives is to consider the value of the cash flows over a period of time and to discount the cost of capital by an appropriate percentage. You can't do this with break-even analyses either because the time to reach the various levels of sales are not indicated. Nevertheless, break-even analysis is a useful technique and should always be included as a part of the marketing plan.

The Balance Sheet, Projected Profit and Loss Statement, and Cash-Flow Projections

A balance sheet is usually calculated for businesses but it can also be calculated for a project. Basically, it is a financial snapshot of two different points in time—the point at which you start and a point

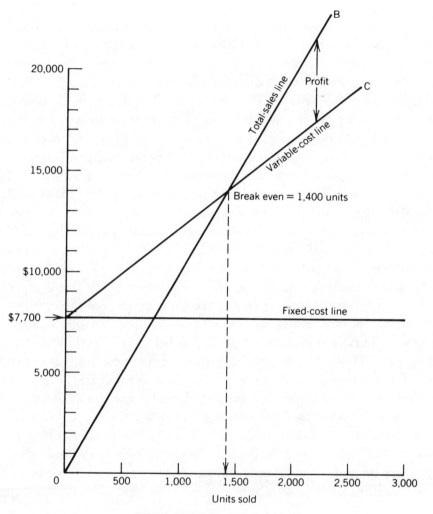

FIGURE 7-5. Break-even analysis chart.

sometime in the future that you select. In Figure 7-6, a balance sheet form is shown for Year 1 and Year 2. You calculate current assets, fixed assets, other assets, current liabilities, and long-term liabilities to arrive at a total net worth. With the marketing plan, this should be done for a time period that seems reasonable for this particular project. It could be simply Year 1 and Year 2, or it could be five years in the future. The same is true regarding the projected profit and loss statement form in Figure 7-7. The projected profit and loss statement is broken down on a monthly basis. You note total net sales from your forecasts done earlier, the cost of sales, and gross profit. You also note controllable expenses and fixed expenses and develop a net profit or loss before taxes for every month. Again, this may be done only for a single year or it can be done for up to five years into the future, depending on the project. This is important because, although the balance sheet may show that after a year you are profitable and after a second year you are even more profitable, it won't show what is happening to you in between the periods you have selected. This is summarized in the cash-flow projections form in Figure 7-8. Here you have cash, income, and expenses on a monthly basis from start-up for a single year or for several years. A cash-flow projection is most important because it will show the availability of cash on a monthly basis. If you need additional cash to keep your project going, it will show when the money will be needed. Obviously this will not only be of great interest to you but also to your potential investors or company finance officers, who want to know not only how much is needed but when.

Balance Sheet

	Year 1	Year 2
Current Assets		
Cash		
Accounts receivable		
Inventory		
Fixed Assets		
Real estate		
Fixtures and equipment		
Vehicles		
Other Assets		
Licenses		
Goodwill		
Total Assets		
Current Liabilities		
Notes payable (due within 1 year)		
Accounts payable		
Accrued expenses		
Taxes owed		
Long-Term Liabilities		
Notes payable (due after 1 year)		
Other		
Total Liabilities		
Net Worth (Assets minus Liabilities)		

Total Liabilities plus Net Worth should equal Assets

FIGURE 7-6. Balance sheet.

Projected Profit and Loss Statement

	Month 1	Month 2	Month 3	Month 4	Month 5	Month 6	Month 7	Month 8	Month 9	Month 10	Month 11	Month 12
Total Net Sales												
Cost of Sales												
Gross Profit												
Controllable Expenses:												
Salaries												
Payroll taxes												
Security												
Advertising												
Automobile												
Dues and subscriptions												
Legal and accounting												
Office supplies												
Telephone												
Utilities												
Miscellaneous												
Total Controllable Expenses												

Fixed Expenses:										
Depreciation										
Insurance										
Rent										
Taxes and licenses										
Loan Payments										
Total Fixed Expenses										
Total Expenses										
Net Profit (Loss) (before taxes)										

FIGURE 7-7. Projected profit and loss statement.

Cash-Flow Projections

	Start-up or prior to loan	Month 1	Month 2	Month 3	Month 4	Month 5	Month 6	Month 7	Month 8	Month 9	Month 10	Month 11	Month 12	TOTAL
Cash (beginning of month)														
Cash on hand														
Cash in bank														
Cash in investments														
Total Cash														
Income (during month)														
Cash sales														
Credit sales payments														
Investment income														
Loans														
Other cash income														
Total Income														
Total Cash and Income														

Expenses (during month)														
Inventory or new material														
Wages (including owner's)														
Taxes														
Equipment expense														
Overhead														
Selling expense														
Transportation														
Loan repayment														
Other cash expenses														
Total Expenses														
Cash Flow Excess (end of month)														
Cash Flow Cumulative (monthly)														

FIGURE 7-8. Cash-flow projections.

SUMMARY

In this chapter you have seen how to forecast for your marketing plan. You have seen how to calculate not only market potential, sales potential, and sales forecasts but also how to forecast costs to develop a project development schedule with costs recorded periodically as needed, how to complete a break-even chart to determine how many units you need to sell to be profitable, how much money you made at any level of units sold, how to complete a balance sheet that indicates the status of your project at the end of various periods of time, and how to calculate a profit and loss statement and cash-flow projections on a monthly basis. No marketing plan can be implemented without financial resources. The forecasts discussed in this chapter will enable you to know what financial resources are necessary, as well as the benefits that will accrue as a result of investing these resources. You are now in a position to calculate important financial ratios and to use them to help determine how efficient your plan is and how beneficial it is to the firm compared with other alternatives. Knowledge of these financial ratios will help you to get resources from those in authority in your company or from outside lenders.

8

IMPORTANT FINANCIAL RATIOS FOR YOUR MARKETING PLAN

The financial ratios in this chapter will help provide the information by which your project may be compared with competing plans on a financial basis. Thus they will not only enable you to better understand the efficiency of the plan you have constructed, but assuming the ratios are favorable, will help you to win support for your project.

MEASURES OF LIQUIDITY

Liquidity is the ability to use the money available in your business. In general, the more liquid, the better the state of financial health. However, this is a bit oversimplified as I will show you later. The ratios intended to measure liquidity in your business will tell you whether you have enough cash on hand, plus assets that can be readily turned into cash, to pay debts that may fall due during any given period. They will also tell you how quickly they can be turned into cash.

THE CURRENT RATIO

The current ratio is possibly the best-known measure of financial health. It answers this question: Does your business have sufficient current assets to meet current debts with a margin of safety for possible losses due to uncollectible accounts receivable and other factors?

The current ratio is computed by using information on your balance sheet. You simply divide current assets by current liabilities; for example, if you consider the sample balance sheet in Figure 8-1, current assets are $155,000 and current liabilities are $90,000; $155,000 divided by $90,000 equals a current ratio of 1.7.

Now you may ask: Is this a good current ratio or is it not? You cannot determine this from the numerical value of 1.7 by itself, even though there is a popular rule of thumb which says that a current ratio of at least two to one is okay. The current ratio very much depends on your business and the specific characteristics of your current assets and liabilities. One major indication, however, is a comparison with other companies in your industry. I'll give you sources for this information in the section "Sources of Ratio Analyses from All Industries."

If after analysis and comparison you decide that your current ratio is too low, you may be able to raise it by the following actions:

1. Increase your current assets by new equity contributions.
2. Try converting noncurrent assets into current assets.
3. Pay some of your debts.
4. Increase your current assets from loans or other types of borrowing which have a maturity of at least a year in the future.
5. Put some of the profits back into the business.

THE ACID TEST, OR "QUICK," RATIO

The acid test, or "quick," ratio is also an outstanding measurement of liquidity. You calculate this ratio as follows: cash plus government securities plus receivables divided by current liabilities.

December 31, 19___

Balance Sheet

Current assets:

Cash	$ 35,000.00	
Accounts receivable	55,000.00	
Inventory	60,000.00	
Temporary investments	3,000.00	
Prepaid expenses	2,000.00	
Total current assets		$155,000.00

Fixed assets:

Machinery and equipment	$ 35,000.00	
Buildings	42,000.00	
Land	40,000.00	
Total fixed assets		117,000.00

Other assets:

None		
Total other assets		0
Total assets		$272,000.00

Current liabilities

Accounts payable	$ 36,000.00	
Notes payable	44,000.00	
Current portion of long-term notes	4,000.00	
Interest payable	1,000.00	
Taxes payable	3,000.00	
Accrued payroll	2,000.00	
Total current liabilities		$ 90,000.00

Long-term liabilities:

Notes payable	$ 25,000.00	
Total long-term liabilities		$ 25,000.00

Equity:

Owner's equity	$115,000.00	
Total equity		$115,000.00
Total liabilities and equity		$272,000.00

FIGURE 8-1. Sample balance sheet for the XYZ Company.

The company shown in Figure 8-1 has no government securities. Therefore the numerator of this figure becomes $35,000 cash plus $55,000 in accounts receivable, or $90,000. This is divided by current liabilities on the same balance sheet of $90,000 to result in an acid test ratio of 1.0.

The quick ratio concentrates on really liquid assets whose values are definite and well known. Therefore the quick ratio will answer this question: If all your sales revenue disappears tomorrow, can you meet current obligations with your cash or quick funds on hand? Usually an acid test ratio of approximately 1.0 is considered satisfactory. However, you must also make this decision conditional on the following:

1. There should be nothing in the offing to slow up the collection of your accounts receivable.

2. The receipt of accounts receivable collections should not trail the due schedule for paying your current liabilities. In checking out this timing, you should consider payment of your creditors sufficiently early to take advantage of any discounts which are offered.

If these two conditions are not met, then you will need an acid test ratio higher than 1.0. It is erroneous to believe that the current or the acid test ratio should always be as high as possible. Only those from whom you have borrowed money would say this is so. Naturally, they are interested in the greatest possible safety of their loan. However, you do not want to have large sums of money lying idle and not earning you additional profits. If you do have idle cash balances and receivables and inventories which are out of proportion to your needs, you should reduce them. The key here is to be conservative enough to keep a safety pad and yet bold enough to take advantage of the fact that you have these resources that can be used to earn additional profits for you. Before you make this decision as to the right amount of liquidity you should consider the two ratios discussed next, average collection period and inventory turnover.

AVERAGE COLLECTION PERIOD

The average collection period is the number of days that sales are tied up in accounts receivable. This number can be calculated by using your profit and loss statement or income statement as shown in Figure 8-2. First, take your net sales which in Figure 8-2 are $1,035,000, and divide this figure by the days in your accounting period, or 365. This equals $2836, the average sales per day in the accounting period. Next, take your accounts receivable which you obtain from the balance sheet, Figure 8-1. Accounts receivable are $55,000. Divide $55,000 by the figure you just calculated ($2836); $55,000 divided by $2836 equals 19. This is the average number of days sales are tied up in receivables. It is also your average collection period.

This tells you how promptly your accounts are being collected, considering whatever credit terms you are extending. It tells you two other things: (1) the quality of your accounts and notes receivable, that is, whether you are really getting paid rapidly or not; and (2) how good a job your credit department is doing in collecting these accounts.

Now the question is whether the figure of 19 days is good or not good? There is a rule of thumb that says the average collection period should not exceed one and one-third times the credit terms offered. Therefore, if your company offers 30 days to pay and the average collection period is only 19 days, you are doing very well. On the other hand, anything in excess of 40 days ($1\frac{1}{3} \times 30 = 40$) would show that you may have a problem.

INVENTORY TURNOVER

Inventory turnover will show you how rapidly your merchandise is moving. It will also show you how much capital you had tied up in inventory to support the level of your company's operations for the period that you are analyzing. To calculate inventory turnover, simply divide the cost of goods sold that you obtain from your income statement, Figure 8-2, by your average inventory. According to Figure 8-2, your income profit and loss statement, the cost of goods sold equals $525,000. You cannot calculate your average inventory from Figure 8-1. You only know that for the period for which the inventory is stated, it equals $60,000. Let's assume that the previous balance sheet indicated that your inventory was $50,000. Then the average inventory for the two periods would be $60,000 plus $50,000 divided by 2, or $55,000. Now, let's see what inventory turnover is: cost of goods sold again was $525,000 divided by $55,000 equals 9.5.

Income Statement		For the year ended December 31, 19___
Sales or revenue:		$1,040,000.00
Less returns and allowances		5,000.00
Net sales		$1,035,000.00
Cost of sales:		
Beginning inventory, Jan 1,19___		250,000.00
Merchandise purchases	500,000.00	
Cost of goods available for sale		750,000.00
Less ending inventory, Dec. 31, 19___		225,000.00
Total cost of goods sold		525,000.00
Gross profit		$ 510,000.00
Operating expenses:		
Selling and general and administrative		
Salaries and wages		180,000.00
Advertising		200,000.00
Rent		10,000.00
Utilities		5,000.00
Other expenses		10,000.00
Total operating expenses		405,000.00
Total operating income		$ 105,000.00
Other revenue and expenses		0
Pretax income		$ 105,000.00
Taxes on income		50,000.00
Income after taxes but before extraordinary gain or loss		$ 55,000.00
Extraordinary gain or loss		0
Net income (or loss)		$ 55,000.00

FIGURE 8-2. Sample income statement for the XYZ Company.

This means that you turned your inventory 9.5 times during the year. Put another way, through your business operations you used up merchandise which total 9.5 times the average inventory investment. Under most circumstances, the higher the turnover of inventory, the better, because it means that you are able to operate with a relatively small sum of money invested in this inventory. Another implication is that your inventory is the right inventory; that is, it is salable and has not been in stock too long. But even here you must consider that too high a figure may be a sign of a problem. Very high inventory may mean that you have inventory shortages and inventory shortages soon lead to customer dissatisfaction and may mean a loss of customers to the competition in the long run.

Is 9.5 a satisfactory inventory turnover or not? Again, the desirable rate depends on your business, your industry, your method of valuing inventories, and numerous other factors that are unique to your situation. Once again, it is helpful to study and compare your turnover rate with that of similar businesses of your size in your industry. Once you have been working and operating for some time, past experiences with inventory turnover will indicate what is good and what is not with less reliance on inventory comparisons.

Frequently it is helpful to analyze not just your total inventory but specific inventory turnover for different products or even groups of products or product lines. This will show you which items are doing well and which are not. You may also prepare turnover analyses for much more frequent periods than a year. Even monthly or weekly periods may be necessary or required for perishable items or items that become obsolete very quickly. Thus you will know to reorder those items which are truly "hot" items early and in plenty of time and you will also know which items you should not order and which items you must order before their value goes down to a point at which you can no longer sell them.

PROFITABILITY MEASURES

Measures of profitability are essential in your business if you are to know how much money you are making, whether you are making as much as you can, or whether you are making money at all. There are several different ratios which will assist you in determining this. These are the asset earning power, return on owner's equity, net profit on sales, investment turnover, and, finally, return on investment (ROI).

Asset Earning Power

Asset earning power is determined by the ratio of earnings before interest and taxes to total assets. From the income statement in Figure 8-2 we can see that total operating profit or income is $105,000.

Total assets from the balance sheet, Figure 8-1, are $272,000. Therefore, $105,000 divided by $272,000 equals 0.39, or 39 percent.

Return on the Owner's Equity

Return on the owner's equity shows the return that you received in exchange for your investment in your business. To compute this ratio you will usually use the average equity for 12 months, if it is available, or, if not, the average of figures from two different balance sheets, your latest and the one before. Return on the owner's equity equals net profit divided by equity. Net profit from Figure 8-2 is $55,000. Equity from Figure 8-1 is $115,000. Assuming the equity from the period before is also $115,000, use this as an average. Therefore, return on the owner's equity equals $55,000 divided by $115,000, which equals 0.48, or 48 percent.

You can calculate a similar ratio by using tangible net worth in lieu of equity. Tangible net worth equals equity less any intangible assets, such as patents and goodwill. If no intangible assets exist, then, of course, the two will be equal.

Net Profit on Sales

The net profit on sales ratio measures the difference between what you take in and what you spend in the process of doing business. Again, net profit was determined to be $55,000. Net sales from Figure 8-2 are $1,035,000. Therefore net profit on sales equals 0.053, or 5.3 percent. This means that for every dollar of sales the company has made a profit of 5.3¢.

The net profit on sales ratio depends mainly on these two factors: (1) operating costs, and (2) pricing policies. Therefore, if this figure goes down, it could be because you have lowered prices or it could be because costs have been increasing at the same time that prices have remained stable.

Again, this ratio should be compared with figures from other similar businesses, and you should consider trends over a period of time. It is also useful to compare net profit on sales ratios for individual products to show which products or product lines should be given additional emphasis and which should be eliminated.

Investment Turnover

This ratio is annual net sales to total assets. In this case net sales of $1,035,000 divided by total assets of $272,000 from Figure 8-1 equals 3.8.

Again, investment turnover should be compared and watched for trends.

Return on Investment (ROI)

There are several different ways of calculating return on investment. It is a very useful method of measuring profitability. One simple way is to take net profit and divide it by total assets. In this case the net profit equals $55,000. Total assets are $272,000. Therefore, $55,000 divided by $272,000 equals 0.20, or 20 percent.

It is desirable here to have the highest net profit for the smallest amount of total assets invested. You can use this rate of return on investment for intercompany and interindustry comparisons, as well as pricing costs, inventory, and investment decisions, and many other measurements of efficiency and profitability. However you use it, always be sure that you are consistent in making your comparisons; that is, be sure that you use the same definitions of net profit and assets invested.

Here are some additional measures of profitability using ROI:

1. *Rate of earnings on total capital employed equals net income plus interest and taxes divided by total liabilities and capital.* This ratio serves as an index of productivity of capital as well as a measure of earning power in operating efficiency.

2. *Rate of earnings on invested capital equals net income plus income taxes divided by proprietary equity and fixed liabilities.* This ratio is used as a measure of earning power of the borrowed invested capital.

3. *Rate of earnings on proprietary equity equals net income divided by total capital including surplus reserves.* This ratio is used as a measure of the yield on the owner's investment.

4. *Rate of earnings on stock equity equals net income divided by total capital including surplus reserves.* This ratio is used as a measure of the attractiveness of common stock as an investment.

5. *Rate of dividends on common stock equity equals common stock dividends divided by common stock equity.* This ratio is used to indicate the desirability of common stock as a source of income.

6. *Rate of dividends on common stock equity equals common stock dividend per share divided by market value per share of common stock.* This ratio is used as a measure of the current yield on investment in a particular stock.

SOURCES OF RATIO ANALYSES FROM ALL INDUSTRIES

To be able to compare your business with other businesses in your industry it is necessary to obtain pertinent data on other businesses. The following are sources of this information:

1. Dun & Bradstreet, Inc., Business Information Systems, 99 Church Street, New York, NY 10007. This firm publishes key business ratios in 125 lines annually. Copies can be obtained free on request.

2. Accounting Corporation of America, 1929 First Avenue, San Diego, CA 92101. This organization publishes *Parameter of Small Businesses* which classifies its operating ratios for various industry groups on the basis of gross volume.

3. National Cash Register Co., Marketing Services Department, Dayton, OH 45409. This firm publishes *Expenses in Retail Businesses* which examines the cost of operations in over 50 kinds of businesses obtained from primary sources, most of which are trade associations.

4. Robert Morris Associates, Philadelphia National Bank Building, Philadelphia, PA 19107. Robert Morris has developed and published ratio studies for over 225 lines of business.

5. The Small Business Administration. The SBA has a new series of reports that provide expenses as a percentage of sales for many industries. Although the reports do not provide strict ratio information, a comparison of percentage expenses will be very useful for your financial management.

6. Trade Associations. Many national trade associations publish ratio studies, including the following:

Air-Conditioning & Refrigeration Wholesalers, 22371 Newman Avenue, Dearborn, MI 48124

Air Transport Association of America, 1000 Connecticut Avenue, NW, Washington, DC 20036

American Bankers Association, 90 Park Avenue, New York, NY 10016

American Book Publishers Council, One Park Avenue, New York, NY 10016

American Booksellers Association, 175 Fifth Avenue, New York, NY 10010

American Carpet Institute, 350 Fifth Avenue, New York, NY 10001

American Electric Association, 16223 Meyers Street, Detroit, MI 48235

American Institute of Laundering, Doris and Chicago Avenues, Joliet, IL 60433

American Institute of Supply Associations, 1505 22d Street NW, Washington, DC 20037

American Meat Institute, 59 East Van Buren Street, Chicago, IL 60605

American Paper Institute, 260 Madison Avenue, New York, NY 10016

American Society of Association Executives, 2000 K Street, NW, Washington, DC 20006

American Supply Association, 221 North LaSalle Street, Chicago, IL 60601

Automotive Service Industry Association, 230 North Michigan Avenue, Chicago, IL 60601

Bowling Proprietors' Association of America, Inc., West Higgins Road, Hoffman Estates, IL 60172

Florists' Telegraph Delivery Association, 900 West Lafayette Boulevard, Detroit MI 48226

Food Service Equipment Industry, Inc., 332 South Michigan Avenue, Chicago, IL 60604

Laundry and Cleaners Allied Trades Association, 1180 Raymond Boulevard, Newark, NJ 07102

Material Handling Equipment Distributors Association, 20 North Wacker Drive, Chicago, IL 60616

Mechanical Contractors Association of America, 666 Third Avenue, Suite 1464, New York, NY 10017

Menswear Retailers of America, 390 National Press Building, Washington, DC 20004

Motor and Equipment Manufacturers Association, 250 West 57th Street, New York, NY 10019

National-American Wholesale Lumber Association, 180 Madison Avenue, New York, NY 10016

National Appliance and Radio-TV Dealers Association, 1319 Merchandise Mart, Chicago, IL 60654

National Association of Accountants, 525 Park Avenue, New York, NY 10022

National Association of Building Owners and Managers, 134 South LaSalle Street, Chicago, IL 60603

National Association of Electrical Distributors, 600 Madison Avenue, New York, NY 10022

National Association of Food Chains, 1725 Eye Street, NW, Washington, DC 20006

National Association of Furniture Manufacturers, 666 North Lake Shore Drive, Chicago, IL 60611

National Association of Insurance Agents, 96 Fulton Street, New York, NY 10038

National Association of Music Merchants, Inc., 222 West Adams Street, Chicago, IL 60606

National Association of Plastic Distributors, 2217 Tribune Tower, Chicago, IL 60611

National Association of Retail Grocers of the United States, 360 North Michigan Avenue, Chicago, IL 60601

National Association of Textile and Apparel Wholesalers, 350 Fifth Avenue, New York, NY 10001

National Association of Tobacco Distributors, 360 Lexington Avenue, New York, NY 10017

National Automatic Merchandising Association, Seven South Dearborn Street, Chicago, IL 60603

National Beer Wholesalers' Association of America, 6310 North Cicero Avenue, Chicago, IL 60646

National Builders' Hardware Association, 1290 Avenue of the Americas, New York, NY 10019

National Electrical Contractors Association, 1200 18th Street, NW, Washington, DC 20036

National Electrical Manufacturers Association, 155 East 44th Street, New York, NY 10017

National Farm and Power Equipment Dealers Association, 2340 Hampton Avenue, St. Louis, MO 63130

National Home Furnishing Association, 1150 Merchandise Mart, Chicago, IL 60654

National Kitchen Cabinet Association, 918 Commonwealth Building, 674 South 4th Street, Louisville, KY 40204

National Lumber and Building Material Dealers Association, Ring Building, Washington, DC 20036

National Machine Tool Builders Association, 2071 East 102d Street, Cleveland, OH 44106

National Office Products Association, Investment Building, 1511 K Street, NW, Washington, DC 20015

National Oil Jobbers Council, 1001 Connecticut Avenue, NW, Washington, DC 20036

National Paper Box Manufacturers Association, 121 North Bread Street, Suite 910, Philadelphia, PA 19107

National Paper Trade Association, 220 East 42d Street, New York, NY 10017

National Parking Association, 1101 17th Street, NW, Washington, DC 20036

National Restaurant Association, 1530 North Lake Shore Drive, Chicago, IL 60610

National Retail Furniture Association, 1150 Merchandise Mart Plaza, Chicago, IL 60654

National Retail Hardware Association, 964 North Pennsylvania Avenue, Indianapolis, IN 46204

National Retail Merchants Association, 100 West 31st Street, New York, NY 10001

National Shoe Retailers Association, 200 Madison Avenue, New York, NY 10016

National Sporting Goods Association, 23 East Jackson Boulevard, Chicago, IL 60604

National Stationery and Office Equipment Association, Investment Building, 1511 K Street, NW, Washington, DC 20005

National Tire Dealers and Retreaders Association, 1343 L Street, NW, Washington, DC 20005

National Wholesale Druggists' Association, 220 East 42d Street, New York, NY 10017

National Wholesale Hardware Association, 1900 Arch Street, Philadelphia, PA 19103

National Wholesale Jewelers Association, 1900 Arch Street, Philadelphia, PA 19103

North American Heating & Airconditioning Wholesalers Association, 1200 West 5th Avenue, Columbus, OH 43212

Optical Wholesalers Association, 222 West Adams Street, Chicago, IL 60606

Paint and Wallpaper Association of America, 7935 Clayton Road, St. Louis, MO 63117

Petroleum Equipment Institute, 525 Dowell Building, Tulsa, OK 74114

Printing Industries of America, 711 14th Street, NW, Washington, DC 20005

Robert Morris Association, Philadelphia National Bank Building, Philadelphia, PA 19107

Scientific Apparatus Makers Associates, 20 North Wacker Drive, Chicago, IL 60606

Shoe Service Institute of America, 222 West Adams Street, Chicago, IL 60606

Super Market Institute, Inc., 200 East Ontario Street, Chicago, IL 60611

United Fresh Fruit and Vegetable Association, 777 14th Street, NW, Washington, DC 20005

United States Wholesale Grocers' Association, 1511 K Street, NW, Washington, DC 20005

Urban Land Institute, 1200 18th Street, NW, Washington, DC 20036

Wine and Spirits Wholesalers of America, 319 North Fourth Street, St. Louis, MO 63102

9

PRESENTING THE MARKETING PLAN

By the time you have reached this chapter you will have all the information necessary to put together a first-rate marketing plan. But now the problem is this. Having done all necessary research and assembled your material, completed the situational analysis and environmental scanning, established goals and objectives and developed marketing strategy and tactics, done necessary forecasting, and developed financial information, it is important not to drop the ball at the very end. The marketing plan must be presented to your target audience in the most professional manner possible. That is the purpose of this chapter—to show you how to present your marketing plan as a physical product and as a formal oral presentation.

THE PHYSICAL PRODUCT

The old saying "You can't judge a book by its cover" may be true, but the problem is that, although everyone agrees with this statement, a professionally-appearing document has a far better chance of success, psychologically, than one that appears to be put together in a haphazard fashion. Therefore it is critical that your marketing plan look as good as it really is. If it does, the psychological advantage is yours, and the reader will proceed from the premise that your plan is professional, well researched, and completely thought through. On the other hand, if the document you present does not have a professional appearance, the contents must overcome a significant psychological disadvantage and disprove the premise that your plan is unprofessional. How can we make our plans look more professional?

First, the plan should be typed by a single typist, and the typing should be neat and free from typographical errors and obvious corrections. A standardized method of typing and collating the different sections of the plan should be used. Which method you choose is usually not critical, unless specified by someone who has asked you to prepare the plan. Standardization, which is always important, includes a form for footnotes, bibliography, and so forth. Sometimes, when several different people work on a single marketing plan, different sections of the plan are assigned to the participants. Although there is nothing wrong with that, one individual should be assigned the task of assembling the overall product to ensure that it is typed consistently. If one coordinator is not assigned, it is not unusual to find sections that are at odds; for example, a conclusion in one section may be nullified by a statement in another or terminology may differ among sections. If the typing is done by different individuals, the marketing plan will have an inconsistent appearance, different styles of type, darkness of imprint, margins that vary, and so forth. Several different style manuals are available at your library. Stick with one of them.

Illustrations and charts should be included as a part of your marketing plan. You must never, however, include illustrations merely to pad the marketing plan nor should you include any unnecessary information. Of course, if information that does not fall easily into the body of the plan is required, it can be added as an appendix. But it is important that you recognize that the information in the appendix is necessary and not simply used to increase the size of the document. There is no minimum length for a marketing plan. Many venture capitalists tend to prefer shorter plans, say 50 pages or less. This is because they review so many marketing and business plans that they prefer to have the essential facts at the beginning and to request additional information only if needed. On the other hand, if you are preparing the plan for yourself or someone else is paying you to prepare it, or you are preparing one as a member of a large corporation, you will probably want to ensure that all the information is available right from the start. This will require at least 50 pages and maybe more than 100. The rule to follow when deciding how long the marketing plan should be is simply to make it long enough to tell your entire story, always considering what your readers will want to know. If you need more pages to cover essential information, use them. On the other hand, if you have covered all the information you feel is necessary for your reader, then stop. Don't pad.

The final point to consider is binding. Some excellent plans are typed neatly and compiled with correct and complete information, yet they still fail to give a professional appearance simply because a cheap binding is used. What amazes me is how easy and inexpensive it is to get a really top-of-the-line binding. Hardcover binding is available from many printers for less than $10. If you are unable to obtain hardcover binding, consider spiral binding. A mechanical means of doing rapid spiral binding is available at many printers. Check in the Yellow Pages of your telephone book for additional sources. Again, the point here is to make your marketing plan look as professional as you can. Your marketing plan should be good and it should look good.

THE FORMAL PRESENTATION

In most cases simply preparing the marketing plan is insufficient. You must also make a formal presentation of your marketing plan to someone else. This may be to individuals who may be interested in funding your plan or to higher management in your company who may be willing to allocate resources to it. In all cases you must first consider the object of your presentation. Usually the object of a marketing plan is to persuade management or investors to allocate resources; that is, money, to enable you to implement your project. Remember that no one is going to give you money for your plan unless they are convinced that it will succeed anu will make money for them. Therefore these individuals will want to know how much money can be made, how much money will be needed from them and when, how long it will be before they will get their money back, exactly what you will do with the money, and why you will succeed with your project. Therefore, although the outline of your marketing plan can be used as described in preceding chapters, some minor changes may be needed for maximum impact. Accordingly, I recommend the following outline for your formal presentation.

I. Introduction. In the introduction you cover the information in your executive summary, including the opportunity and why it exists, the money to be made, the money that's needed, and some brief financial information, such as return on investment, to support the extent of the opportunity as you see it.

II. Why You Will Succeed. In this section you will cover your situational analysis and environmental scanning and the research you did to support it. You should conclude the section with problems and opportunities as well as the projects' goals and objectives.

III. Strategy and Tactics. In this section you will cover the strategy you are going to follow as well as the tactics used to implement the strategy. The main message of this section is the competitive differential advantage that you have over your competition, that unique difference that will allow you to succeed where others may fail.

IV. Forecast and Financial Information. In this section you will cover your forecast, project development schedule, profit and loss statement, and financial ratios and data. This section will contain a detailed description of what you need and when you need it. Sometimes, because of the limited time available for presentation, you may have to cut down on this section and present only the main points. The important financial information, however, should always be available so that in the question-and-answer session that follows you can provide additional data.

V. Conclusion. In this final section of your formal presentation you must restate the opportunity and why you will succeed with it, the money that is required, and the expected return on the investment.

Preparing for Your Presentation

Your first step in preparing for your presentation is obtaining the answers to several important questions. These include the time and date of your presentation, where it is to be held, the time permitted for your presentation, who the audience is, who is in the audience, and the purpose of your presentation. You should also think about the audience's attitude, their knowledge and preconceived notions, anything that requires particular care, and the main points to cover. Probably 99 times out of 100 the purpose of presenting your marketing plan will be to obtain resources. This holds true whether you are an entrepreneur presenting a marketing plan to the loan officer of a bank, a venture capitalist, or someone else who is going to lend you money, or whether you are a member of a company and have been asked to prepare a plan as a potential investment. The exception is a plan that you have prepared as a consultant to an entrepreneur or larger corporation interested in implementing it. In this case your main object is to demonstrate that you have done your job by preparing a plan that your client can use to get resources and eventually to implement.

Think through and write down the answers to these questions, because they can affect what you are going to cover and how you are going to do it.

Your next step is to make an outline of your main and supporting points. To develop this outline you need not follow the outline of the written marketing plan report. Remember that you may wish to change your order of presentation depending on your audience. With different audiences, different sections or topics must be emphasized. If the audience is primarily financial, don't leave out any financial information from your presentation. On the other hand, an engineering audience will probably be more interested in technical aspects of your product, their manufacture, and so forth. Some financial data can be excluded in order to include more technical information. The whole purpose of writing out a new outline is to allow you to make the maximum impact with material that you have prepared.

The following technique is sometimes useful in helping you to prepare your outline and its supporting points. Obtain a number of 3 × 5 filing cards and, without stopping to think, write down everything you think should be emphasized in your presentation, one item to a card. Don't try to coordinate anything at this point. If you have statistics that you think you should include, or anecdotes, quotes, or even jokes, write each on a separate card. Once you have written down as many ideas as you think you can, begin to organize the cards into your main points and supporting points. Statistics will be a supporting point to some main points. So will anecdotes, jokes, and quotes. By using this system you will soon have a stack of cards organized in a logical fashion for your presentation. If you wish to check just how logical it is, once you have your cards arranged as you think they should be, begin to write down the outline of your presentation. Notice that this is a flexible system and that you can move cards around, as well as add cards and points to the outline as new ideas occur.

Note that at no point have I said to write out a speech. Your presentation should never be written out in detail. If you do, you will probably present it that way. Marketing speeches are dull and boring. You want your marketing plan presentation to reflect the work, the accuracy, and the potential and excitement it represents for whoever implements it. This cannot be done with a speech, so leave your presentation in outline form.

Once you have completed your outline you can begin planning for your visual aids.

Planning for Visual Aids

Visual aids can greatly enhance the impact of your presentation and should always be used in making a presentation of a marketing plan. Your basic options are the use of 35-mm slides, overhead transparencies, charts, handouts, or chalkboards. All have their advantages and disadvantages. Let's look at both.

Slides (35-mm). A 35-mm projector and 35-mm slides are easy to carry around. They are eminently transportable. Furthermore the slides can be done in color, they look professional, can be manipulated by the presenter, and yield an extremely professional experience. The disadvantages are the lead time to prepare the slides, the cost, and the difficulty of changing a particular slide once it has been developed. New systems are now available by which 35-mm slides are constructed by computer and then enhanced, in color or otherwise, rapidly and at relatively low cost per unit. However, the equipment required costs several thousand dollars and, of course, you need a computer; therefore this system will not be readily available to everyone.

Overhead Transparencies. Overhead transparencies are as portable as 35-mm slides. The projectors are heavier, however, more cumbersome, and less transportable. There is also a lead time associated with the preparation of overhead transparencies. If camera-ready artwork is available, machines located at many printing shops can construct an instant overhead transparency from your camera-ready copy. With this method the lead time is greatly reduced. Another advantage of an overhead transparency is that you can write on it as you talk. As a result, you can also make changes in the transparency if required. This you cannot do with a 35-mm slide. Although you can talk and operate a projector with overhead transparencies at the same time, this is easier to do with a 35-mm projector, because you must actually be at the overhead transparency projector to make the change from transparency to transparency, whereas a 35-mm projector can be operated from some distance by a remote control device.

Handouts. Handouts are easy to make, because they are reproduced in quantity, even in color if required. Handouts can be changed and new information substituted for the old. But handouts suffer from two major disadvantages. First, if the information is extensive and the audience large, a considerable amount of material must be carried around and distributed. Second, audiences will frequently read ahead in your handout and miss the points you are covering. At the same time, a dramatic sequence of events that you've built into your presentation may be spoiled as the audience reads ahead to your "punch line."

Charts. Charts may be the flip variety or they can be large cardboard or plastic devices that are used in conjunction with your other visual aids. Charts are much less portable than 35-mm slides, transparencies, or handouts. One advantage of a chart, however, is that if you have an artistic bent you may prepare them on your own and thus need not allow as much lead time as with overhead transparencies or 35-mm slides. This places them in the same category as handouts as far as this particular attribute goes. However, if you do prepare your own charts, it is important that it not be done the night before. You need to allow enough time to check them for accuracy, typographical errors, and so forth. If you do them the night before, you are almost certain to make a number of errors.

Chalkboards. Chalkboards on which you write with chalk or plastic boards on which you can write with colored pencils can also be useful during presentations. The major disadvantage is that you cannot prepare your material ahead of time. In this case, the advantage is also the disadvantage, for there is much more drama and spontaneity in having your audience see the point you wish to get across as you write it. However, there are usually so many disadvantages with chalkboards that, at best, they can be used only as an adjunct to your other systems. These include the fact that they are not readily transportable, the material is not permanent, you cannot use the material to key your memory (an advantage with all four other visual systems), and chalkboards may not always be available where you give your presentation.

Whatever system of visual aids you plan on, you should prepare your visual aids immediately, even before you begin to practice for the first time, and not wait until the last moment. My recommendation is that you attempt a presentation in the time you have been allocated at least once. When you are reasonably confident that your presentation will not change in its major points, have your visual aids constructed at once. The reason for this is not only the long lead time—which is a lot longer than you might think, even given a limited number of materials to be reproduced—but also because you want to allow yourself time to proofread the material that is done for you by someone else. I have found after having given hundreds of presentations using visual transparencies, slides, and charts, as well as handouts prepared professionally by others, that in 90 percent of the cases typographical errors will occur. If you wait until the last minute to have your visual aids prepared, you may find that insufficient time is available to correct the errors. So once you know what you want on your visual aids, have them made up at once. You can practice with dummy visual aids while the real ones are being prepared.

Use of Products as Visual Aids. Sometimes the product that is the subject of your marketing plan is available. These products or "feelies" are, in general, very useful for adding interest to your presentation. However, it is important to recognize that if you use products as part of your visual aids, they should be relevant to your presentation. If your product is interesting and the particular twist or unique advantage you have in your product is something worth seeing, then it's worth showing such a product. On the other hand, if your marketing plan is simply to market a product that everyone is familiar with, such as a safety pin, an eraser, or envelopes, don't use the product as a visual aid unless there is some unique aspect that should be demonstrated; do something else with the time you have available.

The Keys to Good Visual Aids

To summarize our discussion on visual aids, I'd like you to think about the following points as you prepare for your presentation.

Make sure you use aids that contain material that is easy to read, without too much information on each. Visual aids are not simply parts of a presentation that must be included. They must make an impact on the audience and reinforce what you say, or make what you say more easily understood. If there is too much information on a single view, your audience will get lost. If the type is too small, your audience will not be able to read what you have prepared.

Pointing techniques. If you are going to use a pointer as an extension of your arm, be careful that when you use it you do not turn your body so as to cut off the view of someone in your audience. The best way to avoid this is to follow this rule: If you are standing to the right of the view of your presentation, then have the pointer in your left hand. This will keep you from turning your back on the audience and cutting off the view of members of the audience who are to your right front. On the other hand, if you are standing to the left of the view, use the pointer in your right hand. In this way, you will not turn your back and cut off the view of individuals in the audience who are on your left front.

Keep your visual aids covered until you use them. Displaying many visual aids simultaneously only causes distractions. It may cause you to lose the interest of your audience, who may become more interested in your visuals than in you. So show one visual. Then, only when you're ready, show the next.

The Practice Sequence

I want to emphasize that you must never memorize anything. If you try to memorize your presentation, you may forget it. Memorization simply isn't necessary. Nor is it necessary to read your presentation. Believe me when I tell you, I learned this lesson the hard way. As a young Air Force officer, I was once asked to make a presentation to 300 science and math teachers on space navigation, a topic in which I had great interest at the time. I had prepared superb 35-mm full-color slides and had spent considerable time writing and honing a one-hour speech which I had written out. I memorized this speech perfectly, word for word, and coordinated it with my very excellent multicolor slides. When the day came I looked out at 300 science and math teachers, I gulped once and could barely remember my name. After several stumbling attempts trying to remember the speech I thought I had memorized perfectly, I reached in my pocket and for the next hour read the speech. What a mistake! Hours of work wasted unnecessarily for a boring speech. After all, I knew the subject matter. By simply flipping through my slides, I could talk to my audience and tell them about each. That really was all that was required for an excellent presentation.

The same is true for you. To give an outstanding presentation of your marketing plan, you don't have to memorize anything and you don't have to bore your audience to death by reading a speech either. You know your subject better than anyone else. Once you are prepared, just going through your presentation as you use your visuals to support what you say will enable you to communicate with your audience for maximum impact. In this way, you will give the best presentation.

If your visual aids are complete during practice, use them. But, if not, write the content of your visual aids on 8½ × 11 sheets of paper and practice with them. You may use the cards that you prepared earlier to help remember the main points. I recommend going through your presentation three times and making adjustments as necessary in order to complete the presentation and get your points across in the time you have been allotted.

If you use cards to supplement what you have displayed on your visual aids to help you remember the main points, do not write more than a few words on the cards. If you do, you will read them. And once you begin to read your cards, you will probably continue to read them. Then you are back to reading a speech. So write just a few words and then talk about those words. Of course, the same is true of the visual aids. They should be sparsely worded for maximum impact. You simply look at the visual aid and speak about it to your audience.

As I fine-tune my presentation, I may add statistics, I may take out a point here or add one there, and I may modify other things I have written. At the same time, I am concentrating on staying within whatever time constraints have been given me. Time is crucial.

The Importance of Controlling Your Time

You must always control your time, and practice within as well as give your presentation in the allotted time, whether this is 15 minutes or several days. Why is this so? The individuals in your audience, no matter how critical and important they feel your presentation will be to them, allot a certain amount of time for it in their schedules. If you exceed this time, even by a few minutes, you will make it more difficult, even impossible, to achieve the objective of your presentation. If you exceed your allotted time by only a few minutes, it may be annoying. If you go over by more than that, this could cause a negative impact on the schedules of people in the audience.

Let me give you a couple of examples to illustrate just how important controlling your time can be. A few years ago a large aerospace corporation was competing for a major government contract with the Air Force. Fifty representatives from the Air Force flew in to receive what was to be a full day's presentation to end no later than 4:00 P.M. The presentation, however, was not well planned by the presenters. By 3:30 P.M. it was clear their full presentation could not be completed as planned within the allotted time. The audience was not given a choice. The presenters plunged on, determined to cover every single one of their overhead transparencies as planned. The presentation was completed more than an hour late. As a result, most of these government representatives missed their return flights. While the presentation was sufficiently important that these representatives would not cut the presentation short, the looks on their faces easily told the story of how they felt about the time overrun. Maybe this was only one factor among a number, but this company did not win the contract, regardless of the quality of the technical proposal or competitiveness in price.

Such mistakes in controlling time are not limited to industry. One practice generally followed in hiring university professors is to require the candidate to make a presentation to the prospective department on some research that he or she has accomplished. Several years ago, a major university reviewed the credentials of a candidate who had graduated from a well-known university in the eastern United States. This individual's background was so outstanding that the members of the department had all but decided to hire the candidate, even before he made a face-to-face appearance. The candidate was asked to make a 30-minute presentation on the research for his PhD dissertation. Initially, the interview visit seemed to be going well. At the appropriate point in the candidate's visit he was asked to make his 30-minute presentation. All 14 members of this department listened attentively as the candidate began because his presentation on his research was interesting and relevant. However, 30 minutes after he started he was still speaking. At 40 minutes professors in the audience began to fidget; several had other meetings scheduled. A few had classes and excused themselves. Forty-five minutes went by, 50 minutes. Finally, at 55 minutes the candidate concluded. This candidate was still hired as a professor by the institution involved. However, the candidate was originally to be hired for a position leading to tenure and promotion, but, because of 25 minutes, the department voted to hire him only on a one-year appointment. After one year, he might be considered for the original position that was to be offered. Twenty-five minutes cost this professor one year in time toward a promotion to the next rank, including pay, allowances, and other fringe benefits.

The lesson is clear. Do not exceed the time that is allotted for your presentation. Practice to make sure that you stay within this time.

Once you have practiced three times and have pretty good control over your presentation, I recommend that you do the presentation twice more, only this time in front of other people. This can mean a spouse, friend, brother, sister, or whomever. The important thing is that we are not looking for a pat on the back but for a real critique. This includes the answers to questions such as: Should I talk louder or softer? Did I use eye contact? Did I talk in a conversational fashion, or did I simply start reading from my cards or visual aids? Did I have a good opener that grabbed the interest of my audience? Did I close my presentation with impact? Did I use supporting matter such as anecdotes or statistics? Was there something particular I said that was liked? Something not liked? If I have visual aids available at this time, I will certainly use them. Were they large enough, and could they be read? Or did they need to be improved in some fashion? Was there anything in my presentation that could not be understood, and, if so, what could I do to make it understandable? Finally, are there any other points or comments or advice that may be relevant?

Questions and Answers and How to Prepare for Them

Questions and answers are going to be a part of every presentation you make on a marketing plan. The first thing you must do is prepare ahead of time. Research has shown that approximately 85 percent of the questions asked can actually be anticipated. So once you have prepared your presentation, think about what questions might be asked by your audience, and prepare for them. You might also have your practice audience ask questions, both to test your preparation for answering them and your ability to think on your feet.

Next have your facts, figures, quotes—all of this information—available. Many astute presenters—who cannot fit all the information they would like into their presentation due to time restrictions—have other visual aids ready and waiting so that when this information is requested it can be immediately used to good advantage. An example might be financial information such as cash flow on a monthly basis. You may not have the time to cover this in your formal presentation. However, it would not hurt to have an overhead transparency or some other visual aid available so that when you are asked a question about these details, you can immediately use your visual aid, demonstrating not only your knowledge, but your preparation for any eventuality.

Remember to keep cool no matter how embarrassing the question or even whether you can answer it. Basically, a four-step procedure in answering questions is recommended. First, restate the question that has been asked. This ensures that the entire audience has heard the question and that you understand it. It also gives you additional time to think about your answer. Second, state your position or your answer to the question. Third, state the supporting reasons for your position. Finally restate your position to make it clear to everyone.

In general, keep your answers brief. If you know the individual who asked the question, use his or her name. If the individual is right and you are wrong about something, admit it. Or, if you don't know something, admit that also. Simply say, "I don't know." Of course, if every other answer is, "I don't know," you can expect your audience to believe that you have not done a very good job of preparing or are not very much of an expert on the marketing plan or on your material.

Never get sidetracked or get in a quarrel with someone who has asked a question. Always be tactful, even with individuals who attack you or your position. Harshly correcting a questioner can turn others in your audience against you even if they agree with your point of view. This is because the audience may be members of the same firm or group, and also because they may resent the manner of your response, especially if the question is innocently, if not tactfully, asked.

Use of the Mental Visualization Technique

For years I prepared for many events by mentally rehearsing them the night before. As I lay in bed thinking about what I was to do the next day, I would go over the entire event in my mind and rehearse it again and again. I never thought much about this, except that it seemed to improve my performance no matter what the event—an athletic event, a test I was going to take, or a presentation I was going to make. Then, on January 13, 1982, the *Wall Street Journal* published a special article entitled, "Why Do Some People Out-Perform Others?" It quoted a psychologist by the name of Charles Garfield who had investigated top performance among business people as well as others. Garfield said that he was most surprised by a trait that he called mental rehearsal, which had meanwhile caught on as a popular concept in sports. According to Garfield, top chief executives would imagine every aspect and feeling of a future presentation, including a successful ending, while less effective executives would prepare their facts and the presentation agendas, but not the psyche. For years now, I have taught this technique to others to help them prepare for presentations, and they report outstanding success with it. All that is necessary is that you take a few minutes before falling asleep the night before your presentation. Visualize everything from greeting your host and your audience to going through your presentation step by step, then a successful ending with smiles and applause all around. Repeat this again and again. You will find that you can go through an entire hour's presentation in a few seconds, and thus you can have as many as 30 or more repetitions of success even before you step on the platform to make your presentation for the first time. I believe this technique has several benefits. First, because you visualize a success again and again, you come to expect a success and, more frequently than not, that is exactly what you will receive as a result of this practice. Secondly, mental rehearsal seems to eliminate excessive nervousness. While all of us may be a little bit nervous when we make a presentation, this is probably good. If we weren't nervous at all, we probably would come across as rather dull and uninteresting. But too much nervousness can cause us to stumble, and may make our audience nervous as well. With mental visualization, you have made your presentation so many times before that when you stand and look at your audience, the sting is gone. It is "old hat." After all, didn't you make the same presentation before the same audience 30 or more times the night before? I highly recommend that you try this technique. From my own experience and the experience of so many others I know that it will work wonders in helping you to present your marketing plan in an interesting way, but without nervousness.

The Keys to Success for Marketing Plan Presentations

The number-one key for making your marketing plan presentation a success is to be enthusiastic about your project. If you aren't enthusiastic, you certainly cannot expect anyone else to be, and they won't be. What happens when you really don't have a great deal of enthusiasm for this project? Perhaps it was not your idea at all. Your boss instructed you to prepare this marketing plan presentation for top management. My recommendation is that if you really aren't interested in the project, then you must act; you must pretend that you are highly interested. This is crucial. Whenever I discuss acting or pretending, I think about the movie *Patton*. In one scene depicting an event during the Battle of the Bulge, things were not going very well for American forces. Patton suddenly turned to an aide and exclaimed, "If any of our commanders retreat, shoot them!" The aide was totally shocked and, in disbelief, he asked, "You really don't mean that?" Patton answered, "It really is not important whether you know whether I really mean it or not. It's only important that I know." Now, in fact, Patton was a tremendous actor. I know this for a fact because Patton's diaries have been published and I have read them. During World War I, Patton was a very young tank commander, commanding the first U.S. tank forces in combat. He wrote to his wife and said, "Every day I practice in front of a mirror looking mean." Patton felt that his mean look saved lives, because it meant his men were more afraid of him than they were of the enemy.

But Patton isn't the only one who recommends acting in order to achieve success. Mary Kay Ash developed a $100 million cosmetic company, and to her salespeople, she recommends, "Fake it 'til you make it." In other words, until you actually have a good day, pretend you're already having one. Or, until you have success, pretend that you are already achieving it. If you do this, if you pretend to be enthusiastic about your product and your project even though you are not, I promise you that this enthusiasm is catching, and that your audience will be enthusiastic as well.

It is extremely important to dress professionally. Appearance does count. As pointed out previously, although you may not be able to judge a book by its cover, psychologically people will attempt to do so. The same goes for your presentation. If you have any doubts about how to dress, the most famous book on this subject is by John T. Molloy, *Dress for Success*, which I highly recommend.

If you have any kind of test to do, or something that must work as a part of your presentation for your marketing plan, it is wise that you practice this test fully, and not just go through the motions. Several years ago, a Navy project engineer made a presentation about an important Navy project. When Navy aviators must eject from aircraft over water, they have a serious problem in getting rid of their parachutes once they have landed in the water. The normal procedure is to climb into a small, one-man life raft that extends 15 feet below the pilot and opens automatically. This must be done while wearing heavy flight equipment, including boots, helmet, and survival gear. Obviously this cannot be done with the parachute, but even more significant is that the chute canopy soon fills with water and can drag the aviator straight down to the bottom. So the suggested method was simply to judge when entrance into the water was about to occur and use an emergency release to get rid of the parachute canopy prior to entrance. The problem was that, the ocean being flat, it is very difficult to judge height. As a result, many aviators who thought they were about to enter the water released their canopies at altitudes of 100 feet or more in the air. This practice had little to recommend it. In order to overcome this problem, the Navy had developed a special squib or light explosive charge that automatically released the canopy when a probe hanging below the pilot contacted water. Thus the canopy was released safely and the pilot would have no problem as he entered the water. The Navy project manager did an outstanding job of presenting—including films of how the system worked, 35-mm slides, and handouts. For the grand finale, he donned a parachute himself and held up a jar of sea water. He then announced before several hundred in the audience that he would introduce the probe into the sea water. He told his audience that they would hear a loud crack as the squib exploded, and that the parachute canopy trailing behind the harness he had donned would immediately separate. The audience prepared themselves, some holding their hands over their ears, and others waiting expectantly. With great drama, he inserted the probe into the sea water. There was a loud silence. Nothing happened. He extracted the probe and inserted it again, and again, and again. Nothing happened. Finally, red-faced as the audience began to snicker, he examined the chute and found out that someone had forgotten to replace a worn-out battery. The point here is that an outstanding presentation was ruined by a demonstration that went awry, a mistake that need not have happened if a full demonstration had been done during the practice stage.

Throughout your presentation you should try to establish empathy or a common bond with your audience. You can do this by being friendly. Remember, the audience is not your enemy. Try to enjoy yourself, and think of yourself as the host of the entire presentation.

The presentation and your written marketing plan report go together. They support one another, and will support your achieving whatever objectives you have set.

SUMMARY

In this chapter we have seen that presenting the marketing plan has two main elements: the written report and the formal presentation. Both are necessary for success—and success is readily obtained by focusing on

preparation

and

professionalism

With preparation and professionalism, you ensure that your excellent content is supported by an excellent package—that your book can be judged by its cover and that the judgment says "the best."

10

IMPLEMENTATION

Regardless of how good your marketing plan is, or how well you have presented it, once you have received the go-ahead you must actually carry out the actions you have planned. Implementation is the final stage in the marketing planning process. During implementation, you can and should use your plan to help you. But the execution of your plan is not automatic. Your plan is not a light switch which, simply turned on, automatically completes every task, tactic, and strategy in exactly the manner you planned. To implement your marketing plan successfully, you must exercise control to ensure that you will reach your planned objectives and goals. To accomplish this you must monitor the implementation of your plan on a periodic basis. Use your project development schedule and measure planned resource allocations against those actually used, along with the time frame in which they were to be used. Measure expected results against actual results. Once implementation has been initiated, things never go exactly as planned. This may be because your planning was not perfect (and what planning ever is?), or it may be because of a change of one or more marketplace environs. Perhaps your competition has responded in an unexpected fashion to various actions you have taken. All of this is normal and simply means that you must make adjustments to get back on track to achieve the objectives and goals you have set.

Conceptually, certain actions are always required in implementation:

1. If you are the manager responsible for the plan's implementation, or some subsection of the plan, take complete responsibility for implementation. This does not mean only responsibility for initiating the actions contained in the plan but, more importantly, responsibility for reaching the goals and objectives contained in the plan.

2. Track all tasks, tactics, and strategies and measure what is planned against what actually happens. Make adjustments as required and do not blindly continue any action simply because it is in your plan.

3. Track the changes in the environs as the implementation of your marketing plan progresses. Changes will sometimes tell you that actions planned for the future should not be taken, or should be altered now. And just as an ounce of prevention is worth a pound of cure, an ounce of change taken now may be well worth a pound of change at a later date, when a foreseeable or predictable threat grows and causes a major problem in implementation.

No marketing plan, regardless of how good it is—with brilliant strategies and clever tactics—can succeed without being implemented. You cannot win your objectives by implementing a poor marketing plan. But you cannot win your objectives by poorly implementing a good marketing plan either. Therefore I wish you the development of an outstanding marketing plan—and I wish you an outstanding implementation as well.

APPENDIX A

SAMPLE MARKETING PLANS

A1: CALIFORNIA TESTING SERVICES

Developed by
STEVE POPKIN
MARK VARNES

CONTENTS

Used with the permission of the authors who developed this plan for a course in Mail Order/ Direct Mail Marketing.

INTRODUCTION

The purpose of this marketing plan is two-fold: (1) to show potential investors and lenders how California Testing Services will operate, why it will be successful, and how the profit structure is determined, and (2) to act as a guiding, measuring, and evaluating vehicle in the implementation of all aspects of California Testing Services.

EXECUTIVE DIGEST

California Testing Services has conducted market research and analysis and has identified a need for an affordable preparatory program for the California State Board of Pharmacy exam. In response to this need, California Testing Services has developed and will market a correspondence program designed specifically for the aforementioned exam. It consists of eight sections and over 5000 sample questions and answers. The price of the program is $295 as opposed to $800 charged by the one competitor in the market.

The company is owned equally by Steve Popkin and Mark Varnes. Both are pursuing Masters of Business Administration degrees and have much applicable professional experience.

The correspondence program will be marketed via mail order. Advertising in trade journals, pharmacy school newspapers, and foreign newspapers will be done to elicit inquiries from potential buyers.

The financial analysis shows that the project requires a small investment, has a high rate of return on investment, low overhead, and low risk.

COMPANY MISSION, SCOPE, AND GOALS

California Testing Services (CTS) is in the test anxiety reduction business. Initially, CTS will strive to be the unit sales leader in preparatory programs for the California State Board of Pharmacy examination by year three. In addition, CTS seeks a client passing rate of 85 percent, a client satisfaction rate of 95 percent, and a product return rate of 10 percent or less. At the conclusion of year one, this initial division will be evaluated for the purpose of determining the feasibility of expanding into selected other states. If the evaluation proves positive, expansion into one additional state is anticipated to begin in year four. If this expansion proves successful, other states will then be studied.

In addition to possibly expanding the pharmacy division, other unsaturated disciplines will be investigated by CTS to determine the feasibility of entering such markets (i.e., psychiatry, nursing, etc.).

The company philosophy is to operate with a minimum amount of risk and overhead.

BUSINESS ANALYSIS

California Testing Services will offer a preparatory correspondence program for the California State Board of Pharmacy exam. The program will include eight separate sections which specifically address the sections on the California State Board of Pharmacy exam (sections are outlined in Exhibit 1). In total there are over 800 pages and 5000 practice test questions in a multiple-choice format. Many questions will appear on the current exam, and most of the remaining ones have been on previous exams (sample questions are shown in Exhibit 2). Included in the program are test-taking techniques and tips.

The program was compiled by Marshall Hankin, doctor of pharmacy and former associate professor of pharmacy at Temple University, School of Pharmacy. Marshall Hankin will assist with the biannual updating of the program. Test questions and information on revised subject matter will be gathered from clients who had just taken the exam. They will be paid a nominal amount. The product is spiral bound with woodgrain vinyl covers. The eight separate sections range from 52 to 137 pages. The price of the program is $295 including tax, shipping, and handling.

EXHIBIT I
TOPIC OUTLINE OF CORRESPONDENCE PROGRAM

Program 100
General pharmacy practice—OTC drug use.

Program 200
Treatment of cardiovascular and respiratory disorders, pharmacology of drugs pertaining thereto.

Program 300
Treatment of gastrointestinal, genitourinary, bone, joints, supportive tissue, dermatologic, neurologic, psychiatric, fluid and electrolytic, and nutritional disorders. Pharmacology of drugs pertaining thereto.

Program 400
Treatment of infections, oncologic, hormonal, metabolic, pediatric, geriatric, obstetrical and gynecologic, toxicologic disorders. Drug abuse. Literature evaluation. Pharmacology of drugs pertaining thereto.

Program 500
Ethics and the law.

Program 600
Pharmaceutical calculations.

Program 700
Pharmaceutics, biopharmaceutics, pharmacokinetics, compounding.

Program 500 Text (500T)
Substantive highlights law.

Program M
Miscellaneous questions and answers.

SITUATION ANALYSIS

Assumptions

The market for new pharmacists in California is relatively stable. There is an adequate number of pharmacists to fill most positions, but the market is not oversaturated. The overabundance of medical school applicants and the limited amount of medical school space has caused a portion of premed students to turn to pharmacy school as an alternative. This is one factor that contributed to the slight but steady increase in pharmacy school graduates during the past five years. This trend is expected to continue for the next five years.

A significant factor in the market is the foreign pharmacist or pharmacy school graduate who immigrates to the United States with hopes of becom-

EXHIBIT 2
SAMPLE TEST QUESTIONS

536. The State Board of Pharmacy may *not:* (FALSE STATEMENT)
    A. Sell copies of its lists of licensees to "junk" mailing services.
    B. License "anyone" to sell hypodermic needles and syringes.
    C. Disclose any or all of its records to the public.
    D. Restrict the sale of any OTC drugs to "sale by pharmacist only" after proper hearings.
    E. Pass regulations which control the physician in his use of drugs.

537. A member of the Board could, if reappointed, serve a term as long as:
    A. Six years
    B. Eight years
    C. Eight and one-half years
    D. Twelve years
    E. No limit

538. An inspector of the State Board of Pharmacy:
    A. Is not a peace officer.
    B. Cannot make arrests without a warrant.
    C. Cannot seize Rx records without a warrant.
    D. Need not be a registered pharmacist.
    E. Is not liable for "false arrest" if "reasonable cause" existed.

539. Members of the California State Board of Pharmacy:
    A. Must be appointed by the Governor from a list of candidates proposed by the California Pharmaceutical Association.
    B. Must be registered pharmacists.
    C. Must have their decisions reviewed by the Director of Professional and Vocational Standards.
    D. Must have their appointments confirmed by the State Legislature.
    E. All of the above are incorrect.

540. Prescriptions may *not* be telephoned to a pharmacy by:
    A. A podiatrist
    B. A veterinarian (D.V.M.)
    C. An appropriately designated employee of a physician
    D. An osteopathic physician
    E. An optometrist

DO NOT WRITE ON THIS PAGE

ing a licensed pharmacist. Each state determines its own eligibility requirements. In 1973, California passed a somewhat permissive law. It requires not only educational equivalency, but also that the applicant have two years of "practical experience" in his or her homeland during the previous five years. Fred Willyerd, State Board executive secretary, observes that the immigrant influx began around 1976, with most immigrating from China,

Japan, India, and the Philippines. Two hundred fifty-eight foreigners took the California licensure exam in 1979 as compared to 142 in 1978, 79 in 1977, and 23 in 1976. Because the failure rate among foreign pharmacists is so high—in June 1979, for example, only 32 of 109 passed—many repeat the test. The great influx of foreign pharmacists has caused tension among United States pharmacists. They claim that foreigners have taken away jobs from American pharmacists and lowered the level of competency. In response to this, legislation was passed in 1980 making it more difficult for foreigners to obtain educational equivalency and be eligible to take the licensure exam. Already the percentage of foreigners enrolling in pharmacy school and taking the licensure exam has dropped significantly. Legislators are now being pressured by foreign lobbyists. The fight seems far from over. The outcome will have a definite effect on the buyer profile and market strategy of California Testing Services. Even with these fluctuations, the actual size of the market remains relatively constant. When there are fewer foreign pharmacists, more American pharmacists are attracted to California; and conversely, when there is an abundance of foreign pharmacists, American pharmacists tend not to migrate to California in as great numbers. Statistics show that more American pharmacists migrate to California than to any other state in the country.

According to Bank of America's *Economic Outlook 1982,* California will experience continued moderate economic growth in 1982. The estimated gross state product will be up 12.5 percent from 1981. This is a 3.5 percent gain after inflation. Employment, personal income, retail sales, and business revenues will all rise moderately. As has been the case since 1973, the state's economic growth will outpace that of the nation as a whole. In addition, service industries will greatly outpace other industry sectors.

Competition

Morris Cody and Associates currently has a monopoly on the preparatory industry for the California State Board of Pharmacy exam. Morris Cody and Associates is basically a one-man operation with a part-time instructor and secretarial service. The company operates from Van Nuys and San Francisco. Morris Cody, the owner and instructor, purchased the business 11 years ago from Dean Brady of the USC School of Pharmacy.

Morris Cody and Associates offers a classroom course held every night for the last two weeks before each exam and Tuesday and Thursday throughout the year. They also offer a correspondence course, or a combination of the two. The materials used in the classroom course are the same as used in the correspondence course. Regardless of which option the individual chooses, the fee is $800. Payment may be made by personal check, Visa, or MasterCard.

Morris Cody and Associates does classified advertising in three pharmacy trade journals (see Exhibit 3). Other than a one-page promotional mail piece sent on request, this is the only advertising done.

The content of the correspondence programs of California Testing Services and Morris Cody and Associates are very similar.

There are two major pharmacy review books that sell for about $25 each; however, they are not specifically geared to the California State Board of Pharmacy exam.

Company Resources

California Testing Services draws on the marketing expertise of Steve Popkin and Mark Varnes. Both partners possess a bachelor's degree in business administration—marketing. In addition, both are currently pursuing master's of business administration degrees. Steve Popkin and Mark Varnes have had formal academic training in mail order marketing and marketing

EXHIBIT 3
QUESTIONNAIRE SURVEY

1. Have you taken a *classroom* review course for the California State Board of Pharmacy Exam?   yes ( )   no ( )
2. If you answered "no" to question 1, were you aware of a classroom review course for the California State Board of Pharmacy Exam? yes ( )   no ( )
3. Have you taken a correspondence course for the California State Board of Pharmacy Exam?   yes ( )   no ( )
4. If you answered "no" to question 3, were you aware of a correspondence course?   yes ( )   no ( )
5. Have you purchased any preparatory books for the California State Board of Pharmacy Exam?   yes ( )   no ( )
6. Have you ever taken the California State Board of Pharmacy Exam before?   yes ( )   no ( )
7. Are you currently a licensed pharmacist?   yes ( )   no ( )
   If yes, in what state are you licensed? _____
8. What pharmacy school did you graduate from? _____
9. Was the California State Board of Pharmacy Exam: (check one)
   ( ) Harder than you had expected.
   ( ) Easier than you had expected.
   ( ) About the same as you had expected.
10. Roughly, what do you feel a fair price is for a correspondence course for the California State Board of Pharmacy? $_____

THANK YOU

a new business. Mark Varnes has professional experience in direct sales, graphic design, and budget administration. Steve Popkin has professional experience in copywriting, direct mail campaigns, and general marketing administration.

California Testing Services employs the pharmacological expertise of Marshall Hankin, PhD, on a contract basis. Marshall Hankin is a licensed pharmacist in California and Philadelphia. He is a former associate professor of pharmacy at Temple University, School of Pharmacy. Marshall Hankin has owned and managed a variety of pharmacies in both California and Philadelphia. Through his experience, Marshall Hankin has gained a concrete understanding of the needs and anxieties of the recent graduate as well as the out-of-state pharmacist. When Marshall Hankin moved to California in 1977, he enrolled in Morris Cody and Associates' classroom course before taking the California State Board of Pharmacy exam. This gave him and California Testing Services a working knowledge of the competition's mode of operation, course content, client attitude, and so on. As previously stated, Marshall Hankin compiled the original correspondence program and will assist in its updating. In addition, he will be contacted for miscellaneous consulting.

California Testing Services will call on Carl Rosen, western regional manager, Division of MasterCard/Visa, City National Bank. Mr. Rosen, a personal friend of one of the partners, has consented to let California Testing Services offer Visa and MasterCard as a merchant through City National Bank.

Market Potentials, Forecasts, Facts

The potential market size for California Testing Services' preparatory program is the number of applicants for the California State Board of Pharmacy exam. A little background is in order. The California State Board of Pharmacy exam is a two-day test that is administered twice a year: once near the end of October and again near the end of June. The testing location alternates between Hayward, California, and Glendale, California. Using 1977 to 1980 figures, the average number of applicants for the October exam is approximately 400, and it rises to approximately 600 in June. Combining the two brings the annual market potential to 1000 units or $295,000 in gross sales. As alluded to earlier, political and environmental factors have an effect on the customer mix but have little effect on the actual size of the market. The past three years' figures show a very slight upward trend in the number of applicants.

California Testing Services' product/service is immune to market saturation and diminishing returns. For the most part, there are a different

1000 people taking the exam annually; thus the demand begins anew each year.

California Testing Services administered a questionnaire survey to persons taking the October 1981 California State Board of Pharmacy exam. The survey was taken at the test location as persons were leaving the testing room. California Testing Services representatives did not identify themselves as such (questionnaire is shown in Exhibit 3). A quota sampling was used with all exam takers meeting the quota requirements. Forty-two responses were gathered. The results of the survey are shown below.

1. 7 percent of respondents had taken a classroom review course.
2. 61 percent of the remainder were not aware of a classroom review course.
3. 16 percent of respondents had taken a correspondence course.
4. 48 percent of the remainder were not aware of a correspondence course.
5. 21 percent of respondents had purchased a preparatory book prior to the exam.
6. 24 percent of respondents had taken the exam previously.
7. 59 percent of respondents were currently licensed pharmacists.
8. No geographical concentration was identified.
9. 27 percent of respondents felt the exam was harder than expected, 54 percent felt it was about the same as expected, and 19 percent felt it was easier than expected.
10. The arithmetic mean for a fair price for the California State Board of Pharmacy exam was $197. The median was $223.

There were not enough respondents to get high confidence-level results; however, there were enough to identify trends, opportunities, and concerns in the market. One major opportunity identified was that if California Testing Services could raise the level of awareness of a correspondence preparatory program, it could increase the industry size and its market share significantly.

Due to the monopolistic nature of the industry, Morris Cody and Associates' sales are the same as total industry sales. From observation, surveys, and actual claims from Morris Cody and Associates, the current industry size is estimated to be approximately 200 units. Of the 200 units, 50 are estimated to be strictly classroom participants and 150 either correspondence or a combination of correspondence and classroom.

The breakdown of State Board applicants by group, as best determined, is 35 percent in-state recent graduates, 20 percent out-of-state recent grad-

uates, 30 percent out-of-state pharmacists, and 15 percent foreign pharmacists. Thirty percent of the aforementioned groups had previously
taken and failed the California State Board of Pharmacy exam.

Market Share

As previously stated, the current size of the California State Board of Pharmacy exam preparatory program industry is approximately 200 units. California Testing Services believes that with a sound marketing effort it can
conservatively increase the industry size to 250 units in year one.

Of the 250 units, California Testing Services forecasts a 40 percent market share, or 100 units. This equates to a 10 percent share of the potential
market. Of the 100 units, an estimated 50 sales will be new sales, purchases
that would not have been made had CTS not been in the market. The
remaining 50 sales will be "taken" from Morris Cody and Associates.

California Testing Services conservatively forecasts sales of 135 and 170
units for years two and three respectively. This represents an estimated 45
and 55 percent market share after allowing for an annual increase in industry size.

There are three separate and one overlapping market segments for the
product/service offered by California Testing Services. These are (1) recent
pharmacy school graduates, in and out of state, (2) currently licensed out-
of-state pharmacists, (3) foreign pharamacists, and, overlapping, (4) applicants who have failed a recent California State Board of Pharmacy exam.

California Testing Services forecasts that 60 percent of its first year sales
will be from out-of-state pharmacists, 30 percent from recent graduates,
and 10 percent from foreign pharmacists. Of these groups, an estimated
20 percent will have taken and failed a previous exam.

Morris Cody and Associates' product/service differentiation is the option
of a classroom course and the availability of presale communication between Morris Cody and the potential client. This is expected to give Morris
Cody and Associates an advantage in the recent in-state-graduate and
foreign-pharmacist segments. It is geographically practical for in-state
graduates to attend classroom sessions. Foreign pharmacists often have a
language communication problem and require extensive personal attention rather than simply written material. In addition, a direct mail piece
that is effective for American potential customers may not be as effective
for foreign potential customers. They may also require personal persua-
siveness before committing to buy. By observation, about half of Morris
Cody and Associates' classroom students are foreign. On the other hand,
in most cases it is very difficult for out-of-state applicants to relieve themselves of obligations and have the time to attend classroom sessions. California Testing Services believes that its price differential will counteract a
portion of Morris Cody and Associates' advantages and will have an ex-

tremely positive effect on the out-of-state market where all things are relatively equal. Within the industry, California Testing Services forecasts (1) 80 percent market share of out-of-state pharmacists, (2) 20 percent market share of in-state recent graduates, (3) 50 percent market share of out-of-state recent graduates, and (4) 30 percent market share of foreign pharmacists.

CURRENT MARKETING ORGANIZATION

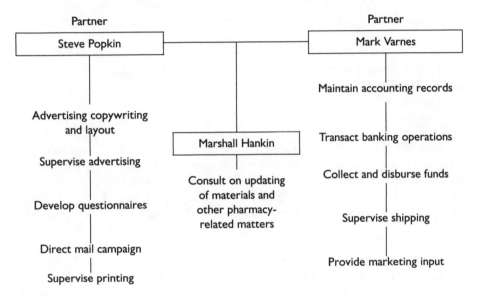

MARKETING OBJECTIVES

Quantitative marketing objectives for years one, two, and three are as follows:

	Year		
	1	2	3
Market share (%)	40	45	55
Inquiries	250	270	325
Unit sales	100	135	170
Closing percentage	40	50	52
Gross sales	$29,000	$39,825	$50,150
Profit before tax	$12,837	$18,409	$23,642

MARKETING STRATEGIES AND PROGRAMS

Advertising

After determining that a mailing list of applicants for the California State Board of Pharmacy exam was not available, California Testing Service chose a two-step advertising approach. The purpose of all its advertising is to motivate potential buyers to send in their names and addresses and receive a direct mail piece giving the details of the offer and an order coupon.

California Testing Services will advertise toward, and elicit sales from, all of the aforementioned four market segments; however, its main thrust and expenditures will be geared toward the out-of-state market.

Out-of-State Pharmacists. To capture this market at the least expense, California Testing Services will do classified advertising in four pharmacy trade journals: *Pharmacy Times, Drug Topics, American Druggist,* and *U.S. Pharmacist.* An estimated 85 percent of those who read pharmacy trade journals read one of these four journals. The charge for an average classified ad in these journals ranges from approximately $35 to $100 with the average being $70. Prices are roughly correlated with circulation (see Exhibit 4 for classified section of *American Druggist* and draft of CTS classified ad). Morris Cody and Associates advertises in the classified section of three of these four trade journals. Each advertisement will be coded for evaluation purposes. This mode of advertising will also touch on all other market segments.

Recent Graduates. California Testing Services will place small display advertisements in pharmacy school newspapers. California has 3 of 72 pharmacy schools: University of Southern California (USC), University of California–San Francisco (UCSF), and University of Pacifica (UOP). Ads will initially be placed in three school newspapers for testing purposes. These schools include USC, UOP, and a third out-of-state school selected on the basis of the size of the school and the California migratory patterns of the area. This test should indicate anticipated demand from in-state local, in-state nonlocal, and out-of-state graduates. It was previously stated that California Testing Services forecasts only a 20 percent market share

EXHIBIT 4
CLASSIFIED ADVERTISEMENT DRAFT

CALIFORNIA BOARD OF PHARMACY EXAM REVIEW: Pass the California State Board of Pharmacy exam—or pay nothing! Be thoroughly prepared to pass the exam, then relax. Most complete and least expensive correspondence course available. You owe it to yourself to find out. For free details, clip this ad and send it with your name and address to: CALIFORNIA TESTING SERVICES. . . .

on in-state recent graduates; however, this represents a greater actual number than does the 40 percent share of out-of-state recent graduates. Initially, advertisements will be placed bimonthly. Depending on the results, the ads may be expanded in coverage and/or frequency, or eliminated.

Foreign Pharmacists. A small display advertisement will be placed in the *World Journal*, a daily Chinese-language newspaper. This newspaper is circulated from San Francisco to San Diego and has the largest readership of any newspaper of its kind. From secondary data and observation of the competition, it was determined that Chinese is by far the predominant nationality of foreign state board applicants. As with the school newspapers, this advertisement will initially appear bimonthly. Depending on the results, it will expand in frequency, remain the same, be eliminated and/or inspire advertising in other foreign languages.

Applicants Who Have Failed a Previous State Board Exam. During each examination, a business/advertising card will be placed on the windshield of each car parked at the testing location. The card will give the company name, services provided, and address to write to for more details. An applicant doesn't know for about six weeks whether he or she passed the exam. In that length of time, a brochure or flyer will often get thrown away or lost in a pile. A business card can be put in a wallet or purse for easy retrieval. In addition, a business card is less expensive and is less likely to elicit objections from test or city authorities.

Brochure. As stated, when a potential buyer sends in his or her name and address, he or she will be sent a brochure. In its brochure, California Testing Services attempts to counter the following potential objections.

1. "$295 is a lot of money."
2. "If you charge so much less than your competition, you must be offering an inferior product."
3. "I don't have that much cash on hand."
4. "I wouldn't buy an expensive item through the mail without seeing it first."

In addition to countering objections, California Testing Services will attempt to elicit customer response by following the AIDA copywriting approach: grab attention, stimulate interest, create desire, encourage action (a rough draft of the brochure copy is shown in Exhibit 5).

A follow-up letter will be sent to a potential customer if an order is not received within two weeks after sending the brochure. Tentatively, the theme of the letter will be anxiety reduction.

EXHIBIT 5
BROCHURE DRAFT

Main
Headline:

PASS THE CALIFORNIA STATE BOARD OF PHARMACY
EXAMINATION—OR PAY NOTHING!!!

Components:
Headline:

DO ANY OF THESE SOUND FAMILIAR?

I want to move to California, but I can't unless I pass the exam.

I've been away from the classroom so long, I don't know if I'll remember enough.

I just graduated, I know the theory, but I don't know what's going to be on the California exam.

I have a family to support; I can't afford not to pass.

IF THEY DO—WE CAN HELP

A team of pharmacists headed by Marshall Hankin, PhD, developed a correspondence program for California Testing Services. We can now offer it to you. The eight separate sections attack the heart of the California State Board of Pharmacy Exam, and will give you confidence entering the testing room.

In total there are over 800 pages and over 5000 questions and answers. Many questions will appear on the actual test. The program is updated after each exam to make sure that you have the most current, accurate material available anywhere. This program was designed specifically to prepare applicants to pass the California State Board of Pharmacy Examination. This is not a book, and cannot be bought in any store.

Headline:

WOULD YOU PAY *$800* FOR A PROGRAM LIKE THIS?

Hundreds of pharmacists have—but you don't have to. Morris Cody and Associates have been offering a very similar correspondence program. At last check it was selling for $800. Through California Testing Services you pay only $295 *including* tax, shipping, and handling. In addition to the cost savings you will, quite frankly, receive a better, more complete program.

Headline:

HOW CAN WE DO IT?

How can California Testing Services offer a program for $295 that sells elsewhere for $800?
ANSWER: We don't have:

A large fancy office building.

Salespeople and secretaries to answer your calls.

Needless business equipment.

What we do have is quality personnel to develop, update, and evaluate the program to be sure that it meets your exact needs.

EXHIBIT 5 continued

Headline:

WOULD YOU PAY $295 THROUGH THE MAIL—SIGHT UNSEEN?

Would a person of above average intelligence send $295 without first seeing the product?

We won't ask you to take our word for the quality of the program, that's why we offer a no risk—double guarantee.

Headline:

NO RISK—DOUBLE GUARANTEE

1. If within 30 days, this program does not meet your expectations, send it back for a complete, no questions asked, refund. You can even postdate your check for 30 days.

2. If for any reason you do not pass the California State Board of Pharmacy Examination, send the program back for a complete refund. Simple enclose a copy of your Consumer Affairs Board of Pharmacy notice. Take up to 90 days after the exam date.

These kinds of guarantees are unheard of in the industry. Our competition doesn't offer even one money-back guarantee. We don't hesitate to offer these guarantees because we believe strongly that this program will be invaluable to you.

Headline:

IF YOU HAVEN'T ALREADY SENT IN YOUR ORDER—READ THIS.

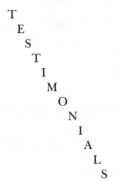

Headline:

DO I HAVE TO SEND A CHECK?

NO. You can send a check or money order, or call toll free 1-800-xxx-xxxx and use your Visa or MasterCard. Either way, we will ship the program to you immediately upon receipt of your order.

Headline:

WOULD YOU INVEST $295 IN YOUR FUTURE?

$295 is still a lot of money, especially these days. But, this $295 can allow you to earn well over $30,000 as a licensed California Pharmacist. That's quite a return on your investment.

EXHIBIT 5 continued

Headline: CALIFORNIA TESTING SERVICES—IT'S WORTH THE PEACE
                OF MIND FOR THE MOST STUDY TIME—ORDER NOW

                    O
                      R
                        D
                          E
                            R
                              F
                                O
                                  R
                                    M

Pricing

As previously stated, Morris Cody and Associates charges $800 and California Testing Services charges $295. A low-price strategy was chosen for several reason.

1. Other than price, there is virtually no product differentiation.

2. Morris Cody and Associates has a reputation, credibility, and personal selling; there must be enough of a price difference to outweigh these advantages.

3. California Testing Services hopes to create a submarket of rational, somewhat price-conscious consumers, rather than compete head to head for existing customer types; the price differentiation will create a new consumer in the market.

4. A strong marketing effort can elicit buyers from untapped areas; however, once Morris Cody and Associates copies the marketing tactics, California Testing Services is back to square 1.

5. Currently Morris Cody and Associates is practicing "skim" pricing in a monopolistic situation. When a competitor enters the market, somewhat of an oligopoly will occur and a response will be elicited (see Figure A1-1). If California Testing Services prices closer to $800, it may spur a "price war" where each competitor is trying to undersell the other. At $295, California Testing Services is at the opposite end of the price range. It would not be feasible for Morris Cody and Associates to compete on a price basis, thus allowing each competitor his own niche in the market place.

6. Protecting the preparatory correspondence program concept and materials is a potential problem. With the emergence of California Testing Services, the high- and low-price ends of the industry are covered. This will make it more difficult and less attractive for another competitor to enter the market.

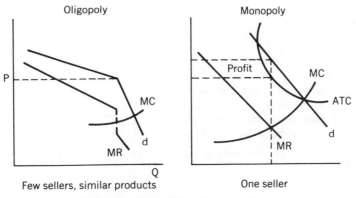

FIGURE A1-1. Oligopoly; monopoly.

7. Surveys have indicated that $800 is well above the initial perceived value for this type of product/service. Two hundred-ninety five dollars is more consistent with perceived value.

8. Oddball pricing ($295 as opposed to $300) is used to promote a "good deal" image.

9. California Testing Services does not believe that the demand for its product is entirely elastic. However, it does feel that, up to a point, a decrease in price will create an increase in sales if accompanied by a sound marketing effort.

A portion of the brochures will be printed with an alternate price, perhaps $395. After the completion of the first six-month business cycle, it will begin being tested for profitability against the control price of $295. Testing will continue until an optimum price is determined.

Distribution Channel

California Testing Services will sell its product via mail order. This choice was based on several factors.

1. Desire to limit the amount of inventory, overhead, and investment.

2. Desire to limit the amount of administrative and selling time.

3. The widespread geographical disbursement of potential customers.

4. The pharmacological expertise lies with someone other than the two general partners.

5. The product is an "unsought good."

Further analysis of the appropriateness of this product for mail order is shown below using Dr. Cohen's mail order product evaluation form. It shows that on almost all points the product is rated very good or excellent.

Mail Order Product Evaluation Form

Instructions: Give each evaluation item
    4 points for an evaluation of excellent
    3 points for an evaluation of very good
    2 points for an evaluation of good
    1 point for an evaluation of fair
    0 point for an evaluation of poor

Multiply the evaluation points times the importance weighting. Only pick new products that have a high point total.

	Importance Weighting		Evaluation Points		Total
I. Marketability					
1. How large is the potential market?	.03	×	1	=	.03
2. How important is the need that the product fills?	.06	×	4	=	.24
3. Can the customer buy the product easily in a store?	.03	×	4	=	.12
II. Profitability					
1. What is the total and yearly profitability estimate?	.06	×	1	=	.06
2. Can the item be sold at 3 to 4 times your cost?	.06	×	4	=	.24
3. Does the product lend itself to repeat business?	.07	×	2	=	.14
4. What is the ratio of total profit to total investment?	.03	×	3	=	.09
III. Investment					
1. How much investment will the project require?	.05	×	4	=	.20
2. How many units must be sold until the investment is recouped?	.04	×	4	=	.16
IV. Legal Consideration					
1. Is the product strictly legal?	.5	×	3	=	.45
2. Is the product completely safe?	.09	×	4	=	.36
3. Can there be any legal repercussion through use or misuse of the product?	.06	×	4	=	.24
V. Mailing					
1. Can the product be shipped and mailed easily?	.06	×	4	=	.24
2. Is the product breakable?	.06	×	4	=	.24
3. Can the product be shipped at low cost?	.07	×	4	=	.28

Grand total 3.09

Advertising and Project Evaluation Criteria

The advertising campaign will begin on March 1, 1982. As shown in the financial analysis, forecasted sales for March are 10 units. Forecasted sales for March through June, the first business cycle, are 60 units. Thirty-one units must be sold to break even for year 1. If on April 1, 1982, 5 units are sold, the project will be continued. If sales are less than 5, the project will be discontinued. If on July 1, 1982, sales are above 30 units, the project will be continued; if it's below, it will be discontinued.

If an advertisement fails to pay for itself at the end of any given month, it will be eliminated. If a newspaper advertisement produces four sales in a given month, it will be increased in frequency and/or size for the next month. In this case, advertisements in similar newspapers will be tested.

California Testing Services believes that quantitative criteria are valuable and necessary. However, it will strive to remain flexible enough to respond to fluctuations and unexpected occurrences in the market.

SCHEDULE OF BUSINESS OPERATIONS: PERT ANALYSIS

Phase 1

  Market survey
  R&D product design
  Plan market research
  Routing (product feasibility)
  Complete prototype model
  Cost estimates
  Preliminary product testing
  Pricing and forecast reports
  Final report

Phase II

  Questionnaires
  Ads in periodicals and newspapers
  Direct mail campaign
  Response from ads and direct mail
  Direct mail brochures
  Orders from customers
  Printing and production of review tests
  Packaging and mailing of product
  Final report

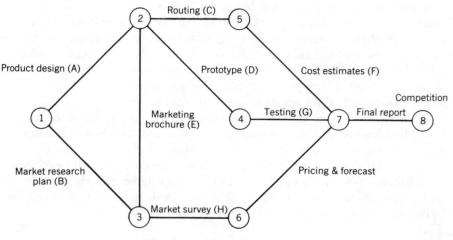

PERT ANALYSIS-PHASE 1

FIGURE A1-2. Pert analysis—phase 1.

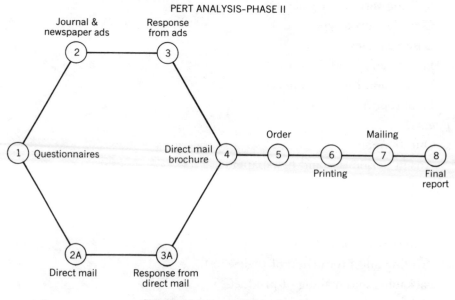

PERT ANALYSIS-PHASE II

FIGURE A1-3. Pert analysis—phase 2.

FINANCIAL ANALYSIS

Projected Years 1, 2, and 3 Income Statements
(Projected in 1981 Dollars)

| | Year | | |
	1	2	3
Total net sales	29,500	39,825	50,150
Cost of goods sold	8,667	11,701	14,734
Gross profit	20,833	28,124	35,416
Expenses	*	*	*
	*	*	*
Advertising	4,200	4,200	4,200
Business registration	75	45	45
Post office box	26	26	26
Postage	60	80	100
Envelopes	150	0	0
Brochures	600	0	600
Follow-up letter	35	0	0
M.C./Visa setup	25	0	0
Product updating	200	200	200
Product returns	2,525	5,164	6,503
Misc.	100	100	100
Total expenses	7,996	9,715	11,774
	*	*	*
	*	*	*
Net profit (loss) before taxes	$12,837	$18,409	$23,642

CONTROLS AND CONTINUITY

Formal records of actual results as compared with forecasted results will be compiled monthly for evaluation purposes. This will allow California Testing Services to to react to small fluctuations and unexpected occurrences in the market.

Biannually, near the end of June and October, this marketing plan will be reviewed in its entirety. Using primary and secondary data, appropriate changes will be made. By November 30 of each year, a written supplement will be submitted identifying necessary amendments in the original marketing plan.

During off seasons, November to March, California Testing Services will investigate company progress and the feasibility of expansion. Medium- and long-range goals and objectives will be determined and evaluated.

Controlling and reviewing the continuity of this plan on a regular basis

Projected Year I Income Statement by Month

	March	April	May	June	July	Aug.	Sept.	Oct.	Nov.	Dec.	Jan.	Feb.
Total net sales	2950	4425	5900	4425	2360	2950	4425	2065	0	0	0	0
Cost of goods sold	868	1302	1735	1302	694	868	1302	607	0	0	0	0
Gross profit	2082	3123	4165	3123	1666	2082	3123	1458	0	0	0	0
Expenses	*	*	*	*	*	*	*	*	*	*	*	*
Advertising	525	525	525	525	525	525	525	525	0	0	0	0
Business registration	75	0	0	0	0	0	0	0	0	0	0	0
Post office box	13	0	0	0	0	0	13	0	0	0	0	0
Postage	6	9	12	9	5	6	9	4	0	0	0	0
Envelopes	150	0	0	0	0	0	0	0	0	0	0	0
Brochure	600	0	0	0	0	0	0	0	0	0	0	0
Follow-up letter	0	35	0	0	0	0	0	0	0	0	0	0
M.C./Visa setup	25	0	0	0	0	0	0	0	0	0	0	0
Product updating	0	0	0	0	100	0	0	0	100	0	0	0
Product returns—15%*	382	574	765	574	306	382	574	268	0	0	0	0
Misc.	12	13	12	13	12	13	12	13	0	0	0	0
Total expenses	1788	1156	1302	1121	936	913	1133	810	100	0	0	0
Net profit (loss) before taxes	294	1967	2863	2002	730	1169	1990	648	(100)	0	0	0

*Product returns are applied to the month in which they are sold.

Break-Even Analysis

Selling price	**$295.00**
Variable costs	
Product reproduction	40.00
State sales tax	17.70
Shipping	5.00
Packaging	2.00
800 tel. # (0.10 × 295) × (0.50)	14.75
MasterCard/Visa (0.05 × 295) × (0.50)	7.38
Total variable costs	$86.78
Gross profit per unit	$208.22
Fixed costs	
Advertising	4,200.00
Business registration	75.00
Post office box	26.00
Postage	60.00
Envelopes	150.00
Brochures	600.00
Follow-up letter	35.00
Updating product	200.00
Misc.	100.00
Total fixed costs	$5,446.00

Total fixed costs ÷ Gross profit per unit = Breakeven quantity

$5446.00	$208.22	26.155

Additional units needed to compensate for 15% product return: 4.62

Adjusted breakeven quantity: <u>31 units</u>

Dollar Requirement for Project Test

Advertising	$525.00
Post office box	$ 13.00
MasterCard/Visa setup charge	$ 25.00
Business registration	$ 75.00
Artwork/typesetting for envelopes and brochure	$250.00
Misc.	$ 50.00
Total	$938.00

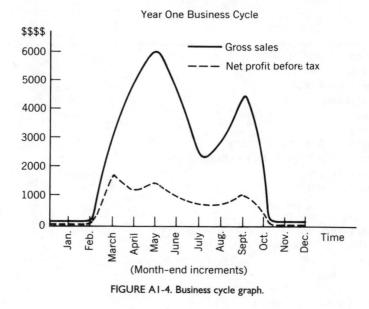

FIGURE AI-4. Business cycle graph.

is extremely important in order to avoid a "marketing myopia" or short-sightedness effect.

CONCLUSION

California Testing Services strongly believes that with an initial investment of $5000 to roughly cover two business cycles, and careful and tenacious administration of its marketing plan, it will become a successful, growing concern.

A2: COLLINS RESTAURANT CONSULTING

Developed by
CHRISTINA LEDEL COLLINS

EXECUTIVE SUMMARY

This marketing plan explains the guidelines and strategies involved in marketing Collins Restaurant Consulting (CRC), a service introduced on the market in December 1984. This company was established in 1983 to perform various tasks in restaurant research, consulting, and planning in California and, in three years, nationwide. Through previous informal studies CRC found a market niche for a personalized restaurant consulting firm, thus conceiving the idea for CRC. CRC's field of expertise includes management, computer science, marketing, sales, advertising, direct mail marketing, and more than 50 years of combined restaurant experience.

Financial resources will be obtained through private investors and the owners. The marketing plan covers the first two years of business. CRC has no fixed overhead and a low-risk plan. The total investment involved in

Used with permission of the author.

the first year of operation is \$62,641, with anticipated costs remaining relatively low and revenues increasing at 50 percent a year.

A table of contents is provided for the reader's convenience in locating details of the marketing plan.

CONTENTS

TABLES

BACKGROUND

Collins Restaurant Consulting is a new, full-service program of training restaurant employees which is now available to the food service industry. As inflation slows to the lowest level in a decade, food service is expected to outperform the economy as a whole in 1983 with a real growth rate of 1 percent.[1] Total food service industry sales will approach $160 billion in 1983 with a real growth higher than in any year since the late 1970s. Fine dining, family, theme/specialty restaurants, coffee shops, and membership clubs all live in interesting times of economic recession (with degrees of regional severity). Increased governmental regulation, a large amount of part-time and student help, coupled with peak unemployment, create a large but potentially demoralized and untrained labor pool for this giant industry. The consumer in 1983 is increasingly demanding, and his or her expectations for fewer meals eaten away from home are higher than ever before. These factors present a significant business opportunity for consulting, training, and seminar workshops specifically focusing on how a restaurant can make a profit on a continuing basis.

How do you increase sales? How do you make customers happy? How do you cut costs? The answer is in the staff. They are the ones who greet the customer with a smile, are going to sell another round of cocktails, sell that appetizer, that extra drink, that bottle of wine, that dessert, that after dinner drink—but only if they have been *trained to do so.* "The key to everything is training!"[2] CRC is designed to help restaurants plan, organize, lead, and control employees. The training concentrates on busboys, bartenders, utility people, fast food servers, cashiers, waiters, waitresses, captains, wine stewards, hosts, hostesses, maitre d's, and valets. The concentration is on service employees, which also includes supervisors and middle management.

The idea for CRC is new. It is a personalized service provided to restau-

---

[1]*Restaurants and Institutions,* (March 15, 1983), p.49.

[2]Gen LaGreca, "The training programs of Inhilco." *Restaurant Hospitality,* (April 1982), p. 51.

rants in need of training on a continuing or one-shot basis. Some larger-scale, well-established hotels and restaurants provide some of the training CRC provides; however most of their training is geared to upper and middle management. CRC offers a full line of service training from telephone voice and etiquette to proper wine opening procedures and analysis of daily sales records. CRC is personalized because CRC becomes an employee of that restaurant, working on its personal, unique problems.

SCOPE AND LIMITATIONS

This marketing plan has a two-fold purpose: to act as a supportive sales tool to potential consumers, and to act as a road map to C. L. Collins, creator of CRC. Research is limited to secondary research and personal experience in the industry. Research was also limited by time constraints.

CRC's long-term plans include consulting in all 50 states. However, due to time constraints, geographic target areas are listed but concentration of market potential is limited to California. Although California has been chosen as the initial target area, CRC will expand as soon as possible after the introduction stage of the product life cycle. California has been chosen because of size, convenience, and market familiarity. This plan is also limited to two-year projections in financial and sales planning.

PART I

Situational Analysis

This section reviews the factors in the present and future business environment. It includes examination of market characteristics, key success factors, competition, market potential, environmental factors, internal resources, problems, and opportunities.

DEMAND AND MARKET ANALYSIS

This market's characteristics are unique but not limited to any particular type of restaurant. A basic characteristic of the market is an ongoing restaurant in business to make money.

Geographic segmentation is nationwide. It includes major cities in the United States. The targeted markets include major metropolitan areas, resort/vacation areas, and entertainment capitals. Areas of concentration are the West Coast and East Coast. Specific cities to be focused on include the greater Los Angeles area, including Westwood, Hollywood, Beverly

Hills, Glendale, Pasadena, Encino, and Malibu. Orange County will also be targeted including the cities of Newport Beach, Laguna Beach, and high-traffic restaurants in that general area. Santa Barbara, Carmel, San Jose, San Francisco, and San Diego will also be included on the West Coast. on the East Coast, areas like New York, Philadelphia, Boston, Chicago, and other major restaurant areas will be included. Other areas of concentration will include Florida, Las Vegas, New Jersey, Reno, Lake Tahoe, Hawaii, and so forth.

Demographically, market segmentation includes fast food chains, mid-price restaurants, coffee shop chains, upscale diners, leisure resort restaurants, fine dining areas, family restaurants, theme/specialty restaurants, and membership club restaurants. The majority of this market will be mid-price restaurants of all types: that is, Mexican, Thai, Spanish, Vietnamese, South American, Scandinavian, Russian, Polynesian, Persian, Moroccan, Middle Eastern, Mediterranean, Lebanese, Korean, Japanese, Italian, Irish, Indonesian, Indian, Hungarian, Greek, German/Austrian, French, English, Continental, Chinese, International, American, kosher, seafood, vegetarian, and so forth. The average customer would be a restaurant that has been in operation for a year or more. The age of the restaurant is not really significant when specifying this market; however, the age of the staff and management does matter and that demographic material has yet to be defined. Generally a younger management team needs more help than an experienced, seasoned team. But occasionally one finds a management team that is older and too set in its ways and needs CRC's help. The age of the service personnel also plays an important role in discipline and motivation; a heavy concentration at the younger or older end of the age spectrum sometimes is the key to behaviorial problems.

Restaurants that have been CRC's customers and request the firm's help in opening a restaurant in a new location are also part of CRC's target market. Restaurants targeted specifically by name include Alice's Restaurant, Big Yellow House, Charley Brown's, Charthouse, Fiasco, Great American Food and Beverage Company, Gulliver's, Hamburger Hamlet, Houlihan's Old Place, Hungry Tiger, Huntington-Sheraton, Lawry's, Lighthouse, Longfellows, Moonshadows, Old World, One West California, The Palm, Playboy Club, Reuben's, Salt Shaker Family Restaurants, Sawmill, Smoke House, Stuart Anderson's Black Angus, Tiny Naylors, Whomphopper's Wagon Works, Marie Callendar's, Rosey's Restaurant. (These restaurants are predominantly located in California.)

Psychologically the consumers have a preoccupation with excellence and the pursuit of excellent performance. They care about their image and reputation portrayed both in the industry and with their customers. CRC's service helps those consumers feel more important, boost self-images, and increase sales, which leads to the bottom line—profit. These restaurants may be in either good or poor financial health; either situation would be examined and helped by this service. CRC would help the problem restaurant get out of the red and into the black, and would help the healthier restaurant increase sales, refine service, detail the entire restaurant, and make it stand out. These restaurants accept major credit cards like Visa, MasterCard, American Express, and Diners Club. They subscribe to publications like *Travel and Leisure, L.A. Magazine, Restaurant Business, Restaurants and Institutions,* and major newspapers. Their management teams, the ones who make the final decision to hire CRC, are innovative. They are open to constructive criticism and have the ability to realize that they might be too close to the restaurants' problems. These managers have above-average energy levels, at least average intelligence, an average level of objectivity, an ability to get along with all kinds of people, the ability to work under pressure, and self-confidence. These restaurants are mostly members of the NRA (National Restaurant Association).

The majority of consumers are responsive restaurants, concerned with their appearance, their employees, and their profits. They have the purchasing power to buy help before they need it, to invest some money in their future now before they go out of business. These consumers are seeking help in specific or general areas that they may have defined or that they have not yet identified.

KEY SUCCESS FACTORS

CRC has defined certain criteria to be very important to the success of its business. In a recent consumer survey conducted by *Restaurant Business* magazine in 1982, the three primary reasons for frequenting a restaurant (including midprice and upscale restaurants) is menu variety/quality, social aspect, and service.[3] Therefore, if the consumer values these factors in a restaurant, the key success factors for CRC are special expertise in menu preparation, food consulting, interior design and publicity, and service technique.

COMPETITION

Three kinds of competition to CRC's service exist to some degree: generic competition, product competition, and direct enterprise competition.

All service items have generic competition because all services are competing with one another for the consumer's dollar. Generic competition exists because the basic alternative to a service such as CRC is the use of

---

[3] *"How life-style shifts will shape our future." Restaurant Business,* (May 1, 1982), pp. 150–175.

in-house resources or doing nothing at all. CRC's objective is a planned advertising campaign to meet that generic competition by supplying consumers (restaurants) with the want-satisfying power—that is, the utility of practicality, convenience, success, and prestige. Those four factors will be the subtle incentives, motivating management to purchase CRC's service.

Product competition varies from the other types of competition. Product competition refers to other types of restaurant consulting, such as books, magazines, self-help plans, restaurant conventions, seminars, and field sales specialized wholesale services. Field sales specialized wholesale services refers to wholesale detail people in the restaurant business. They are salespeople, for example from a wine wholesaler, who carry very specialized, detailed information for a particular issue or area of the restaurant business. If the restaurant does substantial business with that wholesaler, certain services are provided to the restaurant free of charge. Examples of field sales specialized wholesale services include full wine-training programs, full promotional lessons, cooperative advertising budget planning, and so forth, which could satisfy a single restaurant's need. But this is where the application of appeal plays an important role in meeting this competition. One cannot attempt to discount this type of competition, but the primary concern is to identify the alternatives, know they exist, and then create a need in the consumer to be well organized with a prestigious well-rounded service rather than a myopic service that focuses only on one area of the business. Product competition includes personal needs, preferences, and decisions. CRC provides service in varied fields, expertise in all food service, a fair market price versus free service, and confidential service.

The final type of competition is direct enterprise. This type of competition is the most concrete of the three. While product competition is the hardest to identify, direct enterprise competition is established before your company has made its entrance into the market. There are a few consulting and research firms specializing in this area. Restaurant training services such as Inhilco, headquartered in New York's World Trade Center, operates 22 food service units. Over 1000 people service these operations. Gen LaGreca, director of training, has management development courses for middle management and four-day courses that involve decision making, planning, setting objectives, time management, motivation, and monitoring performance. She also has two-day seminars in "training the trainer." In addition, large chain restaurants, especially hotel chains, carry their own sales training force commanding high salaries. There are approximately 200 training directors in the industry, directing training of pizza bakers, pancake flippers, chicken fryers, margarita mixers, doughnut cutters, and even ice cream scoopers. They range in size from single luxury hotels to billion dollar burger chains. Table A2-1 lists the breakdown of training directors involved in different operations:

**TABLE A2-1. Training Directors by Type
of Operation in the Industry[a]**

Operation	Percentage
Full service	30
Fast food	30
Contract management	5
Cafeteria	1
Lodging	15
Military	1
Diversified	18

Table A2-1 reveals the areas on which training concentrated. The Council for Hotel and Restaurant Trainers (CHART) lists the major competitors, their specific area of concentration, and their geographic location. Food service training has come a long way in a short time. The field of employee training today is a growth industry with competition in its infancy.

CRC's differential advantage—what makes its service unique and enables it to stand out from the competition—is based on the recognition that every operation has a set of problems that are uniquely its own—promotional policies, location, size of menu, service tools, personnel, and so forth. CRC scrutinizes *all* areas of work and management, talking to people, and then tailors its program to particular situations and makes them work. Informal market research revealed no other companies presently offering this winning type of a program. This service is well designed and has been proven successful. It is most affordable to the type of consumer previously detailed.

MARKET POTENTIAL

As mentioned earlier, CRC will initially begin business in California. Due to time constraints, this plan will focus on California's market potential. CRC will expand as soon as possible into other target markets previously mentioned under the Market Characteristics section of this plan. Restaurants in the California area are chosen because CRC is headquartered in Los Angeles and the consultants are most familiar with restaurants there.

In the August 1983 edition of *Los Angeles* magazine, 1750 restaurants were listed by price, location, and cuisine; this was the 16th annual restaurant guide published by the magazine. This magazine alone offers CRC 1750 potential clients, all with unique problems or areas of improvement. Each month this magazine continues to list restaurants. This is a potentially large market in itself.

Paul Wallach, a leading restaurant critic in California, published a book entitled *Guide to the Restaurants of California* which lists over 1000 restaurants. This source also provides qualified leads of potential clients. Elmer Dills, KABC talk show host, also has a book of restaurants specifically in California as well as restaurants across the United States. There are also books like *The Menu Guide of Los Angeles, Vols. 1 and 2,* and various other places-to-go-things-to-do type books on the market.

Compiled lists of restaurants broaden market potential substantially. For example, the Automobile Club of California lists many restaurants geographically in their directory for travelers. Private wine masters and restauranteurs are continually writing books and compiling lists of the latest restaurants. This all adds to the list of potential customers for CRC. Within one year CRC hopes to expand to nationwide service. Table A2-2 illustrates a summary of potential growth performance by category of planned growth opportunity.

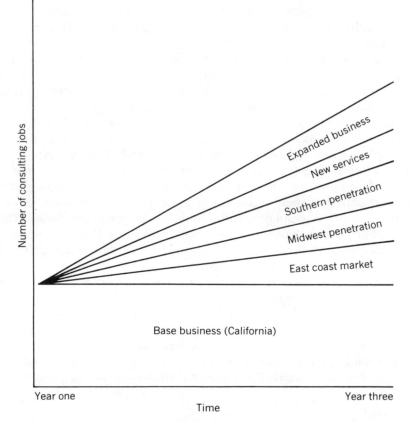

TABLE A2-2. Summary of Potential Growth Performance by Category of Planned Growth Opportunity

ENVIRONMENTAL FACTORS

"The most dominant market trend of the decade will be the maturing of the baby boomers who will trigger a sharp increase in consumer buying power," according to Thayer C. Taylor, senior editor of *Sales and Marketing Management* magazine. The environment surrounding the food service industry is dynamic. Restaurant marketers will be selling to an upscale market in the 1980s as the baby boom generation moves toward the peak income years of the life cycle and as upper-level life-style groups continue to flourish. The 35–44 age group will be the fastest growing segment restaurants must cater to. Because of their sheer numbers and their acquired job experience, the baby boomers will trigger an upward thrust in consumer buying power. The demographics of the industry is changing because of the environment in which restaurants live. For example, the startling changes in households—the key consumer buying unit—which are becoming smaller and forming much later in life than before. A universal sales target previously used was the "typical" family consisting of a working husband, staying-home wife, and one or more children. In 1950 when new values began to stir, such a family accounted for 70 percent of all households.[4]

Between 1960 and 1980, singles rocketed from 13 to 23 percent of all households, female-headed units from 8 to 13 percent of all families and from 13 to 26 percent of all households.[5] Behind these demographic changes, a shift in values has also occurred. New values focus more on self-fulfillment, self-expression, and self-idealization. These new values and thus new buying styles will give some indication as to the types of products these people are looking for, what advertising appeals they will respond to, the kind of interior decorations they will feel most comfortable in, and even the kind of restaurants they will frequent. Restaurants will be forced to polish every aspect of their business and place special emphasis on service, which may be the single biggest differential advantage of the future. Restaurants offering excellent service will appeal to more than one life-style group because every life-style group appreciates service. Thus CRC will help restaurants adjust to this environment.

Another important environmental factor challenging restaurants in the 1980s will be the sweeping electronics revolution created by the computer-on-a-chip, symbolized by the personal computer. The wedding of the computer and TV set will strengthen the trend to at-home leisure and recreation. This means that at-home banking and shopping services will establish a foothold in the 1980s, reducing the number of times people will perform such chores outside the home, and consequently make fewer visits

[4] *Op. cit.,* p. 190.
[5] *Ibid.*

to a restaurant. Faced with this possibility the more sophisticated restaurants will seek help from CRC to devise ways to maintain contact with these elusive consumers. Also CRC will provide services to aid the restaurant in using computers to do some of the restaurant's chores to cut labor costs.

A sudden rise in the cost of living, inflation, or unemployment could obviously cause a dramatic decrease in demand for "want" (versus need) items; that is, in times of economic hardships the frills would be cut out, and restaurants having smaller budgets would basically not have the money to spend on seeking outside help. As disposable income decreases so does the number of trips consumers make to eat out; thus the restaurants' sales decrease and so does CRC's business. Also, a sudden rise in the cost of consumer goods—especially food and liquor—would affect CRC momentarily, because restaurants would be forced to spend more of their dollars on their staples and have less money to spend on training. However, as previously discussed, total food service industry sales will approach $160 billion with a real growth higher than in any year since the 1970s; therefore the environmental factors seem positive for the future.

INTERNAL RESOURCES

CRC will be a privately owned entity. It will be a solely owned corporation of Christina L. Collins and will employ four other consultants to help with workshops and various specialized areas. C. L. Collins' field of expertise is in sales and marketing management. Specialized employees' areas of expertise include industrial psychology, finance, wine and spirits services, culinary services, and human resource development.

CRC offers everything from nuts-and-bolts courses on how-tos, to sales and style courses. It can be a full-function company where the firm would go into the restaurant and run the business for a week, a month, or a quarter. Or CRC could just concentrate on one problem area for a week. The internal strength of CRC stems from over 50 years' combined experience in the industry. CRC's staff has worked for such restaurants as Marie Callendars, Taco Naugles, Lord Charlie's, Charthouse, Chez Sateau, Francois, In-and-Out Burgers, Days Inn, Charlie Brown's, and Rosey's Restaurant.

How did this dynamic team get into the restaurant consulting business? C. L. Collins has a bachelor of science degree in business administration with an emphasis in marketing and a minor in English, and she worked her way through college by being a waitress. She won sales contests in the restaurant and began keeping records of all her sales and analyzing them, figuring out how she could do better, when the president of the company that owned the restaurant talked her into training the other servers. She moved her way up the restaurant management ladder, meeting other dynamic people in the industry. When the restaurant became so finely tuned that it essentially ran itself, she decided to organize a part-time consulting firm. CRC's first success story came from the staff's first project, working for a popular West Cost coffee shop chain. An all-new service staff met for nine sessions entitled "An Introduction to Wine and Service" complete with reviews, exams, videotapes, and role-playing. As a result, the restaurant was rated extraordinary in service by a leading consumer newspaper. CRC organized informally and now, beginning formal business operations with this plan, looks forward to a profitable and exciting future.

PROBLEMS AND OPPORTUNITIES

There are various problems and opportunities involved with the introduction, growth, maturity, and decline stages (the product life cycle) of CRC. This section will discuss the problems and opportunities as they relate to the marketing mix: the product, the price, the place, and the promotion involved.

The product, which is a service, may be adversely affected by a sudden increase in costs associated with running a restaurant. This increase may decrease the amount of available money and willingness to spend money on seeking outside professional help. In addition, a major failure in CRC's history could ruin its reputation, and may alter restaurant buying behavior indefinitely. Therefore CRC must fully scrutinize all commitments and problems before accepting an account with a restaurant. Conversely, opportunities include a good track history of the company, insuring future demand for the service, and a healthy economy with costs of operations remaining relatively the same.

The price may be affected by economic factors such as inflation, recession, depression, and prosperity. In these difficult economic environments, the demand for personal services decreases, and people tend to do jobs for themselves. In a time such as this, demand for consulting service to overcome these problems is on the increase, which will be beneficial to CRC. Another opportunity is the pricing structure that will be implemented, which is a progressive one: the smaller the operation and the fewer employees, the less the cost of hiring CRC. Also, pricing will fluctuate with the size of the job in terms of time, money, and effort involved. Estimates will readily be given to restaurants, and their personal financial condition will be taken into consideration. This pricing could be both a problem and an opportunity, which will be discussed more thoroughly under the marketing strategy entitled Price.

The place may be affected by a lack of availability. The place will usually be the client's restaurant. Because this is a service tailored to a specific restaurant, the facilities must be made available to CRC. With the grand opening of a restaurant and completion of a facility, special accommodations will be arranged. Because CRC is a full-function consulting firm there is a short channel of distribution with relatively few people between the firm and the consumer. CRC will not hire any recruiters or salespeople and will rely directly on advertising and word-of-mouth publicity.

Promotion may be directly affected by a sudden increase in the cost of advertising. The promotion method selected is printed direct response advertising, which will be fully discussed in the marketing strategy under Promotion. Publicity, which is nonpaid advertising, will be an added benefit and opportunity to increase sales volume. Publicity among restaurants is common in this industry.

In order to extend the product life cycle, alternatives have been devised to allow for growth and expansion from California to other tourist states that are highly populated with restaurants. Marketing efforts would be geared toward past performance for many popular California restaurants. Advertising for this segment will be in national restaurant (industry) magazines.

PART II

Marketing Objectives

CRC's goal is to initially obtain a medium request for consulting. The initial communication vehicle selected is a direct mail campaign throughout California. The marketing campaign will begin August 1984 at the California Restaurant Convention held annually at the Los Angeles Convention Center. Objectives in the first year are to complete 50+ consulting jobs at an average cost of $1250. This would yield $63,000 in revenues in year one.

CRC is a special case because of the service nature of the business. In this analysis the basic objective is to produce service contacts leading to final service agreements. A desired goal and secondary objective is to expedite ROI.

Following the first year of operations, CRC plans to expand its market and penetrate other geographical areas beyond California.

TARGET MARKET SEGMENTS

The target market, as previously stated in the section entitled Market Characteristics, is fast food chains, midprice restaurants, coffee shop chains, upscale diners, leisure resort restaurants, fine dining areas, family restaurants, theme/specialty restaurants, and membership club restaurants. The basic "want-satisfying power" or utility (CRC provides) is to help failing businesses get out of the red, to help maintain high sales, and to help successful restaurants stay on top. This is done by keeping the restaurant "polished" and well informed on the state-of-the-art technology and management techniques in the restaurant industry. CRC meets and fulfills every need a restaurant could have.

Further segmentation is limited to geographical location. Additional segmentation is considered futile as the service transcends other boundaries. Such flexibility is available by means of minor alterations and presentation and procedures of the service. Thus this service fits neatly into specific restaurants' schedules.

TARGET VOLUME

CRC's initial sales volume is estimated at 50+ consulting jobs in the first year. This is based on a projection of the total restaurant industry in California, how many restaurants can be reached, and an estimated average time period that each job would require. The total number of restaurants in California alone is approximately 40,050.[6] For the United States in its entirety there are approximately 899,451 food service institutions.[7] California thus has 4.5 percent of the total potential market and becomes the prime location for introducing CRC's services.

Target volume in dollars is based upon projections forecasted from the response rate of the direct mail campaign. Revenue of $63,000 is based on 210 clients with an average sale of $300. This does not imply that 210 clients will each purchase $300 in services, rather the number of clients will range from 1 to 210 and the overall average expenditure will be $300. The estimated 50+ consulting jobs is derived from a conservative estimate of the average expenditure approximating $1250.

The break-even analysis is included in the Profit Analysis section immediately following.

PROFIT ANALYSIS

CRC's profitability and break-even calculations for the first two years of operations are shown in Table A2-3. The third year has been omitted due to statistical invalidity at this time. Analysis of year three is pending further information of a direct response national magazine advertising campaign. Cost assessment has been delayed pending second-year information on tac-

---

[6] *Statistical Abstract of the United States of America 1982.* "Census of Retail Trade," 1977.
[7] *Ibid.*

TABLE A2-3. Profitability and Break-Even Analysis (Stated in Dollars)

Year One:		
Revenue (210 × $300)		63,000
Expenses:		
Direct mail campaign	(5,641)	
Salaries	(50,000)	
Supplies and equipment	(7,000)	
		62,641
		$359
Profit:		
Year Two:		
Revenue (based on 50 percent growth)		94,500
Expenses:		
Direct mail campaign	(5,641)	
Salaries (increase)	(60,000)	
Supplies and equipment (increase)	(15,000)	
		80,641
Profit:		$13,859

tics, involvement, and resources. Please note that said estimates become more reliable the closer they are to implementation.

PART III

Marketing Strategy

This is a detailed specification of the marketing program proposed for CRC. It is divided into four main parts: the product, the price, the promotion, and the place. The basic strategy for marketing CRC's service in the industry is to concentrate on personal improvement, consumer satisfaction, professional image, and quality improvements of restaurants.

THE PRODUCT

CRC has a full line of services and in this case the product is a service: a restaurant consulting service for the food service industry. The product is of high quality and is well packaged. The service package is unique since every operation has a set of problems that is uniquely its own. CRC offers an exceptional array of training seminars accompanied by several supportive functions, such as literature, promotional tips, and how-to books on preparing wine lists, handling purveyors, and so forth. Scheduling options and tailored programs are unique offerings to the specific operation in need, with further differential advantages supplied as needed. The differential advantage is therefore tailoring the service to the customer's needs. Advantages that are difficult to describe are those related to format, style, and those personalized items tailored to provide that special service only CRC offers. The following are examples of some of the products the service offers.

A management development course for middle managers and supervisors is a four-day course that involves decision making, planning, establishing long-range goals, and setting objectives. Other seminars that are in high demand are the time-management seminar and the lecture entitled "Monkeys on My Back," which deals with discretionary time and the lack of such time. Other topics covered in various courses are delegation of work, motivation, communication with employees, discipline, how to monitor performance, and how to criticize constructively.

CRC offers nuts-and-bolts courses on etiquette, style, and grace. Also CRC offers train-the-trainer courses to improve lower management skills. Training also involves newcomers being trained in departments where busboys, bartenders, utility people, servers, cashiers, and cooks are trained. A course for servers and captains is also available which includes learning the menu and selling techniques for describing menu items to customers with enthusiasm.

Incentive and sales techniques are also taught to employees. To emphasize points, courses include the use of videotapes and role-playing, for example, simulated situations with customers and servers. Courses include wine appreciation and food appreciation. A course designed especially for many California restaurants is English as a second language, which draws on talent in the house, because various languages are spoken in an operation and all need to communicate. There are also classes on serving food and wine (placement of glasses, where the ice bucket should stand, how to uncork, etc.).

There are also seminars on house maintenance, how to sell, how to describe, how to serve, and several sessions with the chef, the cooks, and head chef for CRC. Cooking and cleaning tips are recommended, along with basic preparation times and provisions for menu expansion. There are courses in selling and preparing cocktails and courses in after-dinner drinks—cognacs, brandies, armagnacs, eaux de vie, port, and madiera.

All courses, seminars, and lectures are done after a one-week preliminary in-house study conducted by CRC. This time is used for investigating problem areas and for orientating employees by introducing them to Collins Restaurant consultants on a one-to-one basis. The preliminary work is done both to diagnose problems and opportunities and to help CRC learn the extent of work required to facilitate price determination.

The service is unique in that it is guaranteed to do the following in the specific areas of concentration: decrease employee turnover, cut labor costs, cut food costs, decrease employee pilferage (which will come to $53.7 billion a year in 1983[8]), increase morale, increase sales per hour and sales per person, increase wine sales, and, in the long run, increase return customer traffic. This service is the only service on the market that guarantees improvement in specific areas of concentration.

THE PRICE

The price of this service fluctuates substantially based upon the extent of the necessary work. The work may range from a single lecture on a specific topic for a minimum of two hours to full-service takeovers involving up to six months of time. Prices range from $150 up.

The price is flexible and if the CRC management team deems it appropriate, alternative methods of payment can be arranged. This allows for CRC to partake in ventures whose profit potential in the short term is questionable. However, CRC would attain its profits by investing in the long-term benefits attained from CRC's involvement with the establishments (obtaining a percentage of sales, profit, or partnership in the future).

Initial consultation costs include a flat fee of $25. It covers discussion of the estimated costs and terms and writing of an agreement to do business. This nonrefundable service fee is applicable toward a contract. Depending upon location, transportation costs and expenses incurred are to be covered by the client.

Some of the seminars and their associated prices are listed in Table A2-4. Table A2-5 lists some of the courses available and their prices.

TABLE A2-4. Partial List of Available Seminars

Seminar	Price
Hire smart, train hard, manage easy	$200
How to get the Monkeys off your back	$150
Time management	$300
Plan, organize, lead, and control	$275
Don't confuse effort with results	$275
Authority, responsibility, and delegation	$400

[8] Mortimer R. Feinberg, PhD. "Employee stealing on the rise." *Restaurant Business,* (February 1983), pp.

TABLE A2-5. Available Courses

Course	Time Involvement	Price
Preparing 50 proven promotions	2 days	$400
Etiquette, style, and grace	2 weeks	$5000
Human resource development	1 week	$1000[a]
Management, manners, and money	2 days	$300
Wine appreciation I	1 week	$3500[a]
Wine appreciation II	1 week	$5000
Menu and preparation	1 week	$5000[a]
Dining	2 days	$500
Eat and run	2 days	$300
Distilled spirits	2 days	$200

[a]Brief versions available at reduced prices.

Additional courses are available at appropriate costs. Consolidated contracts provide reduced rates and flexible pricing is practiced. All resources and educational material will be provided by CRC, excluding restaurant facilities. This pricing strategy is a normal fluctuating price structure. CRC is not expensive; in the long run the benefits far outweigh the associated short-term costs.

THE PROMOTION

The advertising time frame for CRC will begin in August 1984, at the California Restaurant Convention held annually at the Los Angeles Convention Center. This trade show marks the introduction of CRC's service to the trade. There, CRC will have a drawing to provide the company with a mailing list of California restaurants attending the trade show.

In addition to this list, CRC plans to rent another from a list management company. The list chosen would be acquired through Ash Business List Management located in Canoga Park, California. The director, Carolee Briley, has quoted a price of $35 per thousand with a minimum purchase of 5000 names. CRC plans to do a test mailing of the list in November, and if the list proves to be feasible, a mailing of 30,000 names will be made. The cost of renting a list of this size is $1050. The mailing will consist of a brochure with various success stories about the individuals who run CRC. The mailing would take place at the end of December so that restaurants would receive it the first week in January. Table A2-6 lists associated costs of the direct mail campaign.

The first phase of the advertising will begin at the end of December.

[a]"Operations and technology of food service training today." *Restaurants and Institutions,* (January 1, 1983), pp.

TABLE A2-6. Direct Mail Campaign Cost

1. *Rental Cost of Mailing List* This figure is derived from a cost of $35/m (m = per thousand). This amount of advertising dollars will purchase a targeted mailing list of 21,000 California restaurants, approximately half of the estimated universe (approximately 40,100 restaurants in business in 1977).	$735.00
2. *Direct Mail Piece Costs* A. Letter shop charge is based on $8/m. The expense in total dollars is <u>$168.</u> B. Laser computer personalization is an additional cost incurred above the letter shop fee. This is 5 percent above the base cost. This total amount is <u>$8.40.</u> C. The enclosed response card is an additional 3 percent of the original base letter and envelope charge. The total amount is <u>$5.04.</u> D. Taxation at 6.5 percent of charges is added. The total amount is <u>$11.79.</u>	$193.23
3. *Postage* This lump sum includes the cost of the initial bulk mailing and business reply charges.	$4200.00
4. *Response Testing Cost* This includes testing 10 percent of the original mailing list (2100 names chosen every *n*th name from the list broker).	$512.82
Total	<u>$5,641.05</u>

January and February will be response months. Response is anticipated at 1 percent, which represents 210 restaurants (customers). A customer would have to purchase a mere $26.86 for the direct mail campaign to break even.

These 210 restaurants would represent interested clients willing to purchase the service. After close examination of their purchasing power, and scheduling, the conservative estimate of revenues generated would be $63,000. This figure was based on 210 clients purchasing services at an average cost of $300.

At the end of one year further penetration of the California market would be attempted with a similar mailing in terms of timing, quantity, and costs. At the end of year two, depending on the extent of success, the direct mail campaign will be supplemented by national advertising in industry magazines such as *Restaurant Business, Restaurants and Institutions,* and *Restaurants.* Costs of this campaign cannot be accurately calculated because the future costs, including magazine advertising rates, are not currently available. National magazine ads will be direct response advertisements and would mark the penetration into the entire U.S. market.

THE PLACE

The channel of distribution even in a service situation is very important. A two-level channel of distribution was chosen:

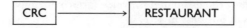

This is compatible with the nonservice industries' two-level channel of distribution that exists between a manufacturer/retailer selling directly to the consumer.

Marketing efforts involved with CRC will begin in December with the direct marketing campaign as the vehicle of communication between CRC and California restaurants. Implementation and follow-up will begin immediately with the appropriate service as needed or requested, as illustrated in Tables A2-4 and A2-5.

The seminars and lectures will actually be conducted in the client's restaurant and the actual place of the service will be in the host restaurant. All equipment that is not in house will be brought into the restaurant by CRC for a fee.

PART IV

Marketing Tactics

This section reviews the how-tos of the marketing strategy. Marketing tactics include necessary tasks and an implementation schedule. This tells CRC how to implement and achieve the marketing strategy.

TASKS

CRC will have a post office box as its mailing address because the owners of the company are the consultants and the majority of the team have other jobs and business ventures. Meetings and discussions are held in one of the consultant's restaurants. Therefore, there are no rental costs for business offices at this time.

CRC is a full-service firm that will be responsible for the following:

1. Receiving, recording, and following up on orders daily.
2. Sending consultants to restaurants.

3. Printing and packaging educational materials.
4. Supplemental costs of running CRC.
5. Legal aspects.

All phases of the business will be shared by all consultants and each new project will be delegated to a specific consultant. That consultant will be the chief of the project in charge of that restaurant and it will be his or her responsibility to delegate work and define needs the rest of the team can fulfill.

Other business logistics of the business plan were discussed in previous sections.

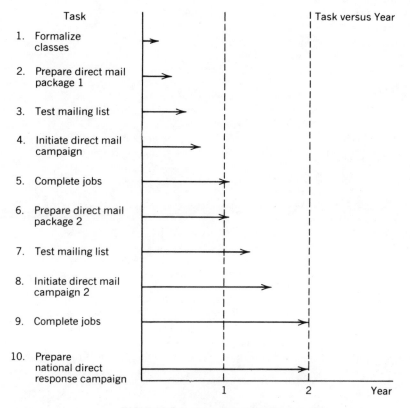

TABLE A2-7. Implementation Schedule

PART V

Conclusion

The total marketing plan concentrates on the logistics involved in marketing CRC service through direct mail marketing techniques for the first two years. At the end of the second year a national direct response advertising campaign will begin through national industry magazines. The plan segments the consumer, analyzes the market, competition, environment, distribution, and problems and opportunities. Lastly the report describes the marketing strategies and tactics involved.

The goal of this marketing plan is to act as a road map to CRC and act as a sales tool to illustrate the various facets involved in marketing CRC. CRC will break even after the first year of operation. CRC will prove profitable after the second year of business.

A3: "LIMIT"—DISPOSABLE ALCOHOL TESTING UNIT

Developed by
SCOTT GILMOUR
STEVEN LUBEGA
ANDREW SMITH
MATT SMITH

CONTENTS

Used with the permission of the authors.

EXECUTIVE SUMMARY

This report presents a detailed marketing plan for introducing a disposable alcohol testing unit (DATU) into the Los Angeles and Orange counties' consumer market.

On the basis of information we gathered during the course of our research, we determined that there is a considerable need for this product and a large potential demand. The number of drunk-driving arrests in Los Angeles and Orange counties last year was 106,585, while the number of drunk-driving occurrences exceeded some 213 million. Following a detailed analysis of our target market, we projected the sale of over 205,000 units, totaling some $197,000 in sales, with profits exceeding $50,000.

Our marketing strategy consists of repositioning a product designed for law enforcement use and promoting it in the consumer market. Market penetration pricing of $1.69 will be used for initial introduction, distributed through existing channels, utilizing agent middlemen and wholesale distributors of sundry items within liquor stores. The product will be sold through grocery and liquor stores, with the primary promotional emphasis on point-of-purchase displays. Planned date of introduction is in May 1983.

INTRODUCTION

In 1978, there were 51,500 traffic fatalities on the nation's highways, 50 percent or some 26,300 of which were caused by drunk drivers. In addition, more Americans died at the hands of drunk drivers during the past two years than were killed in Vietnam during the entire U.S. involvement (13).

Replacement studies by such groups as the National Highway Traffic Safety Administration (NHTSA), the Gallup Poll, and others indicate that 6 out of every 100 (6 percent)) cars you pass on the highway may be operated by a drunk driver, increasing to 10 out of every 100 (10 percent) on the weekends (13).

In an effort to reduce these unacceptable figures, a number of interest groups have sprung up across the country, such as MADD (Mothers Against Drunk Drivers), and have begun a concerted effort to pass tougher drinking and driving laws. Already 27 state legislatures have passed their own versions of "the toughest drunk driving law in the country," while 20 other states have raised the legal drinking age (13).

Clearly, the need exists to find a solution to this problem. For our marketing plan we are proposing a unique approach to this situation. The solution we are offering is a disposable "go–no go" alcohol breath analyzer, ı low-cost, inexpensive one-time-use product that can determine whether a person is legally intoxicated. "Anti-drunk driving crusaders hope that breath-testing devices will become as much a fixture on the social scene as the shaker and stirrer" (13).

The purpose of this marketing plan is to present a viable means of marketing such a product to the general consumer in an effort to reduce the number of alcohol-related accidents that occur on the nation's highways.

SITUATIONAL ANALYSIS

Market Characteristics

Because the product we are proposing to market is unique, the characteristics of our market are not as clear as we would like. The information we came across in our research effort, however, has presented us with some very useful data.

To begin, motor vehicle accidents represent the nation's single greatest killer of people in the under-40 age group, the highest rate occurring between the ages of 16 and 24. Of all causes of death in all age groups, automobile deaths rank fourth after heart disease, cancer, and strokes. Add to that information that 50 percent of all traffic accidents are caused by drunken drivers, and you begin to see the potential market for such a product as ours.

The number of people arrested in the Los Angeles-Orange County area last year for drunk driving was 106,585 (12). Add to that knowledge that only an estimated one drunk driver out of 2000 is actually caught and

arrested, and you really begin to see the potential number of prospects for
our breath analyzer (13).

The Los Angeles marketing area is one of the largest and most powerful
markets in the United States, accounting for at least 40 percent of the population, households, effective buying income, and retail sales of the entire
state of California.

In 1978, there were some 9 million people living within this area, equat-
ing to some 3.5 million households. According to a *Los Angeles Times* market
research "Consumer Trend Analysis" on beer, wine, and distilled spirits,
more than half of all Los Angeles households reported purchasing at least
one type of alcoholic beverage in the preceding 30 days. Figure A3-1 illustrates the purchase incidence of any alcoholic beverage during the prior
30-day periods. Overall, the incidence of purchase was generally higher
for beer than for wine or distilled spirits.

Family income is an important determinant of beverage purchase and
thus would be of concern to us as well. Alcoholic beverage purchases are
more prominent in higher-income households. In 1977, 39.6 percent of all
Los Angeles households earning incomes of $25,000 or more annually pur-
chased an alcoholic beverage within the preceding 30-day period.

Equally important is the fact that fully 47.9 percent of the households
where the age of the household head was under 40 accounted for 64.3

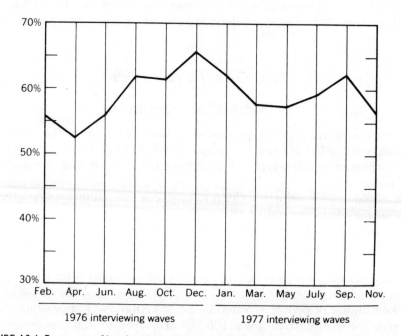

FIGURE A3-1. Percentage of Los Angeles households purchasing any alcoholic beverage in last 30 days.

percent of the beer purchases, 56.2 percent of the wine purchases, and 50.4 percent of the distilled spirits purchases.

Households in which the head has had some college education or more dominated total expenditures for alcoholic beverages. The 59.1 percent of all Los Angeles households where this was the case was responsible for 59.5 percent of the beer purchases, 80.3 percent of the wine purchases, and 73.1 percent of the distilled spirits purchases.

Finally, households headed by someone in a professional or managerial position were the primary contributors to total expenditures on alcoholic beverages. These two occupational groups made up 38.1 percent of all Los Angeles households and were responsible for purchasing 39.7 percent of the beer sold, 56.7 percent of the wine sold, and 50.8 percent of the distilled spirits sold.

Examination of purchase patterns to determine where purchases of alcoholic beverages were made, by type of store, found that the majority of purchases were made at grocery stores, followed by liquor stores, drug stores, discount stores, department stores, and others. The following chart breaks down the specific place of purchase by beverage type:

	Beer (%)	Wine (%)	Distilled Spirits (%)
Grocery store	6.5	60.0	40.9
Liquor store	36.6	37.8	54.5
Drug store	1.2	1.9	2.7
Discount store	2.1	0.9	3.1
Department store	0.7	0.9	0.8
Other	2.8	5.9	2.7
Don't know	—	0.3	1.6

The vast majority of households indicated the male household head was the primary decision maker and purchaser of alcoholic beverages, responsible for 62.5 percent of the beer purchases, 52.2 percent of the wine purchases, and 61.5 percent of the distilled spirits purchases.

Among households purchasing an alcoholic beverage in the preceding 30-day period, about 7 out of 10 reported serving each type once a week or more, with beer (72.7 percent) being more likely to be served on a daily basis than either wine (69.7 percent) or distilled spirits (68.4 percent). Almost two-thirds (65.1 percent) of all Los Angeles households reported serving an alcoholic beverage within the preceding 30-day period, with beer (47 percent) and wine (45 percent) being the most popular. More than 13 percent of these households serve them on a daily basis.

One study concluded that adults in the Los Angeles marketing area are more likely than the average U.S. adult to consume most types of alcoholic beverages and the tendency to consume increases with socioeconomic level: "In this higher-than-average liquor-drinking market, marketers who zero in on Los Angeles adults in the higher-demographic groups are getting the best possible target audience for their products."

Key Success Factors

1. *Limited Competition.* No known competitors exist in the Southern California test market who:
   Distribute a similar product at a low price level, therefore creating a price advantage
   Distribute a disposable device, therefore creating a product portability advantage
2. *Legal Climate.* Currently the trend is heading toward stricter penalties for driving while intoxicated.
   The trend has clearly provided penalties of increasing severity over time (see legal appendix).
3. *Ease of Operation.* The DATU is relatively small—pocket-sized (Figure A3-2).

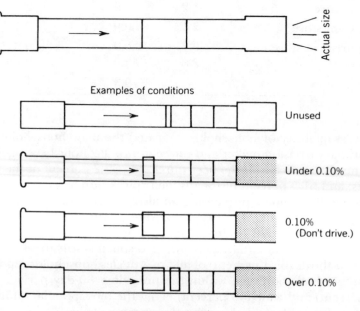

FIGURE A3-2. DATU.

The usage procedure is simple (i.e., blow breath sample into tube and compare color change to calibration on instrument).
4. *Price versus Value.* DATU provides relatively inexpensive protection to drivers who are under the influence of alcohol to some degree.
Value exists in that DATU is significantly less expensive than the potentially negative outcomes of driving while intoxicated:
   a. Loss of license
   b. Legal fine
   c. Loss of life
Price has been designed to be within affordable reach of target market (i.e., under $3).

Competition and Product Comparisons

To date there are no manufacturers who have distributed a DATU to the consumer market. There are three manufacturers in the United States who produce breath-alcohol testing equipment: C.M.I. Incorporated, Minturn, Colorado; Intoximeter Incorporated, St. Louis, Missouri; and Smith and Wesson General Ordinance Equipment Company, Springfield, Massachusetts.

Their major marketing emphasis is toward the law enforcement agencies throughout the United States and abroad. The equipment they produce is used to gain evidential-quality results as to a suspect's breath-alcohol count. The results are used as evidence in the conviction of an intoxicated individual.

These products are very expensive, ranging in price from $300 to over $3500. Their ownership by the general public for self-testing is nonexistent, due to the prohibitive pricing. The competition posed by these manufacturers should be considered potential, rather than direct. Their present market emphasis is due to the expense of their current product line and lack of familiarity with the public consumer market.

The exception to the expensive product lines produced by these manufacturers is the Alcolyser PST (preliminary screening device) produced by Intoximeter Incorporated (Figure A3-3). This device is used by mobile highway patrol and sheriff units throughout the United States. Approximately 1.5 million of these units have been sold to this market. The PST is a disposable, one-time-use device that is portable and reasonably accurate for its intended use. The law enforcement agencies use this device in the field instead of the manual dexterity manipulations to determine a person's ability to drive. The sales of the PST have increased steadily as its application qualities have been recognized. Eventually, the subjective judgment call will be replaced by the PST or a similar product.

In Europe, a similar product has been successfully introduced to the consumer market, with sales of approximately 12 million units. Europe's

Description	The "Alcolyser" is a simple, portable, scientific device for measuring the alcohol content of blood via expired breath. The indication of the Alcolyser detector tube is based on Widmark's reaction principle, with the alcohol in expired breath reacting with the yellow crystals and turning them green.
	For the test, expired air (mixture of tidal and alveolar air) is blown through the tube into a plastic bag in approximately 20 seconds. The Alcolyser will indicate an absolute quantity of alcohol of as little as 5 mg. or an alcohol concentration in blood of 0.3 promille. (30 mg of alcohol per 100 ml of blood.)
	The length of the green stain in the tube is proportional to the blood alcohol concentration. When the green stain extends to the red mark at the center of the tube, then the alcohol level in the blood corresponds to the prescribed limit as indicated on the box label.
Calibration	The Alcolyser detector tubes have been calibrated against direct blood alcohol analysis employing a gas chromatograph with a flame ionization detector.
	The prescribed legal limits of alcohol in the blood vary from one country to another. The Alcolyser range consists of the following calibrated detector tubes:

Alcolyser 50, 80, 100, 125 and
150 mg/100 ml blood.

Precautions	It is important to allow at least 15 minutes to elapse after taking alcoholic drink in order to allow mouth alcohol to disappear. Smoking should be avoided prior to breath test.
Estimation of blood alcohol level	The basis of the determination of blood alcohol via expired breath relies on the established ratio[2] between the alcohol content of blood to that of breath (2100 to 1). Provided the breath test is carried out in accordance with the manufacturers instructions this ratio holds true.
Correlation results	The results given in Table 1 were carried out at Indiana Toxicology, Department of Police Administration, University of Indiana.

FIGURE A3-3. Alcolyser PST (Preliminary Screening Test).

generally harsher penalties for driving under the influence of alcohol have greatly increased the need for this type of product. For example, in Switzerland the penalty for drunk driving is the loss of one's driver's license for five years. Our current laws and penalties are not nearly as severe but are moving in that general direction.

The Alcolyser PST meets our product specifications and will be used for

	BLOOD	ALCO-LYSER	BREATH-ALYSER	BLOOD	ALCO-LYSER	BREATH-ALYSER
	.09	.09	.07	.07	.08	.08
	.06	.08	.07	.04	.04	.03
	.05	.07	.05	.03	.04	.04
	.07	.08	.08	.09	.10	.09
	.11	.12	.12	.06	.08	.06
	.08	.09	.08	.07	.10	.09
	.08	.09	.08	.14	.12	.16
	.07	.08	.07	.07	.09	.09
	.08	.09	.07	.10	.10	.12
TABLE I	.10	.10	.10	.03	.04	.02

Alcolyser screening test calibrated for 0.10%

Summary of Results

(i) Within the limits of accuracy of alcohol detector tubes results show that there is a good correlation between the Alcolyser detector tube and direct blood alcohol estimations.[4]

(ii) When the blood alcohol concentration is at the prescribed limit the Alcolyser gives a reliability of over 90 percent.

(iii) When the blood alcohol level is above the prescribed limit, then the reliability of the "Alcolyser" approaches 100 percent.

(iv) When the blood alcohol level is below the limit, reliability is of the order of 90 percent (just below the limit) but approaching 100 percent when the alcohol level is significantly below the limit.

When used in accordance with the Manufacturer's instructions the Alcolyser can provide a rapid and reliable guide to the alcohol level of the blood.

References

1. Ducie, W. L. and Jones, T. P. Means for detecting breath-alcohol, Pat. No. 1,143,818.
2. Harger, et al. Journal of Biological Chemistry, 1950, 18B, 197.
3. Curry, et al. The Analyst, November, 1966, 91, 742.
4. Jones, T. P. Alcohol and Traffic Safety, 5th International Conference, Freiburg, 1969.

FIGURE A3-3. Continued

the initial introduction to the consumer market. We are repositioning this existing product for use by the general consumer.

Basically, any one of the manufacturers could produce a DATU because the technology is simple and the capital equipment costs are relatively low. Our competitive edge is our expertise in the consumer market and their lack of interest in selling to this market.

Technology

The technology upon which the DATU is based is incredibly simple. It is based primarily upon the scientific principle that deep lung breath and blood alcohol are related in a definite and predictable way.

The DATU is comprised of a glass tube containing potassium dichromate crystals and a catalyst which maximizes the presence of the dichromate ions. We aim to maximize the concentration of the dichromate ion because when one breathes over the crystals, the moisture in the breath dissolves them, at which point both chromate and dichromate ions exist. The dichromate ion, however, has a higher oxidation potential ($E° = 1.33$ volts) than the chromate ion ($E° = -0.13$ volts).

$E°$ represents an oxidation potential measured in volts. More oxidation takes place if the change in energy is greater.

When alcohol is introduced into the DATU, the dichromate ion oxidizes the alcohol (C_2H_5OH). The resultant products are chromic ions (responsible for the change in color). The equation below shows the reaction if a catalyst like sulfuric acid (H_2SO_4) was used (5).

		Alcohol		Chromic Sulfate		Acetaldehyde
$K_2Cr_2O_7$	+	3 C_2H_5OH	–	$Cr_2(SO_4)_3$	+	3 CH_3CHO
Potassium dichromate	+	4 H_2SO_4	+	K_2SO_4	+	7 H_2O
		Sulfuric acid		Potassium sulfate		Water

Legal Environment

The legal environment relating to the sale and consumption of alcoholic beverages in California is to be a crucial variable in our marketing strategy. In fact, the whole raison d'être for our product is embodied in the realization that drinking and driving will in all probability lead to injury of some sort. The recognition of this fact by the law and the consequent penalties are the two factors that make our market viable.

Legally, a person is deemed intoxicated (in California) when their blood alcohol reaches 0.10 percent. It is well recognized, however, that functions critical in driving coordination are impaired quite a bit before the 0.10 percent level. Because "driving under the influence" (DUI) is rightly presumed to represent unreasonable risk both to the driver and to others who may be using the roads, penalties for doing so are becoming stiffer and stiffer. In addition, under California's "implied consent law" (see Legal Appendix), the relevant authorities can require any driver using the highways to submit to an alcohol test (blood, breath, or urine).

If the criminal liability of being intoxicated is frightening, the civil liability is equally so, if not more so. While criminal liability may mean up to three months in jail and $500 in fines, civil liability could easily expose an individual to personal financial ruin.

Under civil liability, specifically under the tort liability of "negligence," the tortfeasor may literally have his or her pants sued off. Prior to 1971, for instance, "a commercial vendor of alcoholic beverages could not be held liable to a *third party* injured by an individual who became intoxicated as the result of the negligent serving of alcoholic beverages" (4).

In June 1971, the California Supreme Court handed down *Vesley v. Sager,* 5 Cal. 3d 153, 95 Cal. Rptr. 623, which opened the door to so-called third-party liability. With the decision in *Vesley* the then-reigning theories which had barred liability (theories relating to proximate and superseding causation) went out the door (4).

It is well recognized, therefore, that one can be held liable for harm caused to another through an intermediate party—a kind of vicarious liability.

Section 430 of the American Restatement of the Law of Torts states that there has to be an adequate causal relationship between the person harmed and the individual who causes the harm (the actor). Additionally, it must be shown that the actor's conduct was negligent before liability can attach:

> The actor's conduct, to be negligent toward another, must involve an unreasonable risk of: (1) causing harm to a class of persons of which the other [plaintiff] is a member and (2) subjecting the other to the hazard from which the harm results. (1)

Section 431 holds that the actor's negligent conduct is a legal cause for harm if it was a substantial factor in bringing about the harm and if "there is no rule of law relieving the actor from liability because of the manner in which his negligence has resulted in harm" (1).

In Section 432, we find that even if there were some other factor operating at the same time as the actor's negligence, which factor in itself would cause the ensuing harm, the actor may not thereby be relieved of substantially causing the harm (1).

Section 435 establishes that foreseeability of the harm is immaterial. In other words, once it has been decided that the actor was negligent, it becomes immaterial whether or not the person actually or reasonably should have foreseen that harm would result from the action so long as the conduct was a substantial cause of the harm(1).

Section 437 states that once it has been established that the actor's negligence is a substantial factor in bringing about harm, it is immaterial, too, that the actor "exercised reasonable care to prevent harm from taking effect." The actor continues to be liable for ensuing harm (1).

What constitutes negligent conduct? According to the Restatement:

> In order that either an act or a failure to act may be negligent, the one essential factor is that the actor realizes or should realize that the act or the failure to act involves an *unreasonable risk of harm* to an interest of another, which is protected against unintended invasion. (1) [*Emphasis added.*]

It seems apparent, therefore, that the legal environment within which we will implement our marketing strategy is ripe for our expolitation.

Social Environment

With regard to the social environment surrounding our breath analyzer and its use to reduce the number of drunk drivers, there is a good deal of activity going on.

At least two major organizations have been formed within the past three years in an effort to provide a vent for public outcry. The persons responsible for founding these organizations, MADD (Mothers Against Drunk Driving) and RID (Remove Intoxicated Drivers), lost loved ones because of alcohol-related accidents. In addition, some 27 states have passed or put into effect tougher drinking and driving laws this year alone, while 20 other states have actually raised the legal-drinking age.

In a recent survey, published in the September 1982 edition of *Glamour* magazine, 60 percent of the respondents said they thought the drinking age should be raised to 21 in all states. In addition, 69 percent said they would not feel safe driving if they had been drinking or riding with a driver who had been. When asked what they would do if they had planned to drive home with someone who had had too much to drink, 7 percent said they would refuse to go, 61 percent said they would insist that someone else drive, and 26 percent said they would call a taxi or go with someone else.

When asked if they thought police should have the right to give breath tests, 89 percent said yes. Finally, 53 percent of the respondents said that drivers who are arrested for drunk driving should have their license revoked for six months to a year, and 89 percent said that all learning drivers should be required to attend classes about the danger of drunk driving.

Problems and Opportunities

1. *Market Characteristics*
   Problem. The actual product demand is unknown.
   Opportunities. The geographic area targeted (Los Angeles and Orange counties) is densely populated. Forty percent of California's population

resides here, allowing ease of covering target market (7).

The average alcohol consumption in this area exceeds the national average (7). This, combined with the fact that freeways are the major source of transportation, creates a large potential for driving while intoxicated.

Existing distribution channels are available through sales representatives who handle liquor and sundry items.

2. *Competition*

   Problem. The technology is simple and easily duplicated.

   Opportunities. Being the first in the market maximizes the chance to become the market leader.

   The consumer market is currently ignored by the competition.

3. *Product Comparisons*

   Problem. DATU is designed for one-time usage, as compared with multiple usage of competitors' higher-priced units.

   Opportunities. The device is small and portable, as compared with other similar units.

   Disposability, as compared with multiple usage of competitors' products, creates convenience.

   DATU is relatively inexpensive, being priced well under competitors' units.

4. *Manufacturing and Technical Factors*

   Problem. DATU has a limited shelf life of approximately six months due to perishability of chemicals employed.

   Opportunities. The simple technology will allow eventual in-house manufacturing.

5. *Environmental Climate*

   Problem. Psychographics with respect to target market attitudes toward admittance of being under the influence of alcohol are unknown. (Will potentially intoxicated drivers react defensively to being told they are "drunk"?)

   Opportunities. There is a trend toward stricter drinking and driving laws (see Legal Appendix).

   The trend has also shown increasing mobilization of action groups (e.g., MADD, or Mothers Against Drunk Drivers).

   The "innkeepers law" is most likely to be reenacted (allows control of patrons' alcohol consumption by placing responsibility on innkeeper for results of drunk drivers' actions).

6. *Internal Resources*

   Problem. DATU requires $30,000 in start-up and introduction costs.

   Opportunities. The existing product manufactured by Intoximeter, Incorporated, meets the need.

   The relatively low cost of the project has a high expected return.

MARKETING OBJECTIVES

Target Market

On the basis of the information presented in our Situational Analysis, we identified the following target market segment as potential product users:

> Males who are members of households where household income exceeds $25,000 annually, are in the 21–40 age group, have had at least some college education, and are employed in professional or managerial positions.

In addition, the ideal purchaser would shop frequently at grocery stores and could be either male or female as the split between sex in purchasing alcoholic beverages in such markets is almost even.

Target Volume in Dollars and/or Units

Once again, on the basis of the information presented in our Situational Analysis, we are projecting the sale of approximately 205,000 units. Arriving at this number involved a complicated and detailed assimilation of data as the following presentation shows:

Percent of households earning $25,000 or more	40.6%
Percent of households less than 40 years of age	47.9%
Percent of households having some college education or more	59.1%
Percent of households where household head is employed in a professional or managerial position	38.1%
Average households in one or more groups	46.4%
Estimated percent of households falling in all categories (as agreed to by L.A. Times Marketing Research Department)	40.0%
Percent of households in all categories (target market)	18.6%
Number of households in market	× 3,417,000
Number of households in target market	635,500
Percent of driving households (2)	× 66.4%
Number of driving households in target market	421,980

Estimated percent of social drinkers who drive while intoxicated (4)	× 15.0%
Number of drinking-driving households in target market	63,297
Average number of occurrences of driving while intoxicated per year (3)	× 65
Number of occurrences of driving while intoxicated by target market, last year	4,114,310
Projected market share captured	× 5%
Projected unit sales	205,700
Unit sales price	0.96¢
Projected total annual sales	$196,800

1. $\dfrac{6{,}250{,}600 \text{ drinking drivers in L.A.-Orange counties}}{9{,}410{,}366 \text{ residents L.A.-Orange counties}} = 66.4\%$

2.

106,585	Drunk-driving arrests
× 2,000	Estimated number of individuals not arrested per every individual arrested (3)
213,200,000	Drunk-driving occurrences in L.A.-Orange counties per year
÷ 1,562,650	Drivers who drink and drive (6,250,600 drivers × 25% estimate (3)
136.39	Number of times each person was driving while intoxicated
× 50%	Estimated split of drunk-driving occurrence between "problem drinkers" and "social drinkers" (3)
68.2%	Rounded to 65

It should be noted that the 5 percent figure for our projected captured share of the market was our best estimate based on the information we came across during the course of our research, as well as our knowledge of market conditions (including input from the manufacturer, a prospective wholesale-distributor for sundry items in liquor stores, and other individuals involved in marketing this product in another area of the country).

Profit Analysis

Projected sales (205,000 units)		$198,850
Less:		

Variable Costs	Unit Cost, $	Total, $
Alcolyser	0.40	82,000
Packaging	0.065	13,325
Labor	0.02	4,100
Promotion	0.08	16,400
Shipping	0.04	10,000
Total variable costs		125,825

Fixed Costs

General and administrative	0.10	$ 20,500	
Total fixed and variable costs			$146,325
Net profit after year one before taxes			$ 50,475

Percent Profit

$50,475 \div $198,850 =		25.4%

Break-Even Analysis

$1x = 0.605x + 20,500$
Approximately 51,900 units
$36,589

STRATEGY

The marketing strategy for the DATU is to introduce the product in an area that is densely populated and has a specified demographic makeup: Los Angeles and Orange counties were chosen on the basis of the large number of drivers and other factors already noted in our Situational Analysis.

Product Strategy

The keystones of our product strategy are based on the following: simplicity, quality, and convenience. The product is extremely simple—both in conception and in use. We believe that to appeal to the average consumer who merely wants to discover the "risk factor" after a few beers, the product has to be simple. The device should be psychologically comforting and not elicit aversion, which it is likely to do if it were complicated.

We believe, and our research confirms, that most people are more interested in knowing whether or not they should drive (go—no go) than in knowing the actual level of their blood alcohol. In fact, our research indicates that knowing the actual level of blood alcohol is psychologically discomforting because it causes apprehension about the physiological effects of the alcohol. We do not want to turn our potential customers off. Neither do we want to scare them away from drinking altogether, for it is from the drinking population that we draw our market.

The simplicity of our product is embodied in one word: *packaging*. Our packaging will carry our message of simplicity par excellence. Thus packaging will fulfill the fundamental marketing concepts of containment and promotion (14). Packaging is especially crucial for us since we are marketing the DATU as a convenience item. As is noted by authorities in the field: "Packaging is usually a more critical element for convenience goods than for shopping or specialty goods" (14).

The second keystone of our product strategy, *quality*, is ensured through the confidence we have in the technology behind the DATU. Quality will become an increasingly important element as sales pick up, because good quality will ensure user-oriented promotion for us through word-of-mouth recommendation.

The third keystone, *convenience*, is reflected by the disposable nature of the DATU. The device will be a one-use item procured at a relative giveaway price. It will be small enough to put in one's pocket, glove compartment, or briefcase and will be easily disposed of once used. There will be no clumsy meters to unsecure and no bags to save. Our product strategy can, therefore, be summarized by the following diagram:

Key Elements	How Achieved
Simplicity	⟶ Packaging/technology
Quality	⟶ Technology
Convenience	⟶ Disposability

Pricing Strategy

Our pricing strategy will complement our product strategy. We want to enter our selected market and achieve maximum level of penetration. We shall, therefore, use a price-penetration strategy: Enter the desired market at a low price and markct the DATU as a convenience item.

Promotional Strategy

Our promotional strategy will be to achieve maximum reach with our message with minimum resource outlay. This strategy is dictated by the limited resources we have on hand. Fortunately, we believe the DATU lends itself to the use of just such a strategy.

The message content of our pitch will be unambiguous. The DATU is designed to give a drinking driver a quick-decision criterion. *The actual decision made must be the driver's.* It will be necessary to embody this in our promotional messages to guard against possible legal liability.

The promotional message will also bring to bear on the driver the possible legal consequences of *not knowing whether he or she has reached the 0.10 percent blood alcohol level.* Thus we will aid the driver in making a "safe" decision. Note should be taken, however, that our message will not be designed to *discourage* the driver from the consumption of alcohol. In fact, our message will be designed to *encourage* the *responsible* consumption of alcoholic beverages.

Because of the minimum outlay approach, we will not advertise via television or print, at the outset. The details of implementation of this strategy are enumerated under Promotional Tactics.

Distribution Strategy

Since the DATU is to be marketed as a convenience item, its distribution is a crucial element. Again we will aim for reach and penetration.

The ultimate consumer of the DATU will be most effectively reached through the retail supermarket and retail liquor stores. Our strategy will be to use a bichanneled approach, on the one hand distributing through wholesale distributors and on the other through agent middlemen.

The distribution channel is presented in Figure A3-4.

Marketing Strategy—A Recoup and a Projection

The entire strategy is product-driven. We believe we have found an unexploited niche in the universe of drinking drivers. Our product is going to satisfy the need which has already been created by stiff legal and social consequences of driving under the influence of alcohol. We see an even rougher horizon: the consequences are to get even tougher.

In the future, we see our sales generated from desire by consumers to know their alcohol level for three reasons:

1. Criminal liability (DUI)
2. Liability of commercial vendors who negligently serve alcohol
3. Liability of hosts (in private homes) who negligently serve alcohol

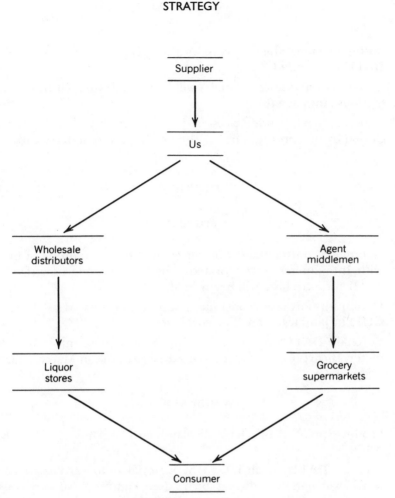

FIGURE A3-4. Distribution channel.

We see a time when insurance companies may actively get in on the market to cover "liquor liability." At present, there are some "general liability comprehensive policies," but many of them exclude liability for harm caused by liquor consumption (4). We also see insurance companies requiring policy holders to keep a kit of breath-analysis devices. In future, therefore, we see a potential for marketing to large institutional buyers—whereupon product changes might be necessary.

As far as our present legal liability is concerned, for harm caused by a drunken driver who may use our product, the following is our strategy:

To negate the legally implied warranty of fitness of the DATU for a particular purpose, we will have clear and unambiguous language stating our nonliability except for the ordinary purpose for which the DATU is intended (6).

The express warranties we make will be in boldfaced, clear, and unambiguous language (6).

We are not liable under present product liability theories for harm caused by our products unless the products were defective (6).

TACTICS

Product

1. Arrange a contractual supply agreement for a minimum of one year with Intoximeter, Incorporated. This will be done now (December 1982) and purchase will begin in March 1983.
2. Obtain support from consumer awareness groups (MADD, RID, and CHP) in January 1983. The cost is zero.
3. Purchase DATU in an initial quantity of 30,000 units from Intoximeter, Incorporated, at a cost of $0.40 per unit, in March 1983.

Promotion

1. Produce point-of-purchase display board in January 1983 (Figure A3-5).
2. Package DATU in shrink to fit material onto cardboard backing which will hang on display board (see Figures A3-6 and A3-7 for illustration). Will occur in March 1983.
3. Contact television, radio, and newspapers in May 1983 for creation of public information news segments. (ABC and CBS television have already shown interest).
4. During DATU introduction in May 1983, employ information leaflets at point of purchase.
5. Use the name "Limit" as trademark of DATU, implying the function of the device (i.e., a person has reached his or her alcohol limit).

Price

1. "Limit" will be priced at $1.69 each (see Figure A3-8 for pricing breakdown).

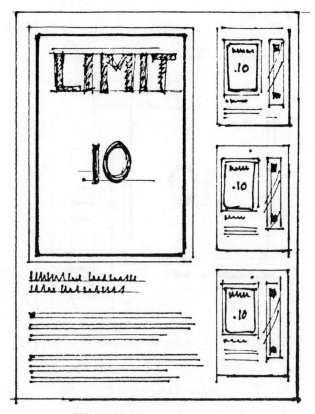

FIGURE A3-5. Point-of-purchase display.

Distribution

1. Distribute "Limit" in Los Angeles and Orange counties in May 1983.

2. Use brokers who distribute alcohol-related products for grocery, drug, and discount stores. This will begin in March 1983, with "Limit" being introduced to retailers for May 1983 delivery. The brokers are paid 25 percent of the wholesale price.

3. Use sundry-item wholesale distributors for liquor store penetration. These will be paid 25 percent of the wholesale price, and the timing is identical to item 2 above.

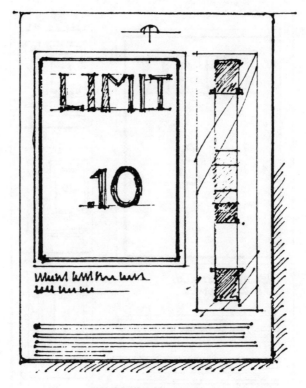

FIGURE A3-6. Hang card.

REFERENCES

1. *American Law Institute Restatement of the Law,* 2nd Torts ed., Vol. 2 St. Paul, MN: American Law Institute Publishers,).

2. *Glamour,* "This Is What You Thought About . . . Raising the Drinking Age," (September, 1982), pp.

3. Mood, J. Linda. "Driving Drunk," *Car & Driver,* (September 1982), pp.

4. *Insurance Company of North America vs. Aaron Shanedling et al.;* 2nd civil suit #51790, Court of Appeal of the State of California, 2nd Appellate District (mimeograph).

5. Interview with William Kalema, PhD (chemical engineering), California Institute of Technology, 1983.

6. Smith, Len Young and Roberson, G. Gale. *Business Law,* 4th ed. St. Paul, MN: West Publishing Co., 1977.

7. "Beer/Wine/Champagne/Distilled Spirits Consumer Trend Analysis," *Los Angeles Times Marketing Research,* 1979.

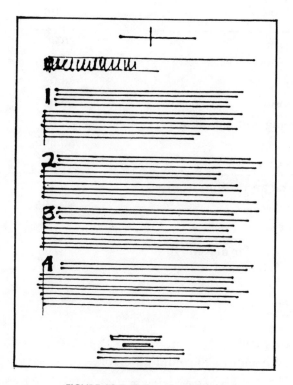

FIGURE A3-7. Back card—directions.

8. Marks, J. "Drinking and Driving: A Ticket to Disaster." *Teen,* (May 1982), pp.

9. Interview with Bud Miller, National Highway Traffic Safety Administration, San Francisco, CA, November 1982.

10. *National Underwriter,* "Joint Action Needed [Editorial Comment]," (October 31, 1981), pp.

11. Piontek, Annmarie B. "Drunk Driver: Challenge to Industry." *National Underwriter,* (September 12, 1980), pp.

12. Interview with Charlotte Rae, State of California Criminal Statistic Program: Uniform Crime Reporting Unit, Sacramento, CA, November 1982.

13. Starr, M. "The War Against Drunk Driving." *Newsweek,* (September 13, 1982), pp.

14. Rewoldt, Stewart H., Scott, James D., and Warshaw, Martin R. *Introduction to Marketing Management.* Homewood, IL: Richard D. Irwin, Inc., 1981.

Variable Costs	Unit	
Alcolyser	$0.40	
Packaging	0.065	
Labor	0.02	
Promotion	0.08	
Shipping and handling	0.04	
	$0.605	
Fixed Cost		
General and administrative	0.10	
Total cost	$0.705	
List Price		$1.69
Less: Retailer margin 40%		0.48
Wholesaler margin	25%	0.24
		0.97
Total cost		0.705
Profit		$0.265
Percent profit		27.3%
Actual profit due to round-off error		25.4%

FIGURE A3-8. Pricing in the consumer market (based on 10,000-unit production runs).

LEGAL APPENDIX

§ 13353. Chemical Blood, Breath, or Urine Tests

(a) Any person who drives a motor vehicle upon a highway shall be deemed to have given his consent to a chemical test of his blood, breath or urine for the purpose of determining the alcoholic content of his blood if lawfully arrested for any offense allegedly committed while the person was driving a motor vehicle under the influence of intoxicating liquor. The test shall be incidental to a lawful arrest and administration at the direction of a peace officer having reasonable cause to believe such person was driving a motor vehicle upon a highway while under the influence of intoxicating liquor. Such person shall be told that his failure to submit to or complete such a chemical test will result in the suspension of his privilege to operate a motor vehicle for a period of six months.

The person arrested shall have the choice of whether the test shall be of his blood, breath or urine, and he shall be advised by the officer that he has such choice. If the person arrested either is incapable, or states that he is incapable, of completing any chosen test, he shall then have the choice of submitting to and completing any of the remaining tests or test, and he shall be advised by the officer that he has such choice.

Such person shall also be advised by the officer that he does not have the right to have an attorney present before stating whether he will submit to a test, before deciding which test to take, or during administration of the test chosen.

Any person who is dead, unconscious, or otherwise in a condition rendering him incapable of refusal shall be deemed not to have withdrawn his consent and such tests may be administered whether or not such person is told that his failure to submit to or complete the test will result in the suspension of his privilege to operate a motor vehicle.

(b) If any such person refuses the officer's request to submit to, or fails to complete, a chemical test, the department, upon receipt of the officer's sworn statement that he had reasonable cause to believe such person had been driving a motor vehicle upon a highway while under the influence of intoxicating liquor and that the person had refused to submit to, or failed to complete, the test after being requested by an officer, shall suspend his privilege to operate a motor vehicle for a period of six months. No such suspension shall become effective until 10 days after the giving of written notice thereof, as provided for in subdivision (c).

(c) The department shall immediately notify such person in writing of the action taken and upon his request in writing and within 15 days from the date of receipt of such request shall afford him an opportunity for a hearing in the same manner and under the same conditions as provided in Article 3 (commencing with Section 14100) of Chapter 3 of this division. For the purposes of this section the scope of the hearing shall cover the issues of whether the peace officer had reasonable cause to believe the person had been driving a motor vehicle upon a highway while under the influence of intoxicating liquor, whether the person was placed under arrest, whether he refused to submit to, or failed to complete, the test after being requested by a peace officer, and whether, except for the persons described in paragraph (a) above who are incapable of refusing, he had been told that his driving privilege would be suspended if he refused to submit to, or failed to complete, the test.

An application for a hearing made by the affected person within 10 days of receiving notice of the department's action shall operate to stay the suspension by the department for a period of 15 days during which time the department must afford a hearing. If the department fails to afford a hearing within 15 days, the suspension shall not take place until such time as the person is granted a hearing and is notified of the department's action as hereinafter provided. However, if the affected person requests that the hearing be continued to a date beyond the 15-day period, the suspension shall become effective immediately upon receipt of the department's notice that said request for continuance has been granted.

If the department determines upon a hearing of the matter to suspend the affected person's privilege to operate a motor vehicle, the suspension herein provided shall not become effective until five days after receipt by said person of the department's notification of such suspension.

(d) Any person who is afflicted with hemophilia shall be exempt from the blood test required by this section.

(e) Any person who is afflicted with a heart condition and is using an anticoagulant under the direction of a physician and surgeon shall be exempt from the blood test required by this section.

(f) A person lawfully arrested by any offense allegedly committed while the person was driving a motor vehicle under the influence of intoxicating liquor may request the arresting officer to have a chemical test made of the arrested person's blood, breath or urine for the purpose of determining the alcoholic content of such person's blood, and, if so requested, the arresting officer shall have the test performed.

Legislative History:

1. Added by Stats 1st Ex Sess 1966 ch 138 § 1.
2. Amended by Stats 1969 ch 1438 § 1, adding "and he shall be advised by the officer that he has such choice" in the second paragraph of subd (a).
3. Amended by Stats 1970 ch 733 § 2.
4. Amended by Stats 1970 ch 1103 § 2, adding (1) "or complete" after "submit to" in the first and fourth paragraph of subd (a); (2) the second sentence of the second paragraph of subd (a); (3) the third paragraph of subd (a); (4) "or fails to complete," in subd (b), and (5) "or failed to complete," wherever it appears in subds (b) and (c).

Former § 13353, relating to the beginning of suspension (based on former Veh C § 307 subd (b)), was enacted Stats 1959 ch 3 and repealed by Stats 1959 c 1996 § 18.4

Collateral References:

Cal Jur 2d Automobiles § 372, Criminal Law § 118, Evidence § 396, Searches and Seizures § 46, Witnesses § 29.

§ 23126. Driving While Intoxicated; Presumption

(a) Upon the trial of any criminal action, or preliminary proceeding in a criminal action, arising out of acts alleged to have been committed by any person while driving a vehicle while under the influence of intoxicating liquor, the amount of alcohol in the person's blood at the time of the test as shown by chemical analysis of his blood, breath, or urine shall give rise to the following presumptions affecting the burden of proof:

(1) If there was at that time less than 0.05 percent by weight of alcohol in the person's blood, it shall be presumed that the person was not under the influence of intoxicating liquor at the time of the alleged offense.

(2) If there was at that time 0.05 percent or more but less than 0.10 percent by weight of alcohol in the person's blood, such fact shall not give rise to any presumption that the person was or was not under the influence of intoxicating liquor, but such fact may be considered with other competent evidence in determining whether the person was under the influence of intoxicating liquor at the time of the alleged offense.

(3) If there was at that time 0.10 percent or more by weight of alcohol in the person's blood, it shall be presumed that the person was under the influence of intoxicating liquor at the time of the alleged offense.

(b) Percent by weight of alcohol in the blood shall be based upon grams of alcohol per 100 milliliters of blood.

(c) The foregoing provisions shall not be construed as limiting the introduction of any other competent evidence bearing upon the question whether the person was under the influence of intoxicating liquor at the time of the alleged offense.

Legislative History:
Added by Stats 1969 ch 231 § 1.

A4: "GIGGLES" TOOTHPASTE

Developed by
KOH CHING HONG
FOO KOK KIN

CONTENTS

Used with permission of the authors.

EXECUTIVE SUMMARY

More and more, Americans are realizing the reality hidden in the old one-liner, "Be true to your teeth and they will never be false to you." Last year alone, Americans spent about $1080 million on 2150 million ounces of toothpaste, an incremental increase of 30.12 percent from 1980's $830 million mark.

In this one billion dollar market, where competing brands are much alike, and where significant technological improvements are hard to come by, toothpaste manufacturers mount their confidence based on minor modifications in product claims, appearances, and flavors. Since all competing brands have the much acclaimed anticavity ingredient fluoride in their products, and since there are not many differences in product packaging (the same traditional tube) except for colors and design, there is little if any product differentiation. However, the biggest selling point among toothpaste consumers, including a large proportion of children, is flavor.

With all these in mind, Giggles has been developed to cater to the growing demand of the young consumers, namely those between 2 and 11 years of age. By creating a revolutionary new packaging or pump dispenser in the shape of animals, children can easily associate with them and will have added incentive to brush their teeth more frequently, which will then indirectly induce parents to buy Giggles for the benefit of their children. In addition, Giggles will be introducing two additional flavors into the market—strawberry and orange—together with the popular flavor of mint.

The marketing objectives and strategy of Giggles, which is scheduled to be on the market in 1984, are given in the following report.

SITUATIONAL ANALYSIS

Demand

Americans are becoming more aware of the importance of maintaining oral hygiene, which was brought about through the vigorous campaigns organized by the American Dental Association (ADA) and several major oral product manufacturers. As a result, this awareness has caused an increase in the demand for oral hygiene products.

Toothpaste, which dominates 56.9 percent of the oral hygiene market, is the second most used health product among the 90.7 percent of the nation's population, with the frequency of use at 89.1 percent.

TGI/SMRB Survey 1982

	Percentage using	Percentage using daily	Exclusive one-brand user
Toothpaste	90.7	89.1	55.4

Using 218 million as total population: 90.7% = 197,726,000 people using toothpaste

Last year, Americans spent about $1080 million on 2150 million ounces of toothpaste. This was an increase of 30.12 percent from 1980's $830 million mark. The toothpaste industry projected the growth rate at 8 percent annually, which will give an estimated $1260 million market in 1984. Market growth in revenue and volume of usage is shown in the Table A4-1 and in Figures A4-1 and A4-2, respectively.

Competition

Market Share. The market shares of various toothpaste brands is shown in Table A4-2.

TABLE A4-1. Market Growth in Revenue and Volume

Year	Revenue in millions	Volume (Millions of Ounces)
1978	$ 650	1400
1979	750	1630
1980	830	1744
1981	1000	2000
1982	1080	2150
1983 (est.)	1166	2322
1984 (projected)[a]	1260	2507

[a]Projection based on 8 percent annual growth.

A4-2. Market Share

	1977	1980	1982
1. Crest	40.0%	36.2%	38.0%
2. Colgate	20.5	18.8	20.0
3. Aim	11.0	10.0	12.0
4. Aqua-Fresh	0.5	13.5	11.0
5. Close-up	7.0	7.3	8.0
6. Gleem	5.0	3.3	3.6
7. Ultra-Brite	5.0	3.2	3.5
8. Pepsodent	3.5	2.7	2.8
9. McLean's	1.5	0.5	0.4
10. Others	6.0	4.5	0.7
	100.0%	100.0%	100.0%

The relative market share for 1982 is illustrated in Figure A4-3.

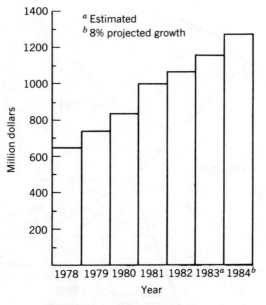

FIGURE A4-1. Market growth: revenue.

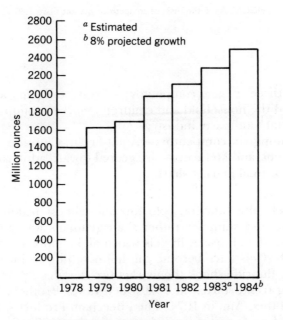

FIGURE A4-2. Market growth: volume.

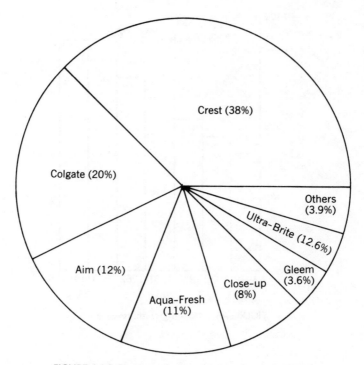

FIGURE A4-3. Pie chart of competition market share 1982.

The top three major competitors—Crest, Colgate, and Aim—are geared toward the household and children's market, commanding 70 percent of the total toothpaste industry.

The remaining six competitors—Aqua-Fresh, Close-up, Gleem, Ultra-Brite, Pepsodent, and McLean's—are geared toward adult consumers, with 29.3 percent of total market share.

Product. Gel—the fanciful, colorful, and almost iridescent kind that seems to glide and shimmer rather than grunt its way out of the tube, involves silicas, the abrasives in gels which allow more sparkling tastes to come through. Gels have become the hottest thing to hit the toothpaste industry since fluoride shook the market two decades ago.

The gelling trend started in 1970 when Lever Brothers came out with Close-up, and then Aim in 1974. Then Beecham Products joined in with a combination of paste and gel called Aqua-Fresh in 1979. So successful was this that in 1981, so as not to lose out in market competitiveness, two industry giants—Procter & Gamble and Colgate-Palmolive, came out with Crest gel and Winterfresh gel, respectively.

In a recent survey of the gel/paste market, gel market share increased from 18.6 percent in 1981 to 37 percent in 1982—a staggering 98.9 percent increase within a year. Industrial experts are predicting the gel market to grow to half the gel/paste market within the next two years. This is not surprising, since gel ingredients make toothpaste sparkle, and most important, its properties hold flavors longer and make them taste better, which is why most manufacturers are shifting into the gel market.

Although the flavor is the most expensive ingredient (followed by the active ingredient and the tube), manufacturers are continuing to put more emphasis on taste. This is because the big selling point these days is taste. Most people choose a toothpaste by its flavor—spearmint is the most popular, followed by peppermint, cinnamon, and wintergreen. Sweetness in the flavor is also a growing trend—the reason, not surprisingly, is children.

Fluoride, which is widely accepted as the ingredient responsible for cavity fighting, is also prevalent in all the competing brands.

The mean prices shown in Table A4-3 are calculated on a survey done in five major supermarkets—Vons, Safeway, Hughes, Ralphs, and Thrifty. All products are based on a family-size, 6.4 fl.oz. tube.

Crest and Aqua-Fresh, selling at $1.69, are pricing their products above all their competitors, and are 25 percent higher than the price leaders, Gleem and Pepsodent.

Promotion. Since most competing brands are pretty much alike and as significant technological improvements are hard to come by, marketers are pegging their hopes on minor changes in product packaging, appearances, scents, or flavors. And companies are spending tens of millions of dollars to advertise those changes and to lure consumers with free samples, price discounts, coupons, and other promotional tools.

TABLE A4-3. Toothpaste Prices

Brand	Price	Type	Size (oz.)	Taste
Crest	1.69	Gel	6.4	Mint
Aqua-Fresh	1.69	Gel	6.4	Mint
Ultra-Brite	1.65	Gel	6.4	Mint
Close-up	1.59	Gel	6.4	Mint
Colgate	1.58	Gel	6.4	Winterfresh
Aim	1.44	Gel	6.4	Mint
Gleem	1.35	Paste	6.4	Mint
Pepsodent	1.35	Paste	6.4	Mint

Leading National Advertisers (LNA), an independent advertising measuring service, estimates that in 1982, $17.9 million was spent on Colgate's television and magazine advertising, and $28.6 million was spent on Crest's. Aim was backed by $16 million, while Close-up advertising expenditures were $11.2 million. These four major competitors spent an estimated $73.7 million on wooing consumers. LNA also reported that an additional 25 percent or more was spent on discounts, coupons, and other incentives.

Brand loyalty among consumers used to be very high, but promotions and advertising have changed that. By using two major media, television and magazines, marketers are reaching out and covering a big portion of the market, each wooing consumers to a particular brand. This huge spending on advertising determines the competitors' market share to a significant degree, and in such a large industry, small changes in market share represent considerable profits.

Market Segmentation. Table A4-4 presents information based on results of an actual benefit-segmentation study of the toothpaste market, and provides valuable understanding of the toothpaste consumer segmentation: demographic, behavioral, and personality characteristics.

Brands heavily favored by the Sensory segment are Colgate, Crest, and Aim, while the Sociables prefer Aqua-Fresh, Ultra-Brite, and Close-up. The Worriers favor Crest and Aim, and the Independents look for brands that are on sale. As in the case of Aim and Crest, they attempt to straddle more than one segment. It is this information that marketers of competing brands utilize to develop a strategy tailored to each segment based on the benefits they seek.

Research and Development. There have been reports that developments are underway for a periodontal toothpaste that removes plaque; toothpaste that shoots out of aerosol cans; and one that does not need mouth rinsing. As most of the toothpaste in the market differs little, manufacturers are increasing their efforts in developing new flavors, new anticavity ingredients, and new appearances for their products. These changes or additions will enable the manufacturers to increase their sales. More toothpastes mean more shelf space. Twice as much shelf space means a bonanza. A new product could very well be the ticket to greater shelf space and profits.

Consumers

The family unit has always been a large market for the toothpaste industry. The family is, of course, an important primary group, as well as a reference group which is acknowledged as injecting important intervening variables in purchasing decisions. It is also widely recognized that suggestions or

TABLE A4-4. Toothpaste Market Segmentation

	Segment Name	
	The Sensory Segment	The Sociables
	Segment characteristic	
Principal benefit sought	Flavor, product appearance	Brightness of teeth
Demographic strength	Children	Teens, young people
Special behavioral characteristics	Users of spearmint flavored toothpaste	Smokers
Personality characteristics	High self-involvement	High sociability
Life-style characteristics	Hedonistic	Active
	Selected marketing recommendations	
Copy tone	Light	Light
Copy depth-of-sell	Superficial and mood oriented. Shorter commercial, higher frequency	Superficial and mood oriented. Shorter commercial, higher frequency
Copy setting	Focus on product	Socially oriented situations
Media environment	Youthful, modern, active; heavy use of TV	Youthful, modern, active; heavy use of TV
Packaging	Colorful	Gleaming white (to indicate white teeth)

	Segment Name	
	The Worriers	The Independent Segment
	Segment Characteristics	
Principal benefit sought	Decay prevention	Price
Demographic strength	Large families	Men
Special behavioral characteristics	Heavy users	Heavy users
Personality characteristics	High hypochondriasis	High autonomy
Life-style characteristics	Conservative	Value-oriented

TABLE A4-4 continued

	Segment Name	
	The Worriers	The Independent Segment
Selected marketing recommendations		
Copy tone	Serious	Rational two-sided arguments. Stress price, product superiority.
Copy depth-of-sell	Intensive. Longer commercials, e.g., 60-second ads	Intensive. Longer commercials, e.g., 60-second ads
Copy setting:		Demonstration & competitive comparison
Media environment	Serious; heavy use of print	Serious; heavy use of print
Packaging	Aqua (to indicate flouride)	

Russell Haley, "Benefit Segmentation: A Decision-Oriented Research Tool." *Journal of Marketing*, Vol. 32 (July 1968), p. 31

advice within a primary group has a greater impact than mass media advertising in changing purchasing decisions.

The purchasing agent of a family unit has a commanding role in product and brand decision and controls the kind of products his or her family members consume. Nevertheless, since the members of the family are users, they do exert considerable influence on the purchaser in making product and brand decisions.

As society changes, so does the consumer's behavior. Such is the case in the household. Forty years ago, purchases of household products were decided by adults, generally the parents. These days, however, children have become a strong influence in household purchasing decisions. Thus more and more products are being created with the large potential market of children in mind, and heavy promotions have been utilized to influence them. Toothpaste is no exception. Fierce competition among toothpaste brands has been won and lost in kids' mouths. Crest, Colgate and Aim now command 70 percent of the total market share just by wooing the demand of the household through influencing of children's demand.

Children, despite the numerous educational campaigns on dental health, still do not realize the importance of brushing their teeth. Also, parents are finding it difficult to motivate their children to brush their teeth regularly.

Regulation

Fluoride, an active cavity-fighting ingredient, is now used in all the toothpaste available in the market. A Food and Drug Administration (FDA) guideline limits fluoride in toothpaste to 1000 parts per million, give or take 10 percent.

Problems

1. Parents are finding it difficult to persuade their children to brush their teeth.
2. Despite numerous dental campaigns, children still do not realize the importance of maintaining oral health.
3. Present toothpaste available in the market has limited flavors.
4. The present traditional tube is not attractive enough to induce children's demand.
5. Children do not have a toothpaste that they can identify as their very own.

Opportunities

1. At 34.8 million (16 percent of the population), children between 2 and 11 continue to be a growing potential market segment.
2. Creating a toothpaste children can identify with, which will give them an incentive to brush their teeth regularly.
3. Introducing new flavors, especially toward the fruity range.
4. Creating new packaging—a pump dispenser that makes it more convenient and fun for the children. It will also prevent wastage and mess.

MARKETING OBJECTIVES

Product Profile

Product name	Giggles
Price	$2.50
Type	Gel
Flavor	Strawberry, orange, spearmint
Size/weight	10.5 fl. oz.

Description   Unique pump dispenser.
                         Comes in animal character packaging
Target market   Children ages 2–11
Appeal to consumers   Gives children a product they can identify with
                         Motivates children to brush their teeth regularly
                         Prevents wastage and mess

Target Market

The target consumers are the following:

Age group   Children
Age range   2–11
Behavioral charac-   Total dependency on parents; fast development
teristics   of thinking ability; peer competition; conscious of
                        being evaluated by others, attends school
Product of interest   Food; toys; clothes; dental care; movies; candy;
                        uniforms; comic books
Role in buying   Influencer; limited decision maker; consumer or
process   user
Amount and source   Very small quantity allowance; gifts
of income
Major sources of   Parents; television; school; peer group; comic
information   books

Giggles is a product that children can identify with as their very own; and through its unique animal character dispensers and sweet flavors, Giggles will be able to satisfy the needs and wants of children.

However, children are dependent on their families, where consumption decisions are often made by the purchasing agent.

Although children these days have greater influence over the consumption pattern of the family, it is the parents who have the authority and final say over the type of goods their family should consume. Conversely, rarely do the parents refuse children's demands when it comes to such things as dental health. Thus, even though the end consumers of Giggles are children, it is also important to motivate the parents to buy our products for their children.

The target purchasing agents are:

Age group   Young parents to middle adulthood
Age range   25–40

Behavioral characteristics	Transition to family-centered behavior; leisure activities centered more at home; safety conscious; picnics; pleasure drives.
Products of interest	Family games; health care services; insurance; gifts
Roles in buying process	Buyer; consumer or user; decision maker; financer.
Social class and income	Middle class; $15,000–$35,000 per year
Major sources of information	Spouse and children; job; close friends; television; newspaper; magazines

Marketing Objectives

Proposed strategies and plans for fiscal 1984 are based on the following basic marketing objectives.

1. To obtain the following sales volume and market share, with a total expenditure of $13,020,000 for advertising and sales promotion.

	Estimated Market Data Fiscal Year 1984
Industry Sales	$1,260,000,000
Giggles sales (in 10.5 fl. ounce unit)	65,100,000
Giggles market share	5.17 pecent
Expenditures (Adv./pro.)	13,020,000
Giggles sales in units	42 million units

(Note: Sales and share figures may not correspond exactly due to minor errors in estimates)

2. To achieve 80 percent national distribution for Giggles by the end of 1984 with the objectives spread over 4 quarters.

Quarter	Percentage of Total Distribution
1	30
2	50
3	70
4	80

3. To develop and test market new packaging and a larger package size in order to ascertain the relative effectiveness of those two approaches in increasing market share.

Break-Even Analysis

$$\frac{\text{Total fixed expenses}}{\text{Unit contribution margin}} = \text{break-even point}$$

$$
\begin{aligned}
\text{Unit contribution margin} &= \text{selling price} - \\
&\qquad \text{variable expenses} \\
&= \$1.55 - .763 \\
&= .787
\end{aligned}
$$

$$\frac{23,675,000}{.787} = 30,082,592 \text{ units}$$

MARKETING STRATEGY

Recommended activities designed to achieve the foregoing objectives are based on the following major points of marketing strategy.

Product Strategy

The main emphasis of our product strategy is on packaging. The attractive and unique package design of Giggles is created to achieve maximum appeal for the targeted market segment. A convenient pump dispenser will control the amount of toothpaste released. This will eliminate the common problem of our target consumers when using the conventional tube, that is, wastage from irregular quantities of toothpaste being squeezed out.

Giggles will be in the form of gel in keeping with changing consumer trends. As our target market ranges in age from 2–11 years old, Giggles will be sweeter than most major brands in the market. To instill confidence in the purchasers, which are identified as parents, Giggles will contain the maximum level of fluoride protection and be endorsed by the American Dental Association.

Another major emphasis is on taste. Three flavors will be offered; strawberry, mint, and orange. The color of the gel will match the flavors to give each product a distinct appeal.

Distribution Strategy

A four-level channel of distribution will be employed to ensure that Giggles will be in the right place at the right time and in the right quantity.

Manufacturer→wholesaler → retailer → consumer

The distribution objective of 80 percent national distribution in 1984 will be spread over four quarters. The strategy to achieve the foregoing objectives is as follows:

1. *First quarter*
   a. To distribute Giggles to all major grocery and drug chain stores. This would ensure breadth of coverage and capitalize on the intensive advertising campaign to create shelf off-take.
   b. Stocking allowances will be offered to retailers to induce them to keep sufficient stock to keep up with anticipated consumer demand.
2. *Second quarter*
   a. Distribution will be extended to smaller independent retail outlets.
   b. Wholesalers and company's sales force will be expanded during this quarter due to wider market coverage.
3. *Third quarter/fourth quarter*
   a. Distribution will be extended further to other remaining retail outlets to achieve the objective of 80 percent national distribution.
   b. More wholesalers will be added to the distribution channel during these two periods.

Sales Force. The main task of the company's sales force is to assist wholesalers in gaining distribution by:

1. Calling on retailers and passing on the orders to the wholesalers.
2. Explaining to retailers the company's stocking allowances.
3. Providing market feedback to improve the distribution channel.
4. Placing promotional materials at point of purchase locations.
5. Obtaining in-store displays through the company's merchandising allowances.

Pricing Strategy

The pricing for Giggles (see Table A4-5) is slightly higher than competitors' brands because of the following:

High introduction cost

High cost of unique packaging

Research and development cost

Prices are expected to remain relatively stable throughout 1984 as we do not anticipate introduction of substitutes by competitors during the year.

TABLE A4-5. Recommended Price Structure

Cost to	Per Unit
Manufacturer cost	$1.32
To Wholesalers	1.55
To Retailers	1.78
To Consumers	2.50

Overall pricing strategy for 1984 is to achieve market share objectives of 5 percent.

Sales Promotion Strategy

The specific objectives of Giggles' 1984 sales promotion program is to stimulate product trial and repurchase. Basic strategy for achieving these objectives is as follows:

1. In order to gain trade support in the forms of in-store display and price features by retailers, emphasis will be placed on direct trade incentive in the form of merchandising allowances.

2. Merchandising allowance support will take the form of contractual payments to retailers for in-store displays. Proposed payments are $10 for a five-case display. In-store display will be carried out only in chain and large, independent outlets.

3. Discount coupons will be strategically placed in newspapers and magazines to encourage consumers to try the product. The coupons will offer consumers 20 cents off the regular retail price. Fifteen million coupons will be mailed during fiscal 1984.

4. During the first quarter of 1984, a sales aid in the form of a children's toothbrush packaged with the toothpaste dispenser will be free with every unit purchased.

5. Free samples will be given to schools' dental programs and to dentists to create greater product awareness, encourage product trial, and gain product acceptance among children.

6. Free samples will also be mailed to selected households.

ADVERTISING

Advertising Objectives

1. To direct advertising to parents as the primary purchase group and to place primary emphasis on children ranging from 2 to 11 years old,

estimated to be 16 percent of the total U.S. population and who exert the primary influence on brand selection by purchaser.

2. To achieve advertising penetration levels as shown below and as measured by a penetration study to be conducted in January 1985 (one year after the launch of the advertising campaign.)

	Awareness Level	Percentage Recalling One or More Sales Points
January 1985	40%	20%

The objectives that appear above are based solely on judgement, since data is lacking that would provide a reliable basis for forecasting annual rates in advertising penetration.

3. To encourage retail trade cooperation by communicating Giggles' brand strength to dealer personnel in buying, merchandising, and store management roles.

Advertising Strategy

Key strategic considerations governing the use of advertising:

1. Advertising support will be sustained throughout the year but will:
   a. Provide peak support during the introduction stage and periods of major promotional activity (January to June).
   b. Be reduced during July–September to evaluate the effectiveness of earlier advertising strategy.
2. The basic copy unit for print advertising will be a full-color page targeted at parents, the primary purchase group.
3. The television copy, in the form of a pool of 30-second commercials, will be targeted primarily at our target market segment—children between 2 and 11 years.
4. Advertising production expenses will be limited to a maximum of 5 percent of the total advertising budget.
5. Five percent of the total promotion budget will be set aside as a general reserve for contigency use.

Copy Strategy

1. Giggles will be sold primarily on the basis of its attractive packaging with the convenient pump dispenser.

2. Copy presentation will also emphasize the three delicious flavors offered by Giggles.

3. The mood of the copy will be casual and friendly, emphasizing the
fun of brushing teeth with Giggles.

4. Copy will recognize the importance of fluoride in preventing cavities.

5. The campaign theme that will be adopted is "If it isn't Giggles it's no
fun."

Media Strategy

Recommended media plans were developed within the framework of these
basic points of media strategy.

1. National consumer magazines will be employed primarily on the basis
of:
   a. Their national coverage.
   b. Their ability to concentrate messages among younger housewives.
2. Local spot television will be employed on a regional basis to:
   a. Permit the brand to apply increased media weight in sales regions
   where potential is greatest.
   b. Create awareness among children more effectively.
3. Significant strategic conclusions regarding the use of each recommended medium include:
   a. Consumer magazines
      i. A minimum of six insertions will be run in each magazine used
      to insure adequate frequency of impression and provide conti-
      nuity of support throughout the year.
      ii. Preferred position space will be used where available at attrac-
      tive rates to increase readership of each advertisement.
   b. Spot television: Thirty-second daytime and weekend morning commercials will be purchased in order to reach children with the greatest possible efficiency.

Media Plan

The principal features of the media plan are:

1. The use of eight consumer magazines that are considered to provide
extensive coverage to the primary purchase group, parents. Each magazine
is scheduled to receive at least six insertions during 1984 (all insertions are
full-page, four-color units). Total exposure is estimated at 130.8 million
and net unduplicated coverage of U.S. households at 55 percent (see promotion budget and exhibit.)

2. The plan also provides for the use of spot television in 100 major markets. These 100 markets will provide coverage of an estimated 70 percent of all households in the United States.

3. Each spot television market will receive 60–100 gross rating points weekly for a total of 26 weeks, which will be divided as follows into four waves of spot activity.

Wave No.	No. Weeks	Weekly GRP	Period in 1984
1	8	100	1/14–1/13
2	6	60	4/1–5/14
3	4	100	7/1–7/31
4	8	60	10/15–12/14

Analysis of Consumer Magazine Coverage

Table A4-6 utilizes W.R. Simmons' 1982 readers-per-copy estimates.

TABLE A4-6. Analysis of Consumer Magazine Coverage

Magazines	48 State Circulation (Millions)	Percentage of U.S. Coverage	Women in Audience (Millions)
Family Circle	7,766	22.6	17,551
Family Weekly	10,851	13.1	10,200
Good Housekeeping	4,800	20.2	15,096
Ladies Home Journal	5,880	17.3	13,465
Parade	19,647	24.0	18,665
People	2,068	10.7	8,396
Reader's Digest	18,283	29.6	23,037
TV Guide	19,181	30.6	23,850

Advertising Costs in Consumer Magazines

Table A4-7 reflects an analysis of advertising costs in consumer magazines.

TABLE A4-7. Advertising Costs in Consumer Magazines

Magazine	Rates per Page Four-Color	Number of Insertions	Total Cost
Family Circle	$49,750	7	$ 348,250
Family Weekly	34,486	6	206,116
Good Housekeeping	36,835	7	257,845
Ladies Home Journal	36,180	6	217,080
Parade	50,150	7	351,050
People	18,950	6	113,700
Reader's Digest	67,610	6	417,000
TV Guide	61,000	6	366,000
			$2,278,501

PROMOTION BUDGET

Summary

Twenty percent of estimated sales for fiscal 1984 is allocated to promotion. Of the total $13,020,000 budget, 70 percent is allocated to advertising and 25 percent to sales promotion, leaving a 5 percent general reserve.

Breakdown of promotion budget:
Advertising—$9,114,000

1. 70 percent on television commercials
2. 25 percent on print ads in consumer magazines
3. 5 percent on production preparation

Sales promotion—$3,255,000

1. 15 percent on merchandise allowances to retailers
2. 30 percent on discount coupons to consumers
3. 15 percent on free toothbrush as sales aid
4. 5 percent on promotional materials
5. 30 percent on free samples
6. 5 percent on miscellaneous expenses

General reserves—$651,000

Proposed Advertising and Sales Promotion Budget

Advertising

Consumer magazines	$2,278,500

Six to seven four-color pages in each of
eight magazines; total exposure of
130.8 million; estimated net
unduplicated coverage of 55 percent of
U.S. households

Spot Television	6,379,800

60–100 gross rating points weekly for
26 weeks in 100 major markets

Production, Preparation

Magazines 91,140	
TV 364,560	455,700
Total Advertising	$9,114,000

Sales Promotion

Merchandise allowances to retailers	488,250
Discount coupons to consumers	976,500
Free toothbrush as sales aid	488,250
Free samples	976,500
Promotional materials	162,750
Miscellaneous Expenses	162,750
Total Sales Promotion	$3,255,000

General Reserves	651,000
Grand Total	$13,020,000

See Figures A4-4 and A4-5 for illustration of these budgets in pie charts.

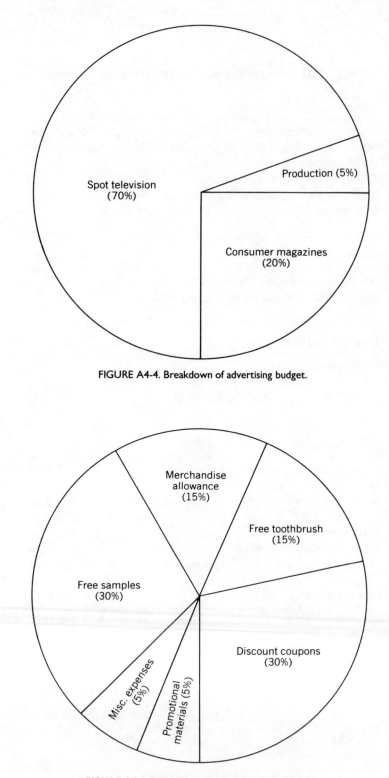

FIGURE A4-4. Breakdown of advertising budget.

FIGURE A4-5. Breakdown of sales promotion budget.

APPENDIX I. Giggles Sales Budget for the Year Ending December 31, 1984

	Quarter				
	1	2	3	4	Year
Expected sales in units	4.2M	8.4M	12.6M	16.8M	42M
Selling price per unit	X $1.55	1.55	1.55	1.55	
	6.51	13.02	19.53	26.04	65.1M

Schedule of Expected Cash Collections

	1	2	3	4	Year
1st quarter sales (6.51m)	3.906M	2.604M			6.51M
2nd quarter sales (13.02m)		7.812M	5.208M		13.02M
3rd quarter sales (19.53m)			11.718M	7.812M	19.53M
4th quarter sales (26.04m)				15.624M	15.624M
	3.906M	10,416M	16.926M	23.436M	54.684M

Note: 60 percent of a quarter's sales are collected in the quarter of sale; the remaining 40 percent is collected in the quarter following.

APPENDIX 2. **Selling and Administrative Expense Budget for the Year Ending December 31, 1984 (M = million)**

	Quarter				
	1	2	3	4	Total
Budgeted sales in units	4.2M	8.4M	12.6M	16.8M	42M
Variable selling and administrative expense per unit*	$ .08	$ .08M	$ .08	$ .08	$ .08
Budgeted variable expenses	$ .336M	$ .672M	$ 1.008M	$ 1.344M	$ 3.36M
Fixed selling and administrative expenses:					
Promotion	$3.906M	$3.906M	$ 2.604M	$ 2.604M	$13.02M
Salaries	1.63M	1.63M	1.63M	1.63 M	6.52M
Insurance	0.13M	–	–	–	0.13M
Miscellaneous	–	–	–	0.13 M	0.13M
Budgeted fixed expenses	$5.666M	$5.536M	$4.234M	$4.364M	$19.80M
Total budgeted selling and administrative expenses	$6.002M	$6.208M	$5.242M	$5.708M	$23.16M

APPENDIX 3. Production Budget for the Year Ending December 31, 1984
(M = millions)

	Quarter				
	1	2	3	4	Year
Expected sales (in units)	4.2M	8.4M	12.6M	16.8M	42M
Plus desired ending inventory of finished goods[a]	.84	1.26	1.68	2.0	2.0
Total needs	5.04M	9.66M	14.28M	18.8M	44.0M
Less beginning inventory of finished goods[b]	–	.84	1.26	1.68	–
Units to be produced[c]	5.04M	8.82M	13.02M	17.12M	44.0M

[a]10 percent of next quarter
[b]10 percent of prior quarter's ending inventory
[c]Estimated

APPENDIX 4. Schedule of Cost of Goods Manufactured

Direct material		$ 9,765,000
Direct labor		11,718,000
Variable manufacturing overhead		
Indirect materials	$1,770,000	
Indirect labor	3,540,000	
Utilities	1,882,000	7,192,000
Variable manufacturing cost		$28,675,000
Fixed manufacturing overhead		
Machine rental	$ 332,000	
Insurance	775,000	
Depreciation (capital equipment)	2,768,000	3,875,000
Total manufacturing cost		$32,550,000

APPENDIX 5. Budgeted Quarterly Income Statement for the Year Ending December 31, 1984

	Quarter			
	1	2	3	4
Sales	$6,510,000	$13,020,000	$19,530,000	$26,040,000
Less variable expenses				
Variable cost of goods sold	2,867,500	5,735,000	8,602,500	11,470,000
Variable selling and administrative expenses	336,000	672,000	1,008,000	1,344,000
Contribution margin	$3,306,500	$ 6,613,000	$ 9,919,500	$13,226,000
Less fixed expenses				
Manufacturing overhead	$ 968,750	$ 968,750	$ 968,750	$ 968,750
Selling and administrative expenses	4,950,000	4,950,000	4,950,000	4,950,000
Net operating income	($2,612,250)	$ 694,250	$ 4,000,750	$ 7,307,250
Less interest expense	125,000	125,000	125,000	125,000
Net income before tax	($2,737,250)	$ 569,250	$ 3,875,750	$ 7,182,250

APPENDIX 6. Budgeted Income Statement for the Year Ending December 31, 1984

Sales		$65,100,000
Less variable expenses:		
Variable cost of goods sold	$28,675,000	
Variable selling and administrative expenses	3,360,000	32,035,000
Contribution margin		$33,065,000
Less fixed expenses:		
Manufacturing overhead	$ 3,875,000	
Selling and administrative expenses	19,800,000	23,675,000
Net operating income		$ 9,390,000
Less interest expense		500,000
Net income before tax		$ 8,890,000
Less income tax (40 percent)		3,556,000
Net income		$ 5,334,000

APPENDIX 7. Marketing Schedule for 1984

Task	JAN 1	FEB 2	MAR 3	APR 4	MAY 5	JUN 6	JUL 7	AUG 8	SEP 9	OCT 10	NOV 11	DEC 12
Distribution	30% of national distribution				50%			70%			80%	
Advertising TV commercial	Wave no. 1			Wave no. 2			Wave no. 3				Wave no. 4	
Discount coupons			Start of coupon campaign									
Stocking allowances	Year-round distribution drive											
Merchandising allowances					Start of in-store display campaign							
On-Pack sales aid—toothbrush												
Sales force							Expansion of sales force to assist expanding distribution					
Wholesalers							Expansion of wholesalers' network					

APPENDIX 8. Sketches of Giggles

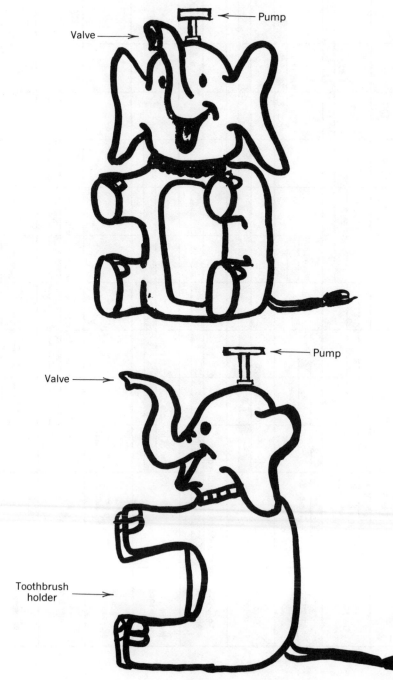

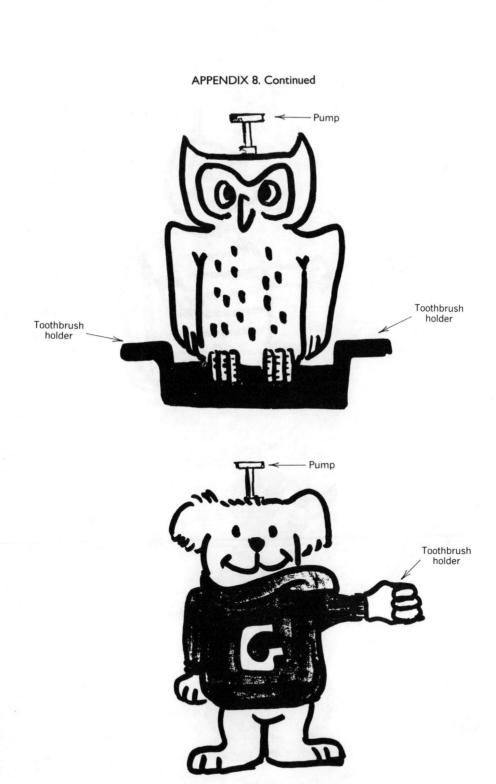

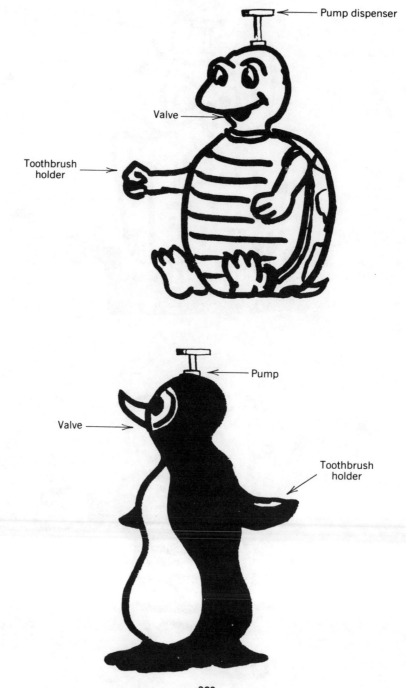

Pump dispenser

Valve

Toothbrush
holder

Pump

Valve

Toothbrush
holder

BIBLIOGRAPHY

Abrams, Bill. "Warring Toothpaste Makers Spend Millions Luring Buyers to Slightly Altered Products." *Wall Street Journal,* (March 5, 1982), pp. 19–21.

Achtert, Mervin. "What is CREST'S lastest strategy?" *Business Week,* (June 20, 1982). pp. 24–29.

Beecham Products Inc. *Annual Report.* 1977–1982

Bower, Jim. "Gels giving pastes a pasting." *Fortune,* (January 15, 1983), pp. 8–12.

Colgate-Palmolive. *Annual Report.* 1977–1982.

Howe, Irving. "The Advertising War of the Toothpaste Industry." *Advertising Age,* (February 24, 1983), pp. 36–38.

Johnson, Bill. "Toothpastes Face Gel Challenge." *Industry Week,* (February 6, 1983), pp. 27–29.

Kanner, Bernice. "The Gelling of America." *New York,* (March 29, 1983), pp. 29–33.

Lever Brothers. *Annual Report.* 1972–1982.

London, David and Albert Della Bitta. *Consumer Behavior: Concepts and Application.* New York: McGraw-Hill, 1979.

Proctor & Gamble. *Annual Report.* 1977–1982.

Rewoldt, Stewart, James Scott, and Martin Shaw. *Introduction to Marketing Management.* Homewood, IL: Richard Irwin, 1981.

Riegelman, Robert. "American Toothpaste War." *Sales and Marketing Management,* (August 16, 1982), pp. 19–23.

Rotbart, Dean. "P & G Wins Dental Group Endorsement For 'New' Crest." *Advertising Age,* (November 25, 1982), pp. 28–30.

Runyon, Kenneth. *Advertising and the Practice of Marketing.* Columbus, OH: Charles Merill, 1977.

Spolsky, Joseph. "Plenty to Smile About." *Wall Street Journal,* (April 15, 1982), pp. 17–22.

Stevens, Richard. "COLGATE'S Winter Fresh. Will it be a Success?" *Wall Street Journal.* (July 30, 1982), p. 8–13.

Wagne, Booth. "CREST'S Secret Formula." *Fortune,* (January 25, 1983), pp.15–16.

Williams, Samuel. "P & G Fighting for Top Share." *New York Times,* (June 30, 1982), p. 7.

SOURCES OF SECONDARY RESEARCH

Following are more than 100 sources based on bibliographies put together by Lloyd M. DeBoer, Dean of the School of Business Administration at George Mason University, Fairfax, Virginia, and the Office of Management and Training of the SBA and published by the Small Business Administration as a part of two booklets, *Marketing Research Procedure* (SBB 9) and *National Directories for Use in Marketing* (SBB 13).

PRELIMINARY SOURCES

This section lists a wide range of reference sources to help locate pertinent materials for specific data. It is a good idea to consult one or more of them before investing substantial time or effort in any kind of market analysis.

Basic Library Reference Sources (SBB-18). SBA. Free. Contains a section on marketing information and guides to research.

Bureau of the Census Catalog. Bureau of the Census, U.S. Department of Commerce. Quarterly, cumulative to annual, with monthly supplements. GPO. Part I lists all publications issued by the Bureau of the Census. Part II lists available data files, special tabulations, and other unpublished materials. Both indexed.

Bureau of the Census Guide to Programs and Publications, Subjects and Areas. Bureau of the Census, Department of Commerce, 1974. GPO. Stock Number 0324–00196. On charts, describes the statistical information available in Census Bureau publications since 1968; defines geographic areas covered, outlines programs and activities. Indexed.

Note: Census data are issued initially in separate, paperbound reports. Publication order forms are issued for reports as they become available and may be obtained from the Subscriber Service Section (Publications), Bureau of Census, Washington, DC 20233, or any U.S. Department of Commerce field office.

Director of Federal Statistics for Local Areas: A Guide to Sources. Bureau of Census, U.S. Department of Commerce. Gives detailed table-by-table descriptions of subjects for almost all types of areas smaller than states. Covers the whole range of local data—social, economic, technical—published by the U.S. government. Bibliography with names and addresses of source agencies. Appendices. Indexed.

Industrial Market Information Guide. Regular monthly column appearing in every issue. Crain Communications, Inc., 740 North Rush St., Chicago, IL 60611. Lists, in 32 market categories, over 600 items of market data annually. Most items available from business publications, government agencies, and other publishers; some material for a limited period.

Measuring Markets: A Guide to the Use of Federal and State Statistical Data. Bureau of Domestic and International Business Administration, Department of Commerce. Revised periodically. Stock No. 003–025–00031. This is an excellent reference which not only describes federal and state government publications useful for measuring markets but also demonstrates the use of federal statistics in market measurement.

Statistical Abstract of the United States. Bureau of Census, Department of Commerce. Annual. GPO. This is the most comprehensive and authoritative data book on the social, economic, and governmental characteristics of the United States. Special features include sections on recent national trends and an appendix on statistical methodology and reliability. Indexed. Appendix IV, *Guide to Sources of Statistics,* is arranged alphabetically by major subjects listing government and private sources.

Statistics Sources: A Subject Guide to Data on Industrial, Business, Social, Educational, Financial, and Other Topics for the United States and Selected Foreign Countries. Gale Research Co., Book Tower, Detroit, MI 48226. Provides thousands of sources of statistics on about 12,000 subjects with 22,000 citations.

CONSUMER MARKET INFORMATION

This section lists references which provide information on products and services bought by individuals or households for home or personal use.

General Data

County and City Data Book. Bureau of Census, Department of Commerce. GPO. A total of 195 statistical items tabulated for the United States, its regions, and each county and state; 190 items for each city; and 161 items for 277 Standard Metropolitan Statistical Areas. Information is derived from latest available censuses of population, housing, governments, mineral industries, agriculture, manufacturers, retail and wholesale trade, and selected services. Also includes data on health, vital statistics, public assistance programs, bank deposits, votes cast for President, and crime.

Statistics for States and Metropolitan Areas. (A preprint from *County and City Data Book*). Bureau of Census, Department of Commerce. GPO. Presents data for 195 statistical items for the United States, its regions, and each state, and 161 items for 277 Standard Metropolitan Statistical Areas.

Statistical Abstract of the United States. Bureau of Census, Department of Commerce. GPO. Includes many consumer market statistics such as income, employment, communications, retail and wholesale trade and services, housing, population characteristics by state and for large cities and standard metropolitan areas. Late editions carry new tables on such topics as gambling, daytime care for children, households with TV sets, federal R&D obligations for energy development, franchised businesses, among others.

A Guide to Consumer Markets. Annual. The Conference Board, Inc., Information Services, 845 Third Ave., New York, NY 10022. Presents a detailed statistical profile of U.S. consumers and the consumer market. Contains data on population growth and mobility, employment, income, consumer spending patterns, production and sales, and prices.

E&P Market Guide. Published annually in fall. Editor & Publisher Company, 575 Lexington Ave., New York, NY 10022. Tabulates current estimates of population, households, retail sales and for nine major sales classifications, income for states, counties, metropolitan areas, and 1500 daily newspaper markets. Also lists specific information on major manufacturing, retailing, and business firms, transportation and utilities, local newspapers, climate, and employment, for newspaper markets. Includes state maps.

S&MM's Survey of Buying Power. Revised annually in july. *Sales and Marketing Management,* 633 Third Ave., New York, NY 10017. Information includes current estimates of population and households by income groups, total effective buying income, retail sales for major retail lines, and market quality indexes; given for all regions, states, counties, and metropolitan areas.

S&MM's Survey of Buying Power—Part II. Revised annually in October. *Sales and Marketing Management,* 633 Third Ave., New York, NY 10017. Gives population, income, retail sales, and buying income figures for television and newspaper markets in the United States and Canada. The data for television markets outline the areas of dominant influence, while the newspaper markets information identifies both dominant and effective coverage areas.

Specific Data

Each of the reference sources listed above under General Data includes at least some *specific* market data. In addition, there are sources of data useful only for the appraisal and management of specific markets. Examples of some of these important market types are listed below.

Automotive Marketing Guide. Motor Age, Chilton Way, Radnor, PA 19089. Number and relative importance (shown as percentage of U.S. total) of automotive wholesalers, franchised car dealers, repair shops, and service stations for counties, marketing areas, and states.

The New Yorker Guide to Selective Marketing. Market Research Department, 25 West 43d St., New York, NY 10036. Identifies and ranks markets for quality and premium-price products and services available in the United States. Includes maps and statistics for 40 top-tier areas of best potential to sell premium-priced products. Gives statistics on high-income families, high-priced car registrations, expensive homes, and various retail sales indices for top 40 and next 20 U.S. markets.

Survey of Industrial Purchasing Power. Revised annually in April. *Sales and Marketing Management,* 633 Third Ave., New York, NY 10017. A comprehensive look at the nation's key industrial markets. Included are a sales road map for the industrial marketer, an evaluation of the top 50 manufacturing counties, and statistics showing manufacturing activity by state, county, and four-digit SIC code.

Sales and Marketing Management Survey of Selling Costs. Revised annually in February. *Sales and Marketing Management,* 633 Third Ave., New York, NY 10017. Contains data on costs of sales meetings and sales training. Metro sales costs for major U.S. markets, compensation, sales-support activities, and transportation. There is also some cost information in the international area.

BUSINESS MARKET INFORMATION

This section lists references for all types of markets other than the consumer (individuals or household for personal use) markets. Some of the sources described in the Consumer Market sections of this appendix also provide data for *business* markets, such as commercial, farm, industrial, institutional, and federal and state governments.

General Data

County Business Patterns. Department of Commerce. Annual. GPO. Separate book for each state, District of Columbia, and a U.S. summary. Reports provide figures on first-quarter employment, first-quarter payroll, annual payroll, number of establishments and number of establishments by employment size class for some 700 different U.S. business and industries by each county in the United States.

County and City Data Book. Bureau of Census, Department of Commerce. GPO. Presents data on housing, population, income, local government financing, elections, agriculture, crime, for states, cities, counties, and 277 Standard Metropolitan Statistical Areas.

Statistics for State and Metropolitan Areas. (A reprint from *County and City Data Book,* 1977). Bureau of Census, Department of Commerce, GPO. Presents data for 195 statistical items for the U.S., its regions, and each state, and 161 items for 277 Standard Metropolitan Statistical Areas.

Statistical Abstract of the United States. Bureau of Census, Department of Commerce. Annual. GPO. Includes national and state data relating to business, industry, and institutional markets, as well as agriculture.

Specific Data

Automotive Marketing Guide. Motor Age, Chilton Way, Radnor, PA 19089. Number and relative importance (shown as a percentage of U.S. total) of automotive wholesalers, franchised car dealers, repair shops, and service stations for counties, marketing areas, and states.

Merchandising: Statistical Issue and Marketing Report. Annual. Billboard Publications, 1 Astor Plaza, New York, NY 10036. Gives retail sales of major appliance types and number of appliance dealers by state and public utility service areas; also gives number of residential utility customers and housing starts by state.

MAPS

This section lists (1) maps that serve merely as a base for market analysis by providing geographic information and (2) maps that themselves display marketing statistics. For ready reference, the maps are listed by publisher's name. Prices are shown when available.

American Map Company, Inc., 1926 Broadway, New York, NY 10023. *Catalog of Cleartype and Colorprint Maps.* Free. The catalog describes the types of maps (including plastic-surfaced maps for crayon presentations and maps on steel to accommodate magnetic markers). Company publishes U.S. base maps for depicting sales, markets, territories, distribution, statistics, and traffic data; detailed state, county, zip codes and township maps; and several types of atlases for use in analyzing national markets.

Rand McNally & Company, P.O. Box 7600, Chicago, IL 60680. Publishes a variety of maps and atlases. This publisher leases a *Commercial Atlas and Marketing Guide* which contains maps showing counties and cities, a road atlas, and statistical data on manufacturing, retail sales, and population. Standard metropolitan areas are shown. Includes a city index with information on transportation facilities, banks, and posted volume and an international section.

Sales Builders, 633 Third Ave., New York, NY 10017. Publishes two sets of nine regional maps (11" × 17") which cover the 50 states and depict either retail sales or industrial sales information. Also publishes two 50-state wall maps (24½" × 38") which have county outlines and depict either the consumer or manufacturing data. For list of prices and order blank, write Sales Builders Division, *Sales and Marketing Management.*

U.S. Geological Survey, Department of the Interior, Washington, DC 20402. Publishes a variety of maps that show state and city areas. The following maps and a list (free) of other available maps may be ordered from the Distribution Section, U.S. Geological Survey, 1200 South Eads St., Arlington, VA 22202.

Map 2-A (54″ × 80″). Shows state and county boundaries and names. State capitals, and county seats in black, water features in blue.

Map 2-B (42″ × 65″). Same as above, without land-tint background.

Map 3-A (42″ × 65″). Shows state boundaries and names. State capitals and principal cities in black, water features in blue.

Map 5-A (24½″ × 38″). Shows state and county boundaries and names, water features in black.

Map 7-A (20″ × 30″). Shows state boundaries and principal cities in black, water features in blue.

Map 11-A (13½″ × 20″). Shows state boundaries and principal cities in black, water features in blue.

Map 16-A (9½″ × 13″). Shows state boundaries and principal cities in black, water features in blue.

Contour Map—Map 7-B (20″ × 30″). State boundaries and principal cities in black, water features in blue, contours in brown.

Outline Map—Map 5-D (24½″ × 38″). State boundaries and names only.

Physical Divisions Map—Map 7-C (28″ × 32″). Physical divisions are outlined in red on the base map. Subdivisions and characteristics of each division are listed on the margin.

LOCATING SOURCES OF NATIONAL LISTS

Other directories, new publications or revisions, may be located in one of the six following sources. Some of the selected directories, as well as the locating guides, are available for reference in public and university libraries.

1. *Mailing Lists.* A major use of directories is in the compilation of mailing lists. Attention, therefore, is directed to another SBA Bibliography (SBB 29), "National Mailing-List Houses," which includes a selected compilation of both general line and limited line mailing-list houses that are national in scope. Also, consult Klein's *Director of Mailing List Houses*—see listings under "Mailing-List Houses" for further description of these two publications.

2. *Trade Associations and National Organizations.* For those trades or industries where directories are not available, membership lists of trade associations, both national and local, are often useful. For names and addresses of trade associations, consult the following directory source— available at most business reference libraries: *Encyclopedia of Associations, Vol I., National Organizations of the United States,* Gale Research Co., Book Tower, Detroit, MI 48226. Published annually. Lists trade, business, professional, labor, scientific, educational, fraternal, and social organizations of the United States; includes historical data.

3. *Business Periodicals.* Many business publications, particularly industrial magazines, develop comprehensive specialized directories of manufacturers in their respective fields. Names and addresses of business periodicals are listed (indexed by name of magazine and by business fields covered) in the *Business Publication Rates and Data* published monthly by Standard Rate and Data Service, 5201 Old Orchard Road, Skokie, IL 60077. Also, for listings of periodicals by subject index, consult the *Standard Periodical Directory,* and for a listing by geographical areas, refer to *Ayer Directory of Publications.* Most libraries have one or more of these directories for reference.

4. *American Directories.* Another source is *Guide to American Directories.* Published by B. Klein Publications, P.O. Box 8503, Coral Springs, FL 33065.

5. *F & S Index of Corporations and Industries.* It is available in most libraries. Indexes over 750 financial, trade, and business publications by corporate name and by SIC code. Published by Predicasts, Inc., 200 University Circle Research Center, 11001 Cedar Ave., Cleveland, OH 44106.

6. *The Public Affairs Information Service.* Available in many libraries, is published weekly, compiled five times a year, and put into an annual edition. This is a selective subject list of the latest books, government publications, reports, and periodical articles, relating to economic conditions, public conditions, public administration and international relations. Published by Public Affairs Information Service, Inc., 11 West 40th St., New York, NY 10018.

DIRECTORIES

The selected national directories are listed under categories of specific business or general marketing areas in an alphabetical subject index.

When the type of directory is not easily found under the alphabetical listing of a general marketing category, such as "jewelry," look for a specific type of industry or outlet, for example, "department stores."

Apparel

Fur Source Directory, Classified. Annually in June. Alphabetical directory of fur manufacturers in New York city area classified by type of fur; names, addresses, and telephone numbers for each. Also lists pelt dealers, fur cleaners, fur designers, resident buyers and brokers, and those engaged in fur repairing, processing, and remodeling. Fur Vogue Publishing Co., 127 West 30th St., New York, NY 10001.

Hat Life Year Book (Men's). Annual. Includes classified list of manufacturers and wholesalers of men's headwear. Hat Life Year Book, 551 Summit Ave., Jersey City, NJ 07306.

Knit Goods Trade, Davison's. Annual. Lists manufacturers of knitted products, manufacturers' agents, New York salesrooms, knit goods wholesalers, chain store organizations, department stores with names of buyers, discount chains, brokers and dealers, and rack jobbers. Davison Publishing Co., P.O. Drawer 477, Ridgewood, NJ 07451.

Men's & Boys' Wear Buyers, Nation-Wide Directory of. (Exclusive of New York Metropolitan Area.) Annually in November. More than 20,000 buyers and merchandise managers for 5000 top department, family clothing, and men's and boys' wear specialty stores. Telephone number, buying office, and postal zip code given for each firm. Also available in individual state editions. The Salesman's Guide, Inc., 1140 Broadway, New York, NY 10001. Also publishes *Metropolitan New York Directory of Men's and Boys' Wear Buyers.* Semiannually in May and November. (Lists same information for the metropolitan New York area as the nationwide directory.)

Teens' & Boys' Outfitter Directory. Semiannually in April and October. (Pocket size.) Lists manufacturers of all types of apparel for boys and students by category, including their New York City addresses and phone numbers; also lists resident buying firms for out-of-town stores, and all trade associations related to boys' wear. The Boys' Outfitter Co., Inc., 71 West 35th St., New York, NY 10001.

Women's & Children's Wear & Accessories Buyers, National Directory of. (Exclusive of New York metropolitan area.) Annually in February. Lists more than 25,000 buyers and divisional merchandise managers for about 5000 leading department, family clothing, and specialty stores. Telephone number and mail zip code given for each store. Also available in individual state editions. The Salesman's Guide, Inc., 1140 Broadway, New York, NY 10001.

Appliances, Household

National Buyer's Guide. Annual. Lists manufacturers and distributors in home electronics, appliances, kitchens. Gives the products they handle, the territories they cover, and complete addresses for each distributor. Dealerscope, 115 Second Avenue, Waltham, MA 02154.

Arts and Antiques

American Art and Antique Dealers, Mastai's Classified, Directory of. Lists 20,000 art museums, with names of directories and curators; art and antique dealers; art galleries; coin, armor, tapestry and china dealers in the United States and Canada. Mastai Publishing Co., 21 E 57th St., New York, NY 10022.

Automatic Merchandising (Vending)

NAMA Directory of Members. Annually in July. Organized by state and by city, lists vending service companies who are NAMA members. Gives mailing address, telephone number, and products vended. Also includes machine manufacturers and suppliers. National Automatic Merchandising Association, 7 South Dearborn St., Chicago, IL 60603.

Automotive

Automotive Affiliated Representatives, Membership Roster. Annual. Free to first seeking representation. Alpha-geographical listing of about 400 member firms including name, address, telephone number, territories covered, and lines carried. Automotive Affiliated Representatives, 625 South Michigan Ave., Chicago, IL 60611.

Automotive Directory of Manufacturers and Their Sales Representatives, National. Annual. Alphabetical arrangement of manufacturers serving automotive replacement market. Where available, includes names and addresses of each manufacturers' representative showing territory covered. W. R. C. Smith Publishing Co., 1760 Peachtree Rd. N.W., Atlanta, GA 30357.

Automotive Warehouse Distributors Association Membership Directory. Annually. Includes listing of manufacturers, warehouse distributors, their products, personnel and territories. Automotive Warehouse Distributors Association, 1719 W. 91st Place, Kansas City, MO 64114.

Auto Trim Resource Directory. November edition; annual issue of *Auto Trim News.* Alphabetical listing of name, address, and telephone number of auto trim resources and wholesalers who service auto trim shops. Has directory of product sources—listed by product supplied—with name and address of firm. Auto Trim News, 1623 Grand Ave., Baldwin, NY 11510.

Credit and Sales Reference Directory. Three times annually. Available only to supplier-manufacturers on annual fee basis. Contains listings of 17,000 automotive distributors in the United States and Canada. Data include name and address of companies, and other pertinent information. Motor and Equipment Manufacturers Assn., MEMA Service Corp., 222 Cedar Lane, Teaneck, NJ 07666.

Home Center, Hardware, Auto Supply Chains. Annually. Lists headquarter addresses, telephone numbers, number and types of stores and locations, annual sales volume, names of executives and buyers. Chain Store Guide Publications, 425 Park Ave., New York, NY 10022.

Jobber Topics Automotive Aftermarket Directory. Annual. Lists 7000 automotive warehouse distributors automotive rebuilders, manufacturers agents, automotive jobbers, associations, and manufacturers. The Irving-Cloud Publishing Co., 7300 N. Cicero Ave., Lincolnwood, Chicago, IL 60646.

Aviation

World Aviation Directory. Published twice a year. Spring and fall. Gives administrative and operating personnel of airlines, aircraft, and engine manufacturers and component manufacturers and distributors, organizations, and schools. Indexed by companies, activities, products, and individuals. Ziff-Davis Aviation Division, 1156 15th St., NW, Washington, DC 20005.

Bookstores

Book Trade Directory, American. Annual. Updated bimonthly. Lists retail and wholesale booksellers in the United States and Canada. Entries alphabetized by state (or province), and then by city and business name. Each listing gives address, telephone numbers, key personnel, types of books sold, subject specialties carried, sidelines and services offered and general characteristics. For wholesale entries give types of accounts, import-export information and territory limitations. Edited by the Jaques Cattell Press. R. R. Bowker Company, 1180 Avenue of the Americas, New York, NY 10036.

Multiple Book Store Owners, Directory of. Annually. Lists over 1000 chains of book stores by state, city, and alphabetically by store within each city. Oldden Mercantile Corp., 560 Northern Blvd., Great Neck, NY 11021.

Building Supplies

Building Supply News Buyers Guide. Annually. Classified directory of manufacturers of lumber, building materials, equipment, and supplies. Cahners Publishing Co., 5 S. Wabash Ave., Chicago, IL 60603.

Business Firms

Dun & Bradstreet Middle Market Directory. Annually in October. Lists about 31,000 businesses with net worth between $500,000 and $1,000,000. Arranged in three sections: alphabetically, geographically, and product classification. Gives business name, state of incorporation, address, telephone number, SIC numbers, function, sales volume, number of employees, and name of officers and directors. Marketing Services Division, Dun & Bradstreet, Inc., 99 Church St., New York, NY 10007.

Dun & Bradstreet Million Dollar Directory. Annually in January. Lists about 46,000 businesses with a net worth of $1 million or more. Arranged in four sections; alphabetically, geographically, line of business, and officers and directors with the same information as detailed in the preceding entry. Marketing Services Division, Dun & Bradstreet, Inc., 99 Church St., New York, NY 10007.

Buying Offices

Buying Offices and Accounts, Directory of. Annually in March. Approximately 230 New York, Chicago, Los Angeles, Dallas, and Miami Resident Buying Offices, Corporate Offices and Merchandise Brokers together with 11,000 accounts listed under its own Buying Office complete with local address and alphabetically by address and buying office. The Salesman's Guide, Inc., 1140 Broadway, New York, NY 10001.

China and Glassware

American Glass Review. Glass factory directory issue. Annually. Issued as part of subscription (13th issue) to *American Glass Review.* Lists companies manufacturing flat glass, tableware glass and fiber glass, giving corporate and plant addresses, executives, type of equipment used. Ebel-Doctorow Publications, Inc., 1115 Clifton Ave., Clifton, NJ 07013.

China Glass & Tableware Red Book Directory Issue. Annually. Issued as part of subscription (13th issue) to *China Glass & Tableware.* Lists about 1000 manufacturers, importers, and national distributors of china, glass, and other table appointments, giving corporate addresses and executives. Ebel-Doctorow Publications, Inc., 1115 Clifton Ave., Clifton, NJ 07013.

City Directories Catalog

Municipal Year Book. Annual. Contains a review of municipal events of the years, analyses of city operations, and a directory of city officials in all the states. International City Management Association, 1140 Connecticut Ave., NW, Washington, DC 20036.

College Stores

College Stores, Directory of. Published every two years. Lists about 3500 college stores, geographically with manager's name, kinds of goods sold, college name, number of students, whether men, women, or both, whether the store is college owned or privately owned. B. Klein Publications, P.O. Box 8503, Coral Springs, FL 33065.

Confectionery

Candy Buyers' Directory. Annually in January. Lists candy manufacturers; importers and U.S. representatives, and confectionery brokers. The Manufacturing Confectionery Publishing Co., 175 Rock Rd., Glen Rock, NJ 07452.

Construction Equipment

Construction Equipment Buyer's Guide, AED Edition. Annual. Summer. Lists U.S. and Canadian construction equipment distributors and manufacturers; includes company names, names of key personnel, addresses, telephone numbers, branch locations, and lines handled or type of equipment produced. Associated Equipment Distributors, 615 West 22d St., Oak Brook, IL 60521.

Conventions and Trade Shows

Directory of Conventions. Annually in January, with July supplement. Contains about 21,000 cross-indexed listings of annual events, gives dates, locations, names, and addresses of executives in charge and type of group two years in advance. *Successful Meetings Magazine,* Directory Dept., 633 Third Ave., New York, NY 10017.

Exhibits Schedule. Annually in January, with supplement in July. Lists over 10,000 exhibits, trade shows, expositions, and fairs held throughout the world with dates given two years in advance. Listings run according to industrial classification covering all industries and professions; full information on dates, city, sponsoring organization, number of exhibits, attendance; gives title and address of executive in charge. *Successful Meetings Magazine,* Directory Dept., 633 Third Ave., New York, NY 10017.

Dental Supply

Dental Supply Houses, Hayes Directory of. Annually in August. Lists wholesalers of dental supplies and equipment with addresses, telephone numbers, financial standing, and credit rating. Edward N. Hayes, Publisher, 4229 Birth St., Newport Beach, CA 92660.

Department Stores

Department Stores. Annually. Lists headquarters address and branch locations, telephone numbers, number of stores, resident buying office, names of executives and buyers for independent and chain operators. Chain Store Guide Publications, 425 Park Ave., New York, NY 10022.

Sheldon's Retail. Annual. Lists 1700 large independent department stores, 446 large junior department store chains, 190 large independent and chain home-furnishing stores, 694 large independent women's specialty stores, and 270 large women's specialty store chains alphabetically by states and also major Canadian stores. Gives all department buyers with lines bought by each buyer, and addresses and telephone numbers of merchandise executives. Also gives all New York, Chicago, or Los Angeles buying offices, the number and locations of branch stores, and an index of all store/chain headquarters. Phelon, Sheldon & Marsar, Inc., 32 Union Sq., New York, NY 10003.

Discount Stores

Discount Department Stores, Phelon's. Gives buying headquarters for about 2000 discount stores, chains, drug chains, catalog showrooms, major jobbers and wholesalers; lines of merchandise bought, buyers' names, leased departments, addresses of leasees, executives, number of stores, and price range. Includes leased department operators with lines and buyers' names. Phelon, Sheldon & Marsar, Inc., 32 Union Sq., New York, NY 10003.

Discount Department Stores. Annually. Lists headquarters address, telephone number, location, square footage of each store, lines carried, leased operators, names of executives and buyers (includes Canada). Also special section on leased department operators. Chain Store Guide Publications, 425 Park Ave., New York, NY 10022.

Drug Outlets—Retail and Wholesale

Drug Stores, Chain. Annually. Lists headquarters address, telephone numbers, number and location of units, names of executives and buyers, wholesale drug distributors (includes Canada). Chain Store Guide Publications, 425 Park Ave., New York, NY 10022.

Druggists—Wholesale. Annually in March. Wholesale druggists in United States with full-line wholesalers specially indicated as taken from the *Hayes Druggist Directory.* Edward N. Hayes, Publisher, 4229 Birch St., Newport Beach, CA 92660.

Druggist Directory, Hayes. Annually in March. List all the retail druggists in the United States, giving addresses, financial standing, and credit rating. Also publishes regional editions for one or more states. Computerized mailing labels available. Edward N. Hayes, Publisher, 4229 Birch St., Newport Beach, CA 92660.

Drug Topics Buyers' Guide. Gives information on wholesale drug companies, chain drug stores headquarters, department stores maintaining toilet goods or drug departments, manufacturers' sales agents, and discount houses operating toilet goods, cosmetic, proprietary medicine, or prescription departments. Drug Topics, Medical Economics Company, Oradell, NJ 07649.

National Wholesale Druggists' Association Membership and Executive Directory. Annually. Lists 800 American and foreign wholesalers and manufacturers of drugs and allied products. National Wholesale Druggists' Association, 670 White Plains Rd., Scarsdale, NY 10583.

Electrical and Electronics

Electronic Industry Telephone Directory. Annual. Contains over 80,000 listings in White and Yellow Page sections. White Pages: name, address, and telephone number of manufacturers, representatives, distributors, government agencies, contracting agencies, and others. Yellow Pages: alphabetical listings by 600 basic product headings and 3000 subproduct headings. Harris Publishing Co., 2057–2 Aurora Rd., Twinsburg, OH 44087.

Electrical Wholesale Distributors, Directory of. Detailed information on almost 5000 listings, including name, address, telephone number, branch and affiliated houses, products handled, etc. Electrical Wholesaling. McGraw-Hill Publications Co., Dept. ECCC Services, 1221 Avenue of the Americas, New York, NY 10020.

Who's Who in Electronics, including Electronic Representatives Directory. Annual. Postpaid. Detailed information (name, address, telephone number, products handled, territories, and so forth) on 7500 electronic manufacturers, 500 suppliers, 3500 independent sales representatives, and 2500 industrial electronic distributors and branch outlets. Purchasing index with 1600 product breakdowns for buyers and purchasing agents. Harris Publishing Co., 2057–2 Aurora Rd., Twinsburg, OH 44087.

Electrical Utilities

Electric Utilities, Electrical World Directory of. Annually in October. Complete listings of electric utilities (investor-owned, municipal, and government agencies in the U.S. and Canada) giving their addresses, personnel, and selected data on operations. McGraw-Hill Publications Co., Inc., Directory of Electric Utilities, 1221 Avenue of the Americas, New York, NY 10020.

Embroidery

Embroidery Directory. Annually in October–November. Alphabetical listing with addresses and telephone numbers of manufacturers, merchandisers, designers, cutters, bleacheries, yarn dealers, machine suppliers and other suppliers to the Schiffli lace and embroidery industry. Schiffli Lace and Embroidery Manufacturers Assn., Inc., 512 23d St., Union City, NJ 07087.

Export and Import

American Register of Exporters and Importers. Annually. Includes over 30,000 importers and exporters and products handled. American Register of Exporters and Importers, Inc., 15 Park Row, New York, NY 10038.

Canadian Trade Directory, Fraser's. Write directly for price. Contains more than 12,000 product classifications with over 400,000 listings from 38,000 Canadian companies. Also lists over 10,000 foreign companies who have Canadian representatives. Fraser's Trade Directories, 481 University Ave., Toronto M5W 1A4, Ontario, Canada.

Flooring

Flooring Directory. Annually in November. Reference to sources of supply, giving their products and brand names, leading distributors, manufacturers' representatives, and associations. Flooring Directory, Harcourt Brace Jovanovich Publications, 1 East First St., Duluth, MN 55802.

Food Dealers—Retail and Wholesale

Co-ops, Voluntary Chains and Wholesale Grocers. Annually. Lists headquarters address, telephone number, number of accounts served, all branch operations, executives, buyers, annual sales volume (includes Canada and special "rack merchandiser" section). Chain Store Guide Publications, 425 Park Ave., New York, NY 10022.

Food Brokers Association, National Directory of Members. Annually in July. Free to business firms writing on their letterhead. Arranged by states and cities, lists member food brokers in the United States and Europe, giving names and addresses, products they handle, and services they perform. National Food Brokers Association, 1916 M St., NW, Washington, DC 20036.

Food Service Distributors. Annually. Lists headquarters address, telephone number, number of accounts served, branch operations, executives, and buyers for distributors serving the restaurant and institutional market. Chain Store Guide Publications, 425 Park Ave., New York, NY 10022.

Fresh Fruit and Vegetable Dealers, The Blue Book of Credit Book and Marketing Guide. Semiannually in April and October. (Kept up to date by weekly credit sheets and monthly supplements.) Lists shippers, buyers, jobbers, brokers, wholesale and retail grocers, importeers and exporters in the United States and Canada that handle fresh fruits and vegetables in carlot and trucklot quantities. Also lists truckers, truck brokers of exempt perishables with "customs and rules" covering both produce trading and truck transportation. Produce Reporter Co., 315 West Wesley St., Wheaton, IL 60187.

Frozen Food Fact Book and Directory. Annual. Free to association members. Lists packers, distributors, suppliers, refrigerated warehouses, wholesalers, and brokers; includes names and addresses of each firm and their key officials. Contains statistical marketing data. National Frozen Food Association, Inc., P.O. Box 398, 1 Chocolate Ave., Hershey, PA 17033.

Grocery Register, Thomas'. Annual. Three volumes. Vol. 1 & 3 or Vol. 2 & 3. Volume 1: Lists supermarket chains, wholesalers, brokers, frozen food brokers, exporters, warehouses. Volume 2: Contains information on products and services, manufacturers, sources of supplies, importers. Volume 3: A–Z index of 56,000 companies. Also, a brand name—trademark index. Thomas Publishing Co., One Penn Plaza, New York, NY 10001.

Quick Frozen Foods Directory of Wholesale Distributors. Biennially. Lists distributors of frozen foods. Quick Frozen Foods, P.O. Box 6128, Duluth, MN 55806.

Supermarket, Grocery & Convenience Store Chains. Annually. Lists headquarters address, telephone number, location and type of unit, annual sales volume, executive and buyers, cartographic display of 267 Standard Metropolitan Statistical Areas (includes Canada). Chain Store Guide Publications, 425 Park Ave., New York, NY 10022.

Tea and Coffee Buyers' Guide, Users' International. Biennial. Includes revised and updated lists of participants in the tea and coffee and allied trades. The Tea and Coffee Trade Journal, 18–15 Francis Lewis Blvd., Whitestone, NY 11357.

Gas Companies

Gas Companies, Brown's Directory of International. Annually in August. Includes information on every known gas utility company and holding company worldwide. Brown's Directory, Harcourt Brace Jovanovich Publications, 1 East First St., Duluth, MN 55802.

LP/Gas. Annually in March. Lists suppliers, supplies, and distributors. Harcourt Brace Jovanovich Publications, 1 East First St., Duluth, MN 55802.

Gift and Art

Gift and Decorative Accessory Buyers Directory. Annually in August. Included in subscription price of monthly magazine. *Gifts and Decorative Accessories.* Alphabetical listing of manufacturers, importers, jobbers, and representatives in the gift field. Listing of trade names, trademarks, brand names, and trade associations. Geyer-McAllister Publications, 51 Madison Ave., New York, NY 10010.

Gift and Housewares Buyers, Nationwide Directory. Annually with semi-annual supplement. For 4673 different types of retail firms lists store name, address, type of store, number of stores, names of president, merchandise managers, and buyers, and so forth, for giftwares and housewares. State editions also available. The Salesman's Guide, Inc., 1140 Broadway, New York, NY 10001.

Gift & Tableware Reporter Directory Issue. Annual. Alphabetical listing by category of each (manufacturer, representative, importer, distributor, or jobber). Includes identification of trade names and trademarks, and statistics for imports, manufacturing, and retail sales. Gift & Tableware Reporter, 1 Astor Place, New York, NY 10036.

Gift Shop Directory. Biennially. List 900 gift shops in the United States. Resourceful Research, Box 642, F.D.R. Station, New York, NY 10022.

Hardware

Hardware Wholesalers Guide, National. Annual. Alphabetical listing of manufacturers of hardware and building supplies. Where available, includes names and addresses of each manufacturer's representative showing territory covered. W.R.C. Smith Publishing Co., 1760 Peachtree Rd. N.W., Atlanta, GA 30357.

Hardware Wholesalers, Verified List of. Lists distributors (wholesale general hardware houses and hardware chain stores) serving the United States and Canada. Also lists manufacturers' agents handling hardware and allied lines. Chilton Co., Chilton Way, Radnor, PA 19089.

Home Furnishings

The Antiques Dealer. Annual directory issue. Issued in September as part of subscription. Lists major wholesale sources by geographical section. Includes special listing for show managers, auctioneers, appraisers, reproductions, supplies, and services. Ebel-Doctorow Publications, Inc., 115 Clifton Ave., Clifton, NJ 07013.

Home Lighting & Accessories Suppliers. Directory issues. Semiannual. Issue in March and October as part of subscription. Lists names and addresses of suppliers to the lamp and lighting industry. Ebel-Doctorow Publications, Inc., 1115 Clifton Ave., Clifton, NJ 07013.

Interior Decorator's Handbook. Semiannually. To trade only. Published expressly for decorators and designers, interior decorating staff of department and furniture stores. Lists from firms handling items used in interior decoration. Columbia Communications, Inc., 370 Lexington Ave., New York, NY 10017.

Hospitals

American Hospital Association Guide to the Health Care Field. Annually in August. Lists registered hospitals, with selected data as well as listings of nursing homes, health related organizations, and professional schools. Includes international, national, regional, and state organizations and agencies. American Hospital Associations, 840 North Lake Shore Dr., Chicago, IL 60611.

Hotels and Motels

Hotel-Motel Guide and Travel Atlas, Leahy's. Annually. Lists more than 47,000 hotels and motels in the United States, Canada, and Mexico; includes room rates, number of rooms, and plan of operation. Also has extensive maps. American Hotel Register Co., 2775 Shermer Road, Northbrook, IL 60062.

Hotel Red Book. Annually in May. Lists hotels in the United States, Canada, Caribbean, Mexico, Central and South America. Includes a section covering Europe, Asia, and Africa. Gives detailed information for each hotel. American Hotel Association Directory Corporation, 888 Seventh Ave., New York, NY 10019.

Hotels Systems, Directory of. Annually in July. Lists approximately 300 hotel systems in the Western Hemisphere, American Hotel Association Directory Corporation, 888 Seventh Ave., New York, NY 10019.

Housewares

Housewares Reps Registry. Annually in May. (Included with subscription to *Housewares.*) Compilation of resources of the housewares trade, includes listing of their products, trade names, and a registry of manufacturers' representatives. Housewares Directory, Harcourt Brace Jovanovich Publications, 1 East First St., Duluth, MN 55802.

Jewelry

The Jewelers Board of Trade Confidential Reference Book. Semiannually in March and September. Supplied only to members subscribing to the agency service. Write directly for prices. Lists manufacturers, importers, distributors, and retailers of jewelry; diamonds; precious, semiprecious, and imitation stones; watches; silverware; and kindred articles. Includes credit ratings. The Jewelers Board of Trade, 70 Catamore Blvd., East Providence, RI 02914.

Liquor

Wine and Spirits Wholesalers, Blue Book of. Annually in December. Lists names of member companies; includes parent house and branches, addresses, and names of managers. Also has register of suppliers, and give state liquor control administrators, national associations, and trade press directory. Wine and Spirits Wholesalers of America, Inc., 2033 M St., NW, Suite 400, Washington, DC 20036.

Mailing-List Houses

Mailing List Houses, Directory of. Lists more than 3000 list firms, brokers, compilers, and firms offering their own lists for rent, includes the specialties of each firm. Arranged geographically. B. Klein Publications, P.O. Box 8503, Coral Springs, FL 33065.

National Mailing-List Houses. (Small Business Bibliography 29). Free. Lists selected national mailing-list houses; includes both general line and limited line houses. Small Business Administration, P.O. Box 15434, Ft. Worth, TX 76119.

Mail Order Businesses

Mail Order Business Directory. Lists more than 6300 names or mail-order firms with buyers' names, and lines carried. Arranged geographically. B. Klein Publications, P.O. Box 8503, Coral Springs, FL 33065.

Manufacturers

MacRae's Blue Book. Annual. In five volumes: Volume 1—Corporate Index lists company names and addresses alphabetically, with 60,000 branch and/or sales office telephone numbers. Volumes 2, 3, and 4—companies listed by 40,000 product classifications. Volume 5—company product catalogs. MacRae's Blue Book, 100 Shore Drive, Hinsdale, IL 60521.

Manufacturers, Thomas' Register of American. Annual. In 14 volumes, Volume 1–7—products and services; suppliers of each product category grouped by state and city. Vols. 9–14—manufacturers' catalogs. Thomas Publishing Co., One Penn Plaza, New York, NY 10001.

Manufacturers' Sales Representatives

Manufacturers & Agents National Association Directory of Members. Annually in July. Contains individual listings of manufacturers' agents throughout the United States, Canada, and several foreign countries. Listings cross-referenced by alphabetical, geographical, and product classification. Manufacturers' Agents National Association, P.O. Box 16878. Irvine, CA 92713.

Mass Merchandisers

Major Mass Market Merchandisers, Nationwide Directory of. (Exclusive of New York metropolitan area). Annually. Lists men's, women's, and children's wear buyers who buy for over 175,000 units—top discount, variety, supermarket, and drug chains; factory outlet stores; leased department operators. The Salesman's Guide, Inc., 1140 Broadway, New York, NY 10001.

Mass Retailing Merchandiser Buyers Directory. Annually. Lists 7000 manufacturers, mass retail chains, manufacturers' representatives, jobbers, and
wholesalers serving the mass-retailing field. Merchandiser Publishing Co.,
Inc., 222 West Adams, Chicago, IL 60606.

Metalworking

Metalworking Directory, Dun & Bradstreet. Annually in May. Published in
one national and five sectional editions. Retail price available upon request.
Lists about 44,000 metalworking and metal-producing plants with 20 or
more production employees. Arranged in four sections: geographically,
line of business, alphabetically, and statistical courts summary. Marketing
Services Division, Dun & Bradstreet, Inc., 99 Church St., New York, NY
10007.

Military Market

Buyers' Guide. Annually. Listings grouped by systems served of suppliers
names and addresses, military representatives, and civilian brokerage firms
that specialize in serving military stores are given. Military Market, 475
School St., SW, Washington, DC 20024.

Nonfood Products

Non-Food Buyers, National Directory Of. Annually. Alpha-geographical listing of 9000 buyers of nonfood merchandise for over 336,000 outlets.
United Publishing Co., 1372 Peachtree St., N.E., Atlanta, GA 30309.

Paper Products

Sources of Supply Buyers' Guide. Lists mills and converters of paper, film,
foil and allied products, and paper merchants in the United States alphabetically with addresses, principal personnel, and products manufactured.
Also lists trade associations, brand names, and manufacturers' representatives. Advertisers and Publishers Service, Inc., P.O. Drawer 795, 300 N.
Prospect Ave., Park Ridge, IL 60068.

Physicians and Medical Supply Houses

Medical Directory, American. Volumes 1–4 gives complete information
about all physicians in the United States and possessions—alphabetical and

geographical listings. Volume 5—Directory of Women Physicians. American Medical Associations, 535 North Dearborn St., Chicago, IL 60610.

Physician and Hospital Supply Houses, Hayes' Directory of. Annually in August. Listings of 1850 U.S. wholesalers doing business in physician, hospital, and surgical supplies and equipment; includes addresses, telephone numbers, financial standing, and credit ratings. Edward N. Hayes, Publisher, 4229 Birch St., Newport Beach, CA 92660.

Plumbing

Manufacturers' Representatives, Directory of. Annually as a special section of the February issue of *The Wholesaler* magazine. Write directly for subscription price. Lists representatives of manufacturers selling plumbing, heating and cooling equipment, components, tools and related products, to this industry through wholesaler channels, with detailed information on each. Scott Periodicals Corp., 135 Addison Avenue, Elmhurst, IL 60126.

Premium Sources

Premium and Incentive Buyers, Directory of. Annual in September. Lists over 16,000 executives for 12,000 firms with title, telephone number, address, and merchandise executive desires to buy in the premium, incentive, and travel fields. The Salesman's Guide, 1140 Broadway, New York, NY 10001.

Incentive Marketing/Incorporating Incentive Travel: Supply Sources Directory. Annual in January. Contains classified directory of suppliers, and list of manufacturers' representatives serving the premium field. Also, lists associations and clubs, and trade shows. Incentive Marketing, 633 Third Ave., New York, NY 10017.

Purchasing, Government

U.S. Government Purchasing and Sales Directory. Booklet by Small Business Administration. Designed to help small businesses receive an equitable share of government contracts. Lists types of purchases for both military and civilian needs, catalogs procurement offices by state. Lists SBA regional and branch offices. Order from Superintendent of Documents, U.S. Government Printing Office, Washington, DC 20402.

Refrigeration and Air-Conditioning

Air Conditioning, Heating & Refrigeration News. Special issue. Lists alphabetically and by products, the names of refrigeration, heating and air-conditioning manufacturers, trade names, wholesalers, and associations in the United States. Business News Publishing Co., P.O. Box 2600, Troy, MI 48084.

Air-Conditioning & Refrigeration Wholesalers Directory. Annually. Lists alphabetically 950 member air-conditioning and refrigeration wholesalers with their addresses, telephone numbers, and official representatives by region, state, and city. Air-conditioning and Refrigeration Wholesalers, 22371 Newman Ave., Dearborn, MI 48124.

Restaurants

Restaurant Operators. (Chain.) Annually. Lists headquarters address, telephone number, number and location of units, trade names used, whether unit is company-operated or franchised, executives and buyers, annual sales volume for chains of restaurants, cafeterias, drive-ins, hotel and motel food operators, industrial caterers, and so forth. Chain Store Guide Publications, 425 Park Ave., New York, NY 10022.

Roofing and Siding

RSI Trade Directory. Annually in April. With subscription to *Roof Siding and Insulation,* monthly. Has listing guide to products and equipment manufacturers, jobbers and distributors, and associations in the roofing, siding, and home improvement industries. RSI Directory, Harcourt Brace Jovanovich Publications, 1 East First St., Duluth, MN 55802.

Selling, Direct

Direct Selling Companies, A Supplier's Guide to. Information supplied by member companies of the Direct Selling Association includes names of contact persons, company product line, method of distribution, and so forth. Direct Selling Association, 1730 M St., NW, Washington, DC 20036.

Direct Selling Directory. Annually in February issue of *Specialty Salesman and Business Opportunities Magazine.* Alphabetical listing of name and address under product and service classifications of specialty sales firms and their products. Specialty Salesmen, 307 North Michigan Ave., Chicago, IL 60601.

Who's Who in Direct Selling. Membership roster of the Direct Selling Association. No charge for single copies. Active members classified by type of product or service. Alphabetical listing gives name, address, and telephone of firm, along with managing official. Direct Selling Association, 1730 M Street, NW, Washington, DC 20036.

Shoes

Chain Shoe Stores Directory. Lists chain shoe stores at their headquarters including officers, buyers, lines carried, trading names of stores, number of operating units. The Rumpf Publishing Co., Div. of Nickerson & Collins Co., 1800 Oakton St., Des Plaines, IL 60018.

Shopping Centers

Shopping Centers in the United States and Canada, Directory of. Annual. Alphabetical listing of 16,000 American and Canadian shopping centers, location, owner-developer, manager, physical plant (number of stores, square feet), and leasing agent. National Research Bureau, Inc., 424 North Third St., Burlington, IA 52601.

Specialty Stores

Women's Specialty Stores, Phelon's. Lists more than 18,000 women's apparel and accessory shops with store headquarters name and address, number of shops operated, New York City buying headquarters or representatives, lines of merchandise bought and sold, name of principal and buyers, store size, and price range. Phelon, Sheldon, & Marsar, Inc., 32 Union Sq., New York, NY 10003.

Sporting Goods

Sporting Goods Buyers, Nationwide Directory of. Including semiannual supplements. Lists over 4500 top retail stores (23 different types) with names of buyers and executives, for all types of sporting goods, athletic apparel and footwear, hunting and fishing, and outdoor equipment. The Salesman's Guide, Inc., 1140 Broadway, New York, NY 10001.

The Sporting Goods Register. (Including jobbers, manufacturers' representatives, and importers). Annual. Geographical listing of firms (name, address, buyers, types of goods sold, and so forth) doing wholesale business in sporting goods merchandise and equipment. Similar data for Canadian firms. Alphabetical grouping of manufacturers' representatives and importers. The Sporting Goods Dealer, 1212 North Lindbergh Blvd., St. Louis, MO 63132.

The Sporting Goods Dealer's Directory. Annual. Lists about 5000 manufacturers and suppliers. Also includes names of manufacturers agents, wholesalers, and sporting goods associations and governing bodies of sports. The Sporting Goods Dealer, 1212 North Lindbergh Blvd., St. Louis, MO 63132.

Stationers

Wholesale Stationers' Association Membership Roster. Annually. Alphabetical listing by company of over 300 wholesaler companies. Wholesale Stationers Assn., 3166 Des Plaines Ave., Des Plaines, IL 60018.

Textiles

Textile Blue Book, Davison's. Annual. Contains more than 18,000 separate company listings (name, address, and so forth) for United States and Canada. Firms included are cotton, wool, synthetic, mills, knitting mills, cordage, twine, and duck manufacturers, dry goods commission merchants, converters, yarn dealers, cordage manufacturers' agents, wool dealers and merchants, cotton merchants, exporter, brokers, and others. Davison Publishing Co., P.O. Drawer 477, Ridgewood, NJ 07451.

Toys and Novelties

Toys, Hobbies & Crafts Directory. Annually in June. Lists manufacturers, products, trade names, suppliers to manufacturers, supplier products, character licensors, manufacturers' representatives, toy trade associations, and trade show managements. Toys Directory, Harcourt Brace Jovanovich Publications, 1 East First St., Duluth, MN 55802.

Wholesalers and Manufacturers, Directory of. Contains information on wholesalers, manufacturers, manufacturers' representatives of toys, games, hobby, art, school, party, and office supply products. Toy Wholesalers' Association of America, 1514 Elmwood Ave., Evanston, IL 60201.

Trailer Parks

Campground Directory, Woodall's North American Canadian Edition. Annually. Lists and star-rates public and private campgrounds in North American continent alphabetically by town with location and description of facilities. Also lists more than 1000 RV service locations. Regional editions available. Woodall Publishing Company, 500 Hyachinth Place, Highland Park, IL 60035.

Trucking

Trinc's Blue Book of the Trucking Industry and Trinc's Five Year Red Book. Retail price upon request. Together these two directories furnish comprehensive statistics on the trucking industry and individual truckers represented by about 3500 Class I and Class II U.S. motor carriers of property. TRINC Transportation Consultants, P.O. Box 23091, Washington, DC 20024.

Variety Stores

General Merchandise, Variety and Junior Department Stores. Annually. Lists headquarters address, telephone number, number of units and locations, executives and buyers (includes Canada). Chain Store Guide Publications, 425 Park Ave., New York, NY 10022.

Warehouses

Distribution Services, Guide to. Annually in July. Lists leading public warehouses in U.S. and Canada, as well as major truck lines, airlines, steamship lines, liquid and dry bulk terminals, material handling equipment suppliers, ports of the world and railroad piggyback services and routes. Distribution Magazine, Chilton Way, Radnor, PA 19089.

Public Refrigerated Warehouses, Directory of. Annually. Free to concerns in perishable food business. Geographical listing of over 750 public refrigerated warehouse members. International Associations of Refrigerated Warehouses, 7315 Wisconsin Ave., NW, Washington, DC 20014.

OTHER IMPORTANT DIRECTORIES

The following business directories are helpful to those persons doing marketing research. Most of these directories are available for reference at the larger libraries. For additional listings, consult the *Guide to American Directories* at local libraries.

AUBER Bibliography of Publications of University Bureaus of Business and Economic Research. Lists studies published by Bureaus of Business and Economic Research affiliated with American colleges and universities. Done for the Association for University Bureaus of Business and Economic Research. Issued annually. Previous volumes available. Bureau of Business Research, College of Business and Economics, West Virginia University, Morgantown, WV 26506.

Bradford's Directory of Marketing Research Agencies and Management Consultants in the United States and the World. Gives names and addresses of more than 350 marketing research agencies in the United States, Canada, and abroad. Lists service offered by agency, along with other pertinent data, such as date established, names of principal officers, and size of staff. Bradford's Directory of Marketing Research Agencies, P.O. Box 276, Department B–15, Fairfax, VA 22030.

Consultants and Consulting Organizations Directory. Contains 5041 entries. Guides reader to right organization for a given consulting assignment. Entries include names, addresses, phone numbers, and data on services performed. Gale Research Company, Book Tower, Detroit, MI 48226.

Research Centers Directory. Palmer, Archie M., editor. Lists more than 5500 nonprofit research organizations. Descriptive information provided for each center, including address, telephone number, name of director, data on staff, funds, publications, and a statement concerning its principal fields of research. Has special indexes. Gale Research Company, Book Tower, Detroit, MI 48226.

MacRae's Blue Book—Materials, Equipment, Supplies, Components. Annual. In five volumes: Vol. 1 is an index by corporations; Vols. 2–4 are a classification by products showing under each classification manufacturers of that item; Vol. 5 contains company catalogs. MacRae's Blue Book Company, 100 Shore Drive, Hinsdale, IL 60521.

Thomas' Grocery Register. Annual. Lists wholesale grocers; chain store organizations, voluntary buying groups; food brokers; exporters and importers of food products; frozen food brokers; distributors and related products distributed through grocery chains. Thomas Publishing Company, One Penn Plaza, New York, NY 10001.

Thomas' Register of American Manufacturers. Annual. In 14 volumes. Vols. 1–7 contain manufacturers arranged geographically under each product, and capitalization or size rating for each manufacturer, Vol. 7 lists brands names and their owners; Vol. 8 lists company addresses, phone numbers, and local offices; Vols. 9–14 contain company catalogs. Thomas Publishing Company, One Penn Plaza, New York, NY 10001.

OTHER SOURCES

U.S. Small Business Administration

The SBA's address is Washington, DC 20416. SBA issues a wide range of management and technical publications designed to help owner-managers and prospective owners of small business. (For general information about SBA, its policies, and assistance programs, ask for *SBA—What It Is,* free on request to nearest SBA office.) Listings of currently available publications (free and for sale) may be requested from SBA, P.O. Box 15434, Ft. Worth, TX 76119, or any of SBA's field offices. Ask for: *SBA 115—Free Management Assistance Publications* and *SBA 115B—For-Sale Booklets.* The lists are free and may be used for ordering the particular series listed, either the free series from SBA, or the for-sale series from the Superintendent of Documents (GPO).

Small Business Bibliography. (8- to 12-page pamphlet.) Each title in this series deals with a specific kind of business or business function, giving reference sources. It consists of an introduction that gives a description of the operation, listing of references applicable to the subject covered. Free.

    Statistics and Maps for National Market Analysis (SBB 12)

    National Directories for Use in Marketing (SBB 13)

    Basic Library Reference Sources (SBB 18)

    Advertising-Retail Store (SBB 20)

Management Aids for Small Manufacturers (4- to 8-page leaflet.) Each title in this series discusses a specific management practice to help the owner-manager of small manufacturing firms with their management problems. Free.

    Using Census Data in Small Plant Marketing (MA 187)

    Locating or Relocating Your Business (MA 201)

    Finding a New Product for Your Company (MA 216)

Small Marketers Aid. (4- to 8-page leaflet.) Each title in this series gives guidance on a specific subject for owners of small retail, wholesale, and service business. Free.

Measuring the Results of Advertising (SMA 121)

Factors in Considering a Shopping Center Location (SMA 143)

Using a Traffic Study to Select a Retail Site (SMA 152)

Using Census Data to Select a Store Site (SMA 154)

Advertising Guidelines for Small Retail Firms (SMA 160)

Small Business Management Series. Each booklet in this series discusses in depth the application of a specific management practice. The series covers a wide range of small business subjects. Prices vary. GPO.

Office of Management and Budget, Executive Office Building, Washington, D.C. 20503.

Standard Industrial Classification Manual. GPO. Gives the definitions of the classifications of industrial establishments by the type of activity in which each is engaged and the resulting Industrial Classification Code. Very useful in classifying data collected from industrial firms so its classification is comparable to data reported by government sources.

Bureau of the Census

The Census Bureau's address is Commerce Department, Suitland, MD 20233. Request list of publications from this bureau. Publication order forms are issued for reports as they become available.

Census of Business: Retail-Area Statistics—U.S. Summary. GPO. Final figures from the Census of Retail Trade, includes statistical totals for each region, state, city and standard metropolitan area—tabulated by type of establishment.

County Business Patterns. GPO. A series of publications presenting first-quarter employment and payroll statistics, by county and by industry. Separate reports issued for each of the 50 states, the District of Columbia, Puerto Rico, and outlying areas of the United States.

County and City Data Book. VGTB. GPO. Contains data for 50 states, 3141 counties or county equivalents, 243 SMSAs, 840 cities of 25,000 inhabitants or more, among others.

Directory of Federal Statistics for Local Areas, A Guide to Sources. GPO. Guide to local area socioeconomic data contained in 182 publications of 33 federal agencies.

Directory of Federal Statistics of States, A Guide to Sources. GPO. Guide to state socioeconomic data contained in more than 750 publications of federal agencies.

Directory of Non-Federal Statistics for State and Local Areas. GPO. Guide to nonfederal sources of current statistics on social, political, and economic subjects for 50 states, the District of Columbia, Guam, Puerto Rico, and the Virgin Islands.

Standard Metropolitan Statistical Areas. GPO. Gives the criteria followed in establishing Standard Metropolitan Statistical Areas. Changes issued periodically as amendments.

Department of Commerce

Direct requests for information to the Department's Domestic and International Business Administration, Washington, DC 20230.

Measuring Markets: A Guide to the Use of Federal and State Statistical Data. GPO. Presents features and measurements of markets, types of useful data published by federal and state governments, case examples of market measurement by use of government data, and bibliographies.

INDEX